VERMONT CASTINGS
MODERN GRILLING

First published in the United States of America by
Quarry Books, a member of
Quayside Publishing Group
33 Commercial Street
Gloucester, Massachusetts 01930-5089
Telephone: (978) 282-9590
Fax: (978) 283-2742
www.quarrybooks.com

ISBN-13: 978-1-59253-328-2
ISBN-10: 1-59253-328-0

10 9 8 7 6 5 4 3 2

Design: Yee Design
Page Layout: QA Solutions India Private Limited
Original recipes by Dwayne Ridgaway, Susan Geiskopf-Hadler,
Jim and Ann Casada, Kate Fiduccia, and Teresa Marrone.

VERMONT CASTINGS

MODERN GRILLING

More than 300 Recipes and Menus for Grilling Year-Round

GLOUCESTER MASSACHUSETTS

QUARRY BOOKS

Edited by Gary Ralph

TABLE OF CONTENTS

INTRODUCTION

THERE HAVE BEEN SO MANY ADVANCES IN

grilling over the past several decades, we now think of our grilling areas as "outdoor kitchens." Not only do grills, with all their features, rival a kitchen's stove, storage space, and counters, but the whole practice of grilling has come of age. Most of us no longer look at grilling as simply tossing a burger on the grill on a hot day. We now think of grilling out of doors as a completely acceptable alternative to indoor cooking. In fact, many of us already think of grilling as the preferred way to cook through the summer and into many of the cooler months of the year, if not year-round. This book is a celebration of modern grilling and all the advances that make grills such an enjoyable part of today's lifestyle.

Outdoor chefs have been working for eons on their recipes and techniques, and many have succeeded in producing grilling classics. Television shows and magazines have been created just for the subject of grilling. The list of foods that can be grilled has expanded to an extent where almost anything, from meat, poultry, and fish to vegetables and fruits, is grist for the grill. The artistry of grilling has been established and shows no signs of fading.

Perhaps the most pronounced advances in grilling have been made over the past decade in the technology of outdoor cooking. Today's grills are marvels of efficiency and versatility. Choosing a new grill may not lift you to the rank of professional overnight, but it can open doors to open-air cooking and make you a very popular person in your home and community.

Where once grills were naked wire grates above beds of lava rocks or bits of charcoal, many are now true kitchens packed with features that go far beyond their cooking surfaces. Consumers have a choice of grills that create heat from wood, charcoal, propane or natural gas, or even from combinations of fuels. And they have options of infrared rotisseries, smokers, warming units, shelves, and storage compartments that emulate or even surpass what we find inside our homes.

AN EVOLUTIONARY LOOK

One of the top grill makers in the world is Vermont Castings, a brand of CFM Corporation, which also makes a wide range of hearth products. A look at some of the components in Vermont Castings Signature Series grills provides a glimpse of the grill's evolution over the past few years. The heart of a grill is its burner, and today's grills may have a number of burners, depending on their price points. Vermont Castings' grills are fueled by natural gas or propane and the company also produces gas smokers.

Side burners allow you to cook pasta and grains
and to prepare sauces to go with the entrée on the grill.

The heat output of a burner is rated in British thermal units, or BTUs. Without getting too technical, a single burner will produce about 28,000 BTUs or more, while a six-burner model will push out about 75,000 BTUs—an incredible amount of heat. A side burner, on which you would place pots, might be rated at 15,000 BTUs in a large grill. Vermont Castings has one-, three-, four-, five-, and six-burner units.

GRILLS IN MANY SIZES

The size of the cooking area is an important consideration. Vermont Castings' economy units begin with primary cooking areas in the neighborhood of 350 square inches (2,258 sq cm). The platform above the main surface is the warming rack and measures about 150 square inches (968 sq cm) in a smaller grilling unit. This adds up to a total cooking surface for a so-called economy grill of about 500 square inches (3,226 sq cm): enough for hamburgers, steaks, franks, salmon chunks, or eggplant strips to feed a family of four hungry people. A high-end grill will have more than twice that amount of cooking space. A Vermont Castings Signature Series grill introduced not long ago measured 750 square inches (4,839 sq cm) on the main surface and 290 square inches (1,871 sq cm) on its porcelain-coated wire warming rack, for a total cooking area of 1,040 square inches (6,710 sq cm). Imagine a really big party with several kinds of foods cooking at once.

FLIPPING, SEARING, AND OTHER TECHNIQUES

Wire racks on the main cooking surface have been replaced in modern grills by aluminum or cast-iron cook grids. Warming racks are still made of wire but, like the better grids, are coated with porcelain to protect them from rust and to ease cleanup. Some of the better cooking racks also have a lip at the rear that helps chefs flip burgers and other foods with flair, not flare-up if food is pushed accidentally onto the burners or charcoal bed.

Innovations such as infrared rotisserie kits, smokers, and side burners that accommodate pots for side dishes enable you to cook in a number of ways. Sear plates are standard or optional equipment in a number of grills and hold in flavor by searing foods outside before cooking their insides to perfection. Griddle plates can be used for cooking bacon and eggs, pancakes, or stir-fries.

Big stainless-steel sear plates provide good distribution of heat across the whole cooking surface.

KEEPING IN THE HEAT

Many grill improvements have been made to enhance cooking by retaining heat within the grill and distributing it evenly to the food.

An extra-deep fire box creates convection-style cooking so food stays moist and the flavor stays in.

Grates are heavy in order to distribute and retain heat. Some grates are made of thick aluminum, while others, like those in Vermont Castings Signature Series grills, are porcelain-coated cast iron. These grates provide even heat distribution so all steaks, chops, and other fare on the grill will cook at the same rate. The hood of the grill is critical for heat retention when closed, as are the ends of the hood known as "end caps." It's also important to have an extra-deep firebox, which will retain heat at its source. Heat retention allows the chef to lower the temperature of the grill to maintain moisture in the foods and to save fuel.

Modern grill makers have considered the benefits of convenience. For instance, they include condiment trays to keep ingredients within easy reach of the grilling chef. A cover on the side burner keeps the wind from blowing smoke into the eyes of the cook and his guests or grit into the cooking pots on the burner.

Tool and towel holders often are found in modern grills. Grease management systems—usually pull-out trays that can be emptied away from the grill—are common in better grills for fast and convenient cleanup.

Grills that retain heat well are more efficient and produce more flavorful food. Look for double-walled lid panels and cast-iron hood end caps that help to keep heat inside the grill where it belongs.

WARM AND HANDY

Other advances in grills include something lacking in many indoor kitchens, a way to keep food warm until it's ready to serve. A top warming rack will keep foods at the peak of flavor, and so will the warming drawers built into many modern grills. These drawers are great for storing breads and buns so they remain toasty.

If roasts and whole chickens are on your menu (and why wouldn't they be?) a rotisserie kit and burner is a must for slow and even infrared cooking.

YOU'RE IN CONTROL

Most people who haven't looked at grills in a few years won't associate controls with grill units. Isn't grilling a matter of throwing a steak on a grate and praying? Not anymore. Electronic ignitions on modern gas grills

A top warming rack helps retain flavor.

have replaced that shot of noxious lighter fluid used to jumpstart charcoal grills while imparting an objectionable taste to food. A single push of a button gets the fire going, while a thermometer on the outside of the grill hood monitors heat for efficient cooking. Vermont Castings also provides what's called a cross-flow ignition system, which allows the chef to use one push of the ignition button to start the flame in a single burner, with each burner firing in sequence afterward.

A night-light is one of the handy features of a modern grill.

-☼-

Not only do heavy porcelain-coated cast-iron cooking grates retain heat for even cooking, but they reduce the chance of foods sticking to the grate.

Control dials on the consoles of higher-end grills provide back lighting to ease cooking at night. Vermont Castings adds pop-up night-lights that rise from the console to illuminate the grilling surface in low- or no-light situations.

GRILLS, GRILLS, AND MORE

While most grills are purchased in cart models, built-in grills are becoming popular in new homes or in refurbished or added decks and patios. These built-in gas grills really are complete, outdoor cooking centers, with options that would make any indoor cook eager to take recipes into the backyard.

Basic grills without the frills are still available, and many are excellent buys at very economical prices. As long as they are solid, dependable, and durable units, small grills will cook food almost as well as the big and much more expensive units do, just not as much at one time and not as quickly. The bigger, well-equipped units represent the cutting edge of grilling. They blend efficiency, convenience, and power to produce some of the best food around. They are focal points at most parties or other gatherings on decks and patios. They have the surface room for a lot of steaks or even a large mixed menu of foods for the variety of tastes among guests.

Grilled food is naturally healthier because fat drips off the food onto the coals or grate, creating smoke that flavors the food above. Many of the dishes prepared with the help of a grill are also healthy because grilling adds extra flavor to low-calorie, high-nutrition foods that might be bland or uninteresting when cooked with other methods. But it's really the variety of foods that can be grilled today that makes grilling rewarding. Learning to grill and expanding on its possibilities creates an excitement to share with family and friends.

FROM BURGERS TO SEA BASS

Improvements in grills, more sophisticated consumer palates, and the greater variety of foods on market shelves have led to an explosion of recipes for outdoor grillers. Long gone are the days when the only foods you threw on the grill were burgers, hot dogs, and chicken breasts. Today's grilling menu runs the gamut from filet steak with a juniper crust to super salads, fantastic fish, and desserts beyond delicious.

NO MORE THE LOWLY BURGER

Hamburgers have gone gourmet in recent years because our palates have grown accustomed to global flavors. Once a lowly meal of ground chuck, today's burgers reach into the heights of gastronomy. And, while some of the classics are found in this book, you will also find the most exotic versions sitting by their sides. All of these delicious burgers can be made on your backyard grills in much less time than it takes to go to the drive-through.

A GALAXY OF MEAT AND POULTRY

Because modern grills have such astounding heat output, retention, and distribution, there is no meat, fish, vegetable, or poultry we can't take out to the patio or deck to prepare. Beef steaks and burgers, pork ribs, and chicken have been joined by lamb chops, lamb meatballs, and lamb burgers; turkey in all variations; and a whole range of game meats and poultry such as venison, elk, pheasant, quail, and even alligator. Modern grilling has married many popular tastes for traditional food with combinations unheard of just a few years ago.

WILD AND WONDERFUL

Grilling or cooking over direct fire began with the cooking of wild game in a cave somewhere. Wild game has returned to the modern menu, and there is no better way to prepare this fare than on the grill. There are recipes for plain and fancy grilling of goose, pheasant, and quail as well as venison, elk, and so on. Imagine a Blue Cheese Venison Steak (page 152) that

begins with searing and is ready for the table in less than fifteen minutes. Whether grilling elk or wild salmon, the modern grill can handle and enhance the foods on which our ancient ancestors once depended.

GRILLING FISH AND SEAFOOD

Fish is a wonderful main course when cooked on the grill. Once messy to make on the grill, delicate fish as well as the meaty tuna, salmon, and swordfish are new favorites thanks to grilling accessories that hold fish together. But don't limit yourself to grilling fish directly on the grate; today's grills are capable of handling any fish dish. Sardines, for instance, can be marinated in a shallow dish set on the shelf of a grill unit, then moved to the grate and cooked over medium-high heat. Prawns can be grilled in a Thai-style sauce, then tossed in a saucepan on a nearby burner with rice for an unusual

jambalaya. How would you like Cedar Planked Fish (page 182), another kind of dish that has become wildly popular in the past decade or so? With a little care in turning, a bass, bream, or mullet can be coated with a wonderful rub and grilled to perfection. The grill has become a marvelous tool for the seafood-loving chef; just consider using the appliance to cook trout wrapped in smoked bacon or different kinds of scallop or shrimp dishes.

UNIVERSAL PIZZA

No food is more universal and more in tune with our times than pizza. More people are making pizza at home and an increasing number are making pizza on their grills. Pizza is the product of a number of ancient cultures but no resident of its birthplace in pre-Renaissance Naples, Italy, would recognize the Hawaiian version with pineapple and ham; the modern pizza takes many forms and one is the grilled pizza.

With an outdoor kitchen, you can prepare most pizza ingredients on the grill and side burner. Make tomato sauce in a large pot on the side burner, and spice it up with red pepper flakes and ground red pepper chosen from the rack on the grill. You can even grill the dough itself. When thin-crust pizza is cooked on a wood-burning grill, it gets the same kind of smoked flavor and crisp crust that it would from a traditional wood-burning pizza oven. For convenience, a gas grill, if large enough to create hot and cool zones, can be used to bake the pizza beginning to end. If the cooking surface is smaller, you can grill the pizza most of the way and finish it in an oven on a pizza stone. Add wood chips to a gas or charcoal grill to get that smoked aroma and flavor that many people like.

MENUS FROM MEXICO

Mexican-inspired foods have become staples in our modern diets. Dishes like burritos, tostados, and fajitas are taken directly from hearty Mexican menus. Most Mexican food can be cooked outside. A burrito, for instance, can be cooked on a grill, using medium-high heat, in less than 30 minutes.

SANDWICH MAKING

In today's busy world, sandwiches are more popular than ever and their variety is mind-boggling. Many sandwiches, including relative newcomers like the panini, can be grilled whole or, at least, the inside ingredients can be cooked on a grill. For instance, consider the Chicken Soprano Panini (page 199)—its main ingredients of chicken and red peppers can be grilled first and topped with provolone, basil, pepperoni, and mozzarella. Once assembled in a ciabatta roll, this marvelous creation can be finished on the grill.

Pita bread has a pouch that makes for a great sandwich. Pita rounds bake quickly, so take care not to burn them. Ciabatta bread also makes a top-notch grilled sandwich.

VEGETARIAN VARIETY

We know how far grilling has come from its early days in our backyards when we look at the number and variety of vegetarian dishes that can be grilled. There's no law that says a kebab, fajita, taco, wrap, or pizza has to contain meat, fish, or poultry. Almost any grilled dish today can have a veggie equivalent. The options on bigger grills allow you to make almost any kind of sauce or salsa to accompany a vegetarian dish. Grill toppings for crostini (toasted bread slices) using tomatoes, zucchini, eggplant, or other vegetables mixed with basil and garlic. Ingredients of vegetarian salads can be cooked on the grill. And for main dishes, try recipes like tacos with grilled peppers, veggie burgers, focaccia with grilled portobello mushrooms, or vermicelli with tomato sauce.

HOW SWEET IT IS

Some home chefs may not associate grilling with dessert preparation. Well, start thinking about grilled pineapple with honey glaze or grilled cake with bananas. Many desserts can be grilled, and recipes for some of the best are included in this book.

IN THIS BOOK

In chapter 1, we'll talk about how to choose your grill and accessories. We'll describe the tools needed to cook almost any dish you can dream of preparing. Chapter 2 covers the care and maintenance of the grill and grilling techniques. Chapters 3 through 12 contain page after page of recipes created by many great professional chefs and by a lot of guys and gals who just love to cook wonderful food outdoors and have contributed their creations to Vermont Castings' Web site collection of recipes (www.myownbbq.com). Vermont Castings has been collecting recipes from grilling fans for a long time and asking other grill users to rate them. Many of their favorites have found their way onto these pages and, hopefully, now into your repertoire. This is a book about the pleasures and the current state of the art of grilling.

CHAPTER ONE

BUYING THE RIGHT GRILL AND ACCESSORIES

THIS CHAPTER DESCRIBES HOW TO CHOOSE THE GRILL THAT

is right for you, your cooking aspirations, your family's lifestyle, your budget, and where you will place your new and proud acquisition. There are two types of grills: charcoal and gas. But, in these two basic categories, there are a long list of models with a seemingly endless list of standard and optional features.

Begin with a realistic look at what you want to do with your grill. Take a close look at your family's lifestyle. Does the family gather for small informal meals or snacks on the deck or patio? If so, you can probably make due with a small- to medium-size grill. Or do you host many large parties? Will you want to feed ten or more people on a frequent basis? Is your yard, deck, or patio large enough to serve as a focal point for many of your social functions? If you're nodding your head, you likely need a large grill.

GAS OR CHARCOAL?

For the most convenient outdoor kitchen, opt for a gas grill. However, purists may be happier with a small charcoal-fired grill regardless of the fact that there seems to be no real difference in the taste of food grilled one way or the other. Charcoal or gas? It's a matter of personal preference, the amount of money you want to spend, and the price and availability of fuel in your area. Over time, the cost of each is almost the same: a gas grill may cost more initially but a charcoal grill may be more costly, depending on the local price of briquettes, and certainly less convenient to operate and clean because of ash buildup and disposal.

Top and bottom vents on a charcoal grill improve airflow and, when closed, put out the fire and save fuel.

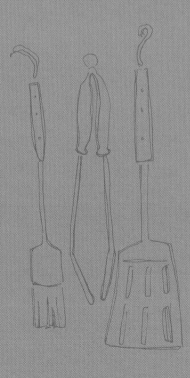

Most gas grills are fueled with either propane, usually from a portable tank, or natural gas, which requires a natural gas line to the deck or patio. A few grills use butane gas. Propane comes in refillable tanks, which have warranties from their makers and not from the grill manufacturer. Many propane grills can be converted to natural gas (NG), or vice versa, if the owner moves or decides to change fuel type after purchase. All Vermont Castings grills are "field fuel convertible" and can be changed from propane to natural gas or vice versa, but grill conversions have to be handled by a licensed technician.

Once you've decided if you want a gas or charcoal grill, the next step is finding a reputable dealer.

SELECTING A DEALER

As with any appliance purchase, seek a reputable dealer in the area. Look for one who displays models within your price range and preferences. A dealer should be knowledgeable and take time to explain the advantages of one brand and model over others in your price range. A dealer also should stock brochures or other easy-to-digest information so a consumer can take materials home to study. The dealer should be able to provide service, spare parts, and options for the grill.

SELECTING A BRAND

If a grill is manufactured by a name-brand maker with a good reputation, the company will be more likely to stand behind its products and be around over the long haul to provide spare parts, service the grill, provide optional add-on features, and assist you with your next grill if you outgrow your initial choice.

CONSIDER WARRANTIES

Look carefully at the grills' warranties to see if there is a long warranty period, including a burner warranty of up to twenty-five years and, on the most expensive units, a lifetime warranty. For instance, for one of

Vermont Castings' most economical grills, the warranty for cast-aluminum parts against burn-through, rust, and structural failure, excluding paint, neglect, or abuse, is seventy-five years from date of purchase. The burner warranty provides for either free or prorated replacement for up to twenty-five years. Other parts are covered for five years, except for paint. Many large grills have lifetime warranties.

Look for a long or even lifetime warranty if buying a large grill like the five-burner unit from Vermont Castings.

PUTTING IT TOGETHER

At a dealer, carefully examine the components of the grills. Most grills are made from stainless steel but the grade of steel will vary depending on price. Select the highest quality of stainless steel you can afford by pressing against the sides of competing units and asking the dealer for specifications on each grill under consideration. The lid of the grill should be heavy and close tightly. Most grills are made from die-cut parts: check the fit of parts to see that they are tight and that the grill is sturdy and durable.

It is usual to assemble parts of the grill after you get the unit home, such as legs and side shelves, but make sure the assembly is easy and the parts fit well.

A tool set made for your grill is an excellent option or feature to ask for from your grill dealer.

NO-STICK SURFACES

Modern grill cooking surfaces have porcelain-enamel coating, which is baked rather than sprayed on. This coating will protect the metal underneath and will keep foods from sticking to surfaces. Grates can be plated with nickel or made of stainless steel. In Vermont Castings Signature Series grills, cooking grates and other parts are cast iron covered with baked-on porcelain enamel for superior heat distribution and retention. Regardless of materials, cooking grates should be solid and heavy to retain and distribute heat evenly.

SAFE HANDLING

The grill's handle will be made of metal, wood, or plastic and should stay cool to the touch. Test the handle to make certain your hands and arms will remain clear of a hot surface when you are raising or lowering the lid of the grill. Some handles are bent away from the grill to facilitate safe and comfortable lifting and lowering of the lid.

CLEANUP

Look for a charcoal grill with a pan that makes the job of collecting and disposing of ashes easy and less messy. In a gas grill, a grease-management system is a must. This usually takes the form of a tray that collects grease and that can be removed easily for disposal of the grease away from your deck or patio.

MULTIPURPOSE GRILLS

Economy grills are basic units, fine for cooking steaks, chicken breasts, and many other foods over direct heat or for cooking small quantities of food over indirect heat. Moderately priced and expensive grills are really four cookers in one. With the lid open, they are grills on which to sear steaks, chops, and burgers. With the lid closed, they are ovens for baking, roasting, or warming a large variety of dishes. With the addition of a rotisserie burner and kit, grills use infrared cooking to prepare succulent roasts, whole chickens, and other incredible fare. Equip a grill with a side burner or two and you have a stovetop to cook anything from pasta and corn on the cob to lobster and sauces. Multipurpose grills are truly outdoor kitchens.

Steaming vegetables is easy: just place a steamer tray in a large saucepan, add 2 inches (5 cm) of water to the depth of the second knuckle of your index finger, and place the pan on the side burner over medium-high heat. Add vegetables, cover the pan tightly, and cook until fork-tender.

BEYOND THE BASICS

Economical gas grills have a single burner and may have ceramic or other briquettes to aid heat distribution and reduce the possibility of flare-ups. Small grills may also sear and use indirect heat to cook food. Large grills have up to six burners. A choice for fairly frequent grilling within most budgets is a gas model with three or four burners. While a single burner can achieve a heat of about 500°F (260°C) or more within a relatively short time under a closed lid, a number of independent burners allows you to control cooking heat with great precision. Not every dish is grilled over direct flames; many food items are cooked with indirect heat. The cook should have the ability to turn off or reduce heat from some burners while keeping others at full flame. In a charcoal grill, indirect cooking is achieved by moving coals to a particular part of the grill, keeping the heat at an angle to food, so it's the overall size of the charcoal grill that is important when considering both direct- and indirect-heat cooking.

Technically speaking, grilling is not barbecuing. Grilling refers to cooking food over direct heat, whereas barbecuing means cooking food slowly with indirect heat. The words are interchangeable for most people today, and modern grills can both grill and barbecue to produce wonderful meals.

BTUs are one indication of the power of the grill, but good construction, heavy cooking grates, and a good lid are just as important in determining how much heat stays in the unit, how heat is distributed, and how much fuel you will use when you cook for a large group. A higher BTU rating is especially important to maintain cooking temperatures if you grill in cooler weather.

A hinged cooking grate is handy when adding coals to a charcoal fire.

A warming drawer is another useful accessory to add to your outdoor kitchen.

Rotisserie

To roast a whole chicken to golden brown deliciousness or to create a red meat roast that will have guests begging for thirds, you will need a rotisserie in your grill. More expensive grills will have a rotisserie burner and kit—comprising a motor, spit, and brackets—as standard, whereas such features are optional at lower price points. Look for a grill with this feature or to which you can add a rotisserie burner and kit at a later date, once you have mastered basic grilling techniques and recipes.

To move a grill around the deck or patio, heavy-duty casters make the job safe and smooth.

Control Dials

Controls are very important, particularly in a gas grill. You can light a charcoal or gas grill electronically with the push of a button, so there is no reason anymore to risk burning yourself with a match, twist of paper, or squirt of lighter fluid to ignite your grill fire. Beyond battery-operated electronic ignition, look for a degree-

calibrated temperature gauge mounted on the outside of the unit. A gauge is essential to finding when your grill has heated to an optimum temperature and in adjusting the heat when using your grill as an oven. As well, many moderate-priced to expensive gas grills will have dial controls to adjust the flames of individual burners.

Some modern grills have illuminated control dials so you can adjust your flames with precision even after dark. Some Vermont Castings Signature Grills also come with a pop-up LED night-light to illuminate the cooking surface of the grill so the chef can see what he or she is cooking long after sundown.

The Smoker

Some people consider the smoker to be as important as the grill itself. Fueled by charcoal, electricity, or gas, a smoker holds a container of water-soaked wood chips. Some grills have smoker boxes as standard equipment, whereas others offer smokers as options.

Vermont Castings Signature Series includes a sophisticated gas smoker that is double walled, stainless steel, and has an output of 17,500 BTUs. Inside the box are four cooking grids, with a total of 1,033 square inches (6,664 sq cm) of cooking area.

To control the smoke there are three adjustable dampers. The door of the unit has a silicon gel door gasket to maintain optimum and consistent cooking temperatures. This gas smoker also includes an electronic ignition, a durable cast-iron wood-chip box, and a powder-coated grease pan with four grease baffles to ease grease collection.

Cooking over charcoal alone does not produce a smoky flavor in your food. If you prefer this kind of outdoor taste, consider buying a model with a smoker box to vary the flavors imparted by choosing different woods to heat in the unit. For instance, you can use mesquite, hickory, or pecan wood to give a pungent smoked flavor to beef, lamb, or pork. Oak, maple, and alder wood chips will give a moderate flavor to fish, poultry, and pork. Apple, pear, and cherry wood will give a mild smoked flavor to poultry, fish, or vegetables.

Aprons, mitts, and brushes aren't just for show; they help keep the chef and the workspace clean and safe.

Apart from optional and standard equipment on the grill itself, you can outfit yourself with all the cooking accessories you'll need to be a master chef. Get a deep fryer for french fries and a griddle for pancakes. Handheld tools such as a spatula and a long-handled

fork will make flipping a breeze. Don't forget the accessories such as mitts, aprons, a grill cover, and, of course, a great cookbook like this one, because, after you have chosen your grill and your tools, it is all about the food.

To prepare entire meals right at the grill, the cook will need side tables and condiment holders as well as side burners that accommodate cooking pots for dishes and ingredients like pasta, beans, and chili.

CHOOSING FEATURES

A charcoal grill can be bought for a very small amount of money and a basic gas grill won't break most budgets, but don't expect a great many features or a large cooking area on an economy model.

The chart on page 22 lists most of the key features on modern, moderately priced to expensive grills. Some features are usually included as standard items whereas others are offered more often as options. This chart may help you decide on the grill features you want, depending on your lifestyle, location, budget, and expectations.

A thermometer on the outside of the hood is a modern touch on your grill.

FEATURE COMPARISON FOR BUYING GRILLS

FEATURE	STANDARD	GREAT FEATURES
Stainless-steel main burners	Propane or NG gas grills or charcoal grill	3–6 gas burners
Main burner's BTUs	Gas grills: usually between 37,500 and 75,000 BTUs, depending on number of burners	Higher BTUs in cooler climates and for bigger feasts
Primary cooking area	From about 400 to 750 square inches (2,581 to 4,839 sq cm)	Bigger cooking areas for larger families and party givers
Porcelain-coated wire warming rack	From about 150 to about 300 square inches (968 to 1,935 sq cm)	Bigger warming area for larger families, party givers, or extensive menus
Total cooking area	From about 550 to 1,050 square inches (3,548 to 6,774 sq cm)	Bigger cooking areas for more extensive outdoor cooking
Porcelain-coated cast-iron or other cooking grates	Heavy, coated grates are standard in most good grills. May be iron, steel, or aluminum	Iron, coated with porcelain, conducts heat best and is easier to clean
Sear plates	A newer item in some grills. Usually in stainless steel	A good option if not standard
Electronic ignition system	Standard in good gas grills. Charcoal igniter may be electronic, gas, or other	Very handy and safer than other igniters
Porcelain-coated or stainless-steel hood construction and end caps	Hood or lid should be heavy, tight-fitting, and durable. End caps help retain heat.	End caps may come in black or colors.
Porcelain-coated black base oven	Oven base should be deep for heat retention and coated for easy cleaning.	
Enclosed or open cart design	An enclosed cart design keeps storage clean and safe.	
Cart	Most are stainless steel in good grills	
Sides and doors	Most sides and doors are stainless steel. Doors can be single or double.	
Lid handle	Heavy duty, of metal, wood, or plastic and shaped to keep hands away from hot hood	
Heavy-duty commercial casters	Safer and easier to move the cart	Heavy-duty wheels are safer and more durable.
Infrared rear rotisserie burner	From 15,000 to about 20,000 BTUs	If not standard, rotisseries are good to add. Inquire whether rotisserie unit can be added later.

FEATURE	STANDARD	GREAT FEATURES
Rotisserie kit	Motor, spit, and brackets	Standard and optional but cannot be added to some units later
Control panel	On front of gas grill with control for each burner. Some charcoal grills will have a temperature gauge.	Backlit dials are handy for after-dark cooking, but are not included in all grills.
Light@Night cooking light	Example of a brand-specific feature. A pop-up LED light to illuminate cooking surface.	Very handy to illuminate whole cooking surface after dark
Tool holders	May be built into side shelves as standard	Very handy if offered as an option
Stainless-steel condiment trays	May be standard	Very handy if offered as an option
Stainless-steel side shelving	Often standard	Very handy if offered as an option
Cast-iron griddle plate	Usually optional but may be standard	Handy if you like cooking eggs, pancakes, waffles, etc.
Warming drawer	May be standard	Very handy if offered as an option
Grease management	Usually a tray to collect grease. May be removed from front or back of grill for disposal of grease. Most often standard	A must
Side burner and cover	1 or 2 burners of about 15,000 BTUs to accommodate pots. Usually stainless steel with enamel-coated grates. May be standard or optional. Cover protects burner from wind when open, dirt or rain when closed.	Handy if you like cooking everything in the same place without running back and forth to the indoor kitchen while preparing pasta, boiling veggies, etc. At least make sure you can add option later.
Towel bar	Handy and standard in a few grills	Handy but not essential
Tank pull-out tray	Optional in some liquid propane grills; standard in others	Handy to save your back and fingers from tank accidents
Propane or natural gas	Standard in all gas grills but only some can convert from one gas to the other. Some charcoal grills have gas igniter system.	
Grill cover	A must for a clean grill. Optional for some good grills; standard for others	Very handy to keep your grill clean and protected when not in use

CHAPTER TWO
CARING FOR YOUR GRILL AND GRILLING TECHNIQUES

Grilled Chicken Wings with Sweet Mustard Grilling Sauce, page 146

AN OUTDOOR GRILL IS AS EASY TO USE AS YOUR INDOOR

stove or other cooking appliance. Like your kitchen stove, a grill requires proper installation, regular cleaning, reasonable care, and, above all, a regard for safety. If you follow the basics, all will be easy and quick, leaving lots of time and energy for the enjoyment of outdoor cooking.

The most popular grills today are fueled by propane gas, or liquid propane (LP). You can use propane safely, but it is a fuel, so it should be treated with respect.

PROPANE

A normal Type 1 connection system, the common system on most consumer tanks, will not allow gas to flow until a good connection has been made, will shut off the flow of gas when a certain temperature has been reached, and will limit the flow of gas to conserve fuel and to aid safety.

Propane comes in pressurized tanks and, if released, can vaporize gas into the air. Read your owner's manual for specific directions on carrying, refilling, using, and replacing LP tanks.

When filling and transporting your LP tank:

- Transport only one cylinder of propane at a time and then only in an upright position, with the control valve turned off and the POL plug in place.
- Don't carry a cylinder in the passenger area of your vehicle and/or leave it in a car trunk or other area that will be exposed to sun, because high heat will cause gas to vent from the tank valve.
- Use a cylinder cap on the cylinder valve outlet during transport and when the cylinder is not connected to the grill.
- Don't stick any foreign object into the valve outlet or you risk damaging the back check and causing leakage.
- Have your LP cylinder filled or repaired only by a qualified gas dealer and inform the dealer, when filling, if your cylinder is new or used.
- Caution the dealer not to fill the cylinder to more than 80 percent of capacity.
- Ask the dealer to check that the relief valve is in working order after filling and that there are no leaks

When storing a cylinder of LP gas:

- Don't use the fuel cylinder enclosure in your grill to store your grill cover or other items.
- Don't store your cylinder in any building or enclosed area; keep it, and your grill, in a well-ventilated area out of the reach of children and pets.

NATURAL GAS

A natural gas line to your grill location must be installed by a qualified gas installer or licensed plumber. Don't try to install a natural gas line by yourself. Follow manufacturer instructions to attach your grill to the natural gas line.

CHARCOAL

Charcoal grills require the same degree of care as gas grills. When using charcoal:

- Store starter fluid away from heat sources and out of the reach of children.
- Always burn charcoal in a well-ventilated area because the fuel gives off deadly carbon monoxide gas.

GAS GRILL INSPECTION

Whether you have a propane or natural gas grill or charcoal grill with a gas ignition system, get into the habit of inspecting the grill before every use and certainly when you take it out of storage after a period of time. Be sure to:

- Check connections when the grill is cool to make certain they are undamaged, not rusted by food drippings and moisture, and tight.
- If you smell gas or find a damaged or rusted part, test your fuel supply connections by applying a soap-and-water solution to connections and watching for bubbles.
- Perform a leak test each time the gas-supply cylinder is connected to the regulator and at least once each year.
- Inspect the gas supply hose regularly and replace the hose if there are cuts, excessive abrasion, or wear.

SETTING UP YOUR GRILL

It's easy to set up your grill if you follow the directions in your user manual. In general:

- Never use an outdoor grill in a house, garage, cottage, boat, camper trailer, tent, or other enclosed area, or you risk a buildup of deadly carbon monoxide or a fire.

- Avoid setting up your grill under a ceiling or other cover or near combustible material or walls that might be affected by heat.
- Choose a level spot for your grill and avoid facing its cooking surfaces into the wind.
- Leave space around your grill so the flow of air for combustion and ventilation is not blocked.
- Don't use charcoal briquettes in a gas grill.
- Don't use natural gas in a grill designed for propane gas or vice versa.
- Don't use lighter fluid, kerosene, gasoline, or other improper starter fluid in a charcoal grill.

An additional quick disconnect fitting on your grill is likely for an optional side burner.

SAFE HABITS

Safety when using your grill is not only a priority, it's common sense. Form good habits by following these basic precautions:

- Avoid moving your grill while cooking and don't leave it unattended.
- Don't leave any combustible materials like plastic, wood, or paper on or near a grill surface.
- Wear a protective mitt when cooking and serving.
- Don't lean on the side table of any grill or place more than about fifteen pounds of weight on the table.
- Place a drip pan under the grill.
- When starting a charcoal-grill fire, apply starter fluid directly to the coals, then reseal the starter-fluid container and put it away safely; never add starter fluid to burning charcoal.

For safe cooking:

- Use a long-handled spatula or tongs to turn your food.
- Stand to one side of the hot grill when opening the lid.

- Don't place any part of your body directly above the cooking area.
- Lift the lid handle slowly in case of a grease flare-up.

Check your extinguished charcoal grill until it has completely cooled or soak the coals with water, but do it carefully to avoid steam and spattering.

PREPARING YOUR GRILL

Congratulations, you've purchased a new grill and attached your filled gas cylinder or gas line, and you can't wait to try it out. Try to temper your enthusiasm for a few minutes and take these steps to break in your grill:

1. Operate the grill with lid closed on a low setting for about 15 minutes to burn away oil and new-paint smell.
2. Check the burner flame by carefully looking below and through the air-supply openings in the grill bottom, keeping the lid closed. A good flame should be blue coming from the burner holes with some yellow tips. Some yellow tips on flames up to 1" (2.5 cm) in length are acceptable as long as no carbon or soot deposits appear. If flames are almost all yellow in color, rather than bluish red, and irregular, the oil residue may not be completely burned off, or the venturi—the tubes through which gas is supplied—may not be properly positioned over the holes.
3. Allow the grill to cool. If necessary, reposition the venturi tubes over the valve by following the instructions in your owner's manual.

CLEANING YOUR GRILL

By keeping your grill clean, you not only practice good cooking hygiene, you protect your grill from blockages and from rust due to water in grease, propane, and other sources. Follow these steps to clean your grill after use:

1. Using a gas grill, turn the burner-control knob(s) to off.

2. Stand away from the grill.
3. Allow the fire to burn out.
4. After the fire is out and the gas grill is cool, shut off the fuel-supply valve at the fuel source.
5. Wipe the inside of the lid while warm with soapy water to remove carbon buildup.
6. Inspect and clean the burner regularly, removing grill components from a gas grill bottom if necessary to get to the burner inside.
7. If using a gas grill, check for damage to the gas cylinder, cylinder valve, gas-supply hose, burner valve, and burner, and replace damaged parts with factory-authorized parts before operating the appliance again.
8. After cooking on a charcoal grill, allow the ashes to cool for forty-eight hours or carefully soak them with water. Wrap cooled ashes in foil and place them in an empty noncombustible container for disposal. Clear ash and residue before cooking again on your charcoal grill.

Cleaning Internal Parts

Parts of your gas grill might become clogged or coated with cooking residue, outside dirt, or the nests and webs of insects. Blockages may affect the supply of gas and the look of the flame from the burners. Here's how to clean the main internal parts of your gas grill:

- Use a wire bristle brush to clean the burner surface.
- Use a straightened paper clip to remove debris from the small burner ports.
- If you suspect the venturi tubes are blocked by webs or other debris, disconnect the fuel source, detach and remove the burner from the grill bottom, and inspect the venturi tubes. To clean them, insert a long pipe cleaner or spray water into the tubes to loosen and remove blockages. Use care to avoid damaging the screens in the tubes.
- Clean blocked valve orifices behind the control panel valves by unscrewing the orifices from the

rear of the gas-control valve; wash them out and blow air through the small end holes. Replace the orifices into the valve ends when dry and replace the burner assembly into the grill bottom after it is clean, making sure the valve orifices are inside the venturi tubes. Secure the burner to the grill bottom, and reconnect igniter wires.

- When finished cleaning the parts of your grill, replace all parts inside the grill, reconnect the fuel cylinder to the grill, and inspect the condition and position of the gas-supply hose.

COOKING SURFACE CLEANUP

After cooking a fabulous meal, you should clean your cooking surfaces. Here are the basics of cooking cleanup on any kind of grill:

- Burn off the cooking residues in the grill. You can do this just after cooking or before you begin to cook the next time. Just fire up the grill or keep it burning, shut the lid, and set your control knobs to their highest setting for five to fifteen minutes. If you have ceramic briquettes, turn them over before you burn off. Replace these briquettes if they become saturated with grease.
- Use a brass bristle brush to clean remaining residue off porcelain cooking grids.
- Wash grids or grates and other parts of the grill with mild dish soap, a scrub brush, and hot water. Don't allow water to get into burner holes of a gas grill.

Be sure to read your owner's manual for the dos and don'ts of cleaning your grill. You'll learn what to use to clean your grill and what not to use, how to collect and dispose of grease from drippings, and how to keep the parts of the fuel system clean.

Apply a light coating of cooking oil to your cooking grids before grilling to prevent foods from sticking and leaving caked-on deposits on your grill grates.

BASIC TROUBLESHOOTING

Before using your grill or following any of these tips, read all warnings and safety precautions in your owner's manual.

The following tips should help you overcome many of your grill's most common ailments:

- Burner will not light or stay lit or has a yellow flame:
  1. Lack of fuel: Check your LP tank valve to make sure it is turned one to one and a half turns to on and check your natural-gas valve to make sure it fully on. Refill your propane tank or charcoal supply.
  2. Air in tank because it was not purged before filling: Return your tank to an authorized service station for purging and refilling.
  3. Burner venturi are clogged with spider webs or nests: Clean inside venturi tubes with a small wire brush or pipe cleaner.
  4. Burner venturi misaligned on orifices: Move venturi to proper position.
  5. Clogged or blocked orifices, or burner ports: Clean with a straight pin or paper clip and blow out.
  6. Crimped fuel-supply hose: Uncrimp hose.
  7. Faulty regulator or damaged hose: Double-check for proper and snug connections and replace parts if necessary.
  8. Burner is plugged by food particles, grease, or seasoning: Turn the grill into the wind and place the burners on high to burn off residue or let the burner cool and clean with brush, mild soap, and water, keeping water out of burner orifices.
  9. Igniter malfunction: Check for loud click when igniter is activated; check for spark in collector box. Be sure igniter knob is snapped into place on stem and if still no clicks, replace the igniter knob and igniter. Check wire connections and if still no spark, replace collector box assembly.

- Grill is not hot enough, grill gets too hot, or heat is uneven:

    1. Improper lighting procedure: Look closely at the burner flames to see if they are at least 1" (2.5 cm) long. If not, check blocked venturi (#3); clogged orifices or burner ports (#5); or connections (#7). If you have extremely cold or windy conditions, you should turn your grill to shield your cooking from the wind.

    2. Grease flares up: Trim fat from meat, reduce amounts of sauce or basting. Reduce your cooking temperature. If this does not solve the problem in a gas grill, you may have a damaged orifice or regulator. Replace damaged parts.

    3. Grease flare-ups in a charcoal grill: Move the cooking grid up and spread out the coals.

- Grill hums, whistles, or pops:

    1. Whistling noise: You have a malfunctioning regulator or damaged orifice and hear liquid propane passing through the parts. Repair damaged or malfunctioning parts.

    2. Humming noise: This is usually caused by liquid propane passing through the regulator and is noticed mostly in the spring or summer when the gas in your tank expands in hot temperatures. You may have an overfilled tank or the tank is upside down and turned on its side. Usually this noise will go away during use or you can have an LP dealer bleed some propane from the tank. Replace the hose or regulator if the sound persists and the regulator shows a leak when tested.

    3. Smell of gas: If you smell gas at any time, turn off your connections and check for leaks by applying soapy water to connections and watching for bubbles. With all parts assembled, turn the control knobs to off and open the tank valve. Check the hose and regulator connection, the dual valves, and the venturi tubes. Tighten connections and replace parts in which you find leaks.

If you can't resolve a problem, call the manufacturer's or dealer's service center for advice or consult their Web site.

GRILLING TECHNIQUES

Your modern grill is a four-in-one product, or more, depending on options. You can use your grill to sear steaks and other foods; to bake, roast, and warm like an oven; to slow cook rotisserie-style; and to cook in a pot on a stovetop side burner. Modern grill burners can be positioned to cook on either side or both sides of the grill at one time, making almost any cooking style possible.

Cook similar portion sizes together so that they all cook evenly.

STARTING TO GRILL

Before you light any grill, coat the cooking grids with cooking oil to prevent food from sticking.

Do not use gasoline or kerosene to start a fire in a charcoal grill. The wrong kind of fire starter can give your food a bad taste. Ask your dealer for a recommendation and buy the proper starter.

1. Thaw frozen meat and poultry before cooking. You can cook frozen fish and vegetables without thawing, but you risk cracking porcelain finishes by placing frozen food on very hot grates. Trim excess fat to reduce the amount of grease that will drip on your heat source and cause flare-ups. Don't leave cooking food unattended, even while slow-cooking.

2. Preheat the grill with the lid closed for five or ten minutes before cooking. Cook with the lid down whenever possible. While many people love the sight of an open grill with leaping flames and sizzling food, a closed lid will keep the grill temperatures even, save expensive fuel, improve the flavor of your food, and reduce flare-ups.

3. When using a charcoal grill, pile the coals in a pyramid, light them with a starter fluid, and let the flames die out and the coals become red with a gray ash covering before arranging the coals

around the grill bottom. If using direct heat, spread the coals in an even layer a couple of inches thick. For indirect cooking, leave a cool area with no coals—usually the center—sloping coals up to the sides of the oven.

High heat in your grill ranges from 450°F to 550°F (230°C–290°C), medium heat from 350°F to 450°F (180°C–230°C), and low heat from 250°F to 350°F (120°C–180°C). See the Cooking Time Chart (pages 272).

OPEN AND SHUT

Cooking over direct heat can be done with the lid of your grill open and the food placed right over the heat source. For indirect cooking, move the food away from the direct heat and close the lid. Both methods may be used to cook the same meal; for instance, the cook might sear chops or sausages first over high heat before moving the items to the cooler side of the grill and closing the lid to finish cooking the insides. Indirect heat cooks food evenly from all sides once the lid is closed. Use indirect cooking for foods that will take more than about half an hour to prepare, such as roasts; whole chickens, fish, and turkeys; and slabs of ribs.

Use tongs to turn foods on the grill. Never pierce foods while they are cooking on the grill, as this will dry them out.

MATCHING FOOD TO HEAT

Every food has an ideal cooking method and range of heat. For instance, a good chef wouldn't cook a potentially tough cut like pork shoulder or beef brisket over a direct fire; these meats should be cooked slowly, with indirect heat. A whole chicken can't be cooked over direct heat and should be roasted slowly, but a chicken breast can be cooked quickly over direct heat. Well-marbled beef steaks can be cooked over high temperatures because of their fat content, but venison has no marbling. Choice venison is usually cooked quickly to medium-rare, whereas larger cuts require slower cooking with indirect heat. Oily fish can be

grilled over direct heat at low or medium settings, but lean fish will cook better and stay together when cooked in foil or other wrappings. Follow each recipe carefully to match your ingredients to the heat of the grill.

THE GOOD AND BAD OF FLARE-UPS

You will want some flare-ups, caused by grease dripping onto hot coals or burners, because these will provide some flavor to your foods. But you definitely do not want too many flare-ups, which will burn and char your food. You can add a small pan of water to your grill to help keep meats moist, and replace the water as needed. You can have a spray bottle of water handy to douse flare-ups, but this may cause steam and spatters of hot water or grease, so be very careful. Always use any appliance with some degree of caution. A major grease fire can cause a hazardous situation as well as damage to the grill.

Charcoal briquettes are more popular than lump charcoal because of their even heat, but lump charcoal provides a smoky flavor. Mix the two for longer heat and more flavor.

COOKING TIMES

Leave room around your food items so they will cook evenly. It's very important, when using a charcoal grill, to move food toward or away from the grill's hot zone and to move coals around to regulate cooking intensity. To increase the heat of a charcoal grill, move the coals closer together; to reduce the heat, spread them out and partly shut the vents. Add more charcoal to a grill to keep it hot for more than about an hour, but don't pile the new charcoal on the old because this will dampen the heat. Put new charcoal around the edges of the burning coals.

Get to know your grill because individual grills may behave in slightly different ways. Cooking times in recipes will be approximate and you may want to adjust them to suit your own grill and methods.

Charcoal is ready for grilling when it has a light coating of gray ash.

HEAT SETTING

To seal in flavor and produce the right seared look for foods, set your flame to high. After searing, you will reduce your heat setting to finish the food. The best setting for finishing steak, chops, and burgers is medium, whereas the best setting for finishing a roast and rotisserie foods is low. Use the low setting to finish cooking seared thick steaks to a juicy, tender end result.

To keep the flavor in your food:

- Add salt to food after cooking to prevent drying out.
- Brush naturally lean meat, poultry, or fish with cooking oil or margarine.
- Cook small pieces of tender foods in foil.
- Apply barbecue, tomato, or sugar-based sauces no sooner than the last ten minutes of cooking.

When browning meat and cooking meals like hot dogs and burgers, use direct heat, placing your food directly over the flame. Keep an eye on your food so it doesn't burn when using this quick method.

Large dishes such as turkeys, big chickens, roasts, or ducks, are cooked over direct heat but on a low setting and in a foil pan with a corrugated bottom, with water added as needed.

If you are stir-frying food or cooking other food in a skillet, don't overdo the oil you add to the pan and limit the direct heat you use.

Some foods will burn more easily over high heat and require slow cooking. You can cook these foods over indirect heat. In a charcoal grill, this means moving your charcoal to one side of the grill and placing your food away from the direct heat. In a gas grill, adjust the burners so you have a hot zone and a cool zone for indirect cooking. Indirect cooking is slower but produces tender meats, poultry, and fish. Indirect cooking also reduces flare-ups.

Indirect heat can be used to cook meals in casseroles in ovenproof or foil pans. And, using a larger gas grill, you can use different settings for your burners to cook two or even more foods at once.

When adding briquettes to a charcoal grill, bury them in the lit coals and open the lid to let the new coals heat.

SMOKING PERMITTED HERE

If you like a smoky taste to your food, you can add wood chips to your charcoal grill or gas grill, following manufacturer's directions. In general, small wood chips are wrapped in aluminum foil and small holes are punched in the foil. The package is set on the burner element. Chips from wood like apple will give a mild flavor to food, whereas mesquite and hickory will give more robust flavors. You can purchase a smoker unit as an addition to your existing grill, with your new grill, or as a separate appliance.

CHAPTER THREE
SAUCES, MARINADES, RUBS, AND MORE

Peach and Pineapple Salsa with Fresh Tarragon, page 59

MOST PEOPLE GRILL OR BARBECUE FOOD BECAUSE THEY LIKE

the flavor it gives to their dishes. Sauces, marinades, rubs, or mops enhance this flavor by tenderizing meat, holding in moisture and juices, and adding delightful tastes that accent and complement those of the main ingredients. There are thousands of choices in these accompaniments, ranging from popular prepared products available at any supermarket to exotic preparations from specialty stores and makers to hundreds of great recipes like these. By the way, a mop, also called a baste or a sop, is a thin liquid applied several times during cooking over direct heat, to reduce moisture loss, and it's just one more category in this long list of delightful enhancers.

While mops are used for basting while cooking, marinades are used beforehand to protect food from high heat and to make them tasty, tender, and juicy. Don't let food, particularly fish or other kinds of seafood, sit in marinade longer than the instructions say or it may become mushy.

Rubs include dry ingredients such as salts, sugars, garlic, spices like black pepper or cayenne, herbs like oregano, or chile powder. Rubs can be applied the night before cooking or several days before to enhance the taste of meats. Despite the name, rubs are not rubbed into meats but simply used to coat the food. In general, rubs draw excess moisture out of meats like brisket and produce a tasty, attractive crust on grilled meats.

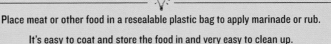

Place meat or other food in a resealable plastic bag to apply marinade or rub.
It's easy to coat and store the food in and very easy to clean up.

Sauces are the kings of flavor enhancers. There are many prepared sauces in the stores, but some of the best are kept as military-style secrets by grilling chefs. Sauces can be used while cooking or for dipping cooked food. Some sauces emulate the flavor imparted by cooking over wood chips. For instance, some sauces give a hickory, mesquite, or other wood-smoked flavor to meats, fish, or poultry, with hickory the most popular of these flavors. There are honey- or tomato-flavored sauces and on and on. The recipes in this chapter are for accompaniments that go well with a variety of dishes.

Apply sugar-based sauces such as commercial barbecue sauces
only during the latter stages of cooking, to prevent charring.

Spicy Tomato Sauce

YIELD: 4 CUPS (940 ML)

- ¼ cup (60 ml) olive oil
- I medium yellow onion, chopped finely
- 4 cloves garlic, minced
- I teaspoon (1.2 g) crushed red pepper flakes
- ¼ teaspoon (0.5 g) cayenne pepper
- ¾ cup (175 ml) dry red wine
- 2 (28-ounce [785-g]) cans whole peeled tomatoes
- I (28-ounce [785-g] can tomato sauce
- I tablespoon (16 g) tomato paste
- I tablespoon (4 g) minced fresh oregano
- ⅓ cup (13 g) packed fresh basil leaves, torn roughly
- ½ teaspoon (0.4 g) minced fresh thyme
- 2 teaspoons (9 g) sugar
- 2 tablespoons (10 g) freshly grated Parmesan cheese
- Salt and freshly ground black pepper, to taste

PREP:

In a large stockpot, heat the olive oil over medium-high heat; add onion, garlic, red pepper flakes, and cayenne pepper, and sauté until onions are just tender, about 3 minutes. Add red wine and reduce by half, then add the canned tomatoes, crushing with back of spoon. Add tomato sauce and tomato paste, and combine. Bring to a boil, then reduce heat to low; add oregano, basil, and thyme, and simmer for 30 minutes, stirring occasionally. Stir in sugar and Parmesan cheese, and cook for an additional 15 minutes. Season with salt and black pepper. Use immediately, or cool completely and refrigerate for up to 1 week. The sauce may also be frozen: once it is cool completely, place in airtight bags or containers and freeze for up to 2 months.

Basic Tomato Sauce

YIELD: 4 CUPS (940 ML)

- 2 (28-ounce [785 g]) cans best-quality peeled plum tomatoes with juice
- 4 cloves garlic, peeled and coarsely chopped
- I tablespoon (18 g) coarse salt
- I tablespoon (13 g) sugar
- ⅓ cup (80 ml) extra-virgin olive oil
- I cup (40 g) loosely packed fresh basil leaves
- 2 tablespoons (32 g) tomato paste
- ¼ teaspoon (0.5 g) black pepper
- 2 teaspoons (2 g) dried oregano
- ¼ cup (60 ml) red wine

PREP:

Place all the ingredients in a large saucepot. Bring to a boil, then stir and boil for about 5 minutes, crushing the tomatoes with the back of a spoon while stirring. Reduce heat and simmer for 20 minutes, stirring occasionally. Use immediately, or refrigerate for up to 5 days. This sauce can be made, chilled, and then frozen in air-tight containers for up to 3 months.

Fresh BBQ Sauce

YIELD: 4 CUPS (940 ML)

- 1½ pounds (680 g) plum tomatoes
- 2 tablespoons (28 ml) canola oil
- 1 medium yellow onion, chopped
- 2 tablespoons (16 g) grated fresh gingerroot
- 2 tablespoons (28 g) fermented black beans, rinsed
- 4 cloves garlic, minced
- 2 serrano chiles, seeded and minced
- ¼ cup (60 ml) rice wine vinegar
- ¼ cup (60 ml) soy sauce
- 2 tablespoons (40 g) honey
- Ground black pepper, to taste

PREP:

Place several quarts of water in a stockpot on the stovetop and bring to a boil over high heat. Place the tomatoes in a blanching basket and put the basket in the water, or simply drop the tomatoes into the boiling water. Within a minute or two, when the tomato skins begin to split and pull away from the flesh, remove the tomatoes with a slotted spoon to a bowl of cold water. When the tomatoes are cool enough to handle, peel off the skins and coarsely chop. Set aside.

Place the canola oil in a large skillet on the stovetop over medium-high heat and add the onion, ginger, fermented black beans, garlic, and serrano chiles. Cook for 8 to 10 minutes, stirring frequently. Add the tomatoes, reduce the heat to medium-low, and continue to cook for about 15 minutes. Add the rice wine vinegar, soy sauce, honey, and black pepper, and cook for an additional 5 minutes. Remove from the heat and place in a food processor. Blend until smooth. Keep refrigerated until needed. This sauce will hold over in the refrigerator for about 2 weeks.

Quick Barbecue Sauce

YIELD: ABOUT 1⅓ CUPS (315 ML)

- 1 cup (235 ml) bottled chile sauce
- ¼ cup (60 ml) olive oil
- 1 tablespoon (15 ml) lemon juice
- 1 tablespoon (15 ml) Worcestershire sauce
- 2 teaspoons (9 g) sugar
- 3–4 cloves garlic, minced

PREP:

Mix ingredients well.

Sumptuous BBQ Rib Sauce

YIELD: 6 CUPS (1.4 L)

- 2 cups (490 g) applesauce
- 2 cups (480 g) ketchup
- 1 cup (225 g) brown sugar
- ½ cup (120 ml) real maple syrup
- 3 cloves garlic
- 2 medium onions
- 2 celery stalks
- 1½ tablespoons (9 g) dehydrated chicken stock
- 1 teaspoon (3 g) dry mustard
- ½ cup (120 ml) boiling water

PREP:

Mix the applesauce and ketchup together in a large bowl. Add the brown sugar and maple syrup.

Chop the cloves of garlic finely and add to the mixture. Cut the onions and the celery into small cubes, then add to the mixture and stir well.

Add the chicken stock and dry mustard to the boiling water. Mix well until fully dissolved. Cool slightly and then add sauce to the mixture. Stir well until completely mixed.

Pour over the ribs, covering them well.

Refrigerate for a minimum of 1 hour before cooking.

Lynchburg Special BBQ Sauce

YIELD: 4 CUPS (940 ML)

- 1 large head of garlic, oven-roasted (see below)
- 3 tablespoons (45 ml) olive oil
- 1 cup (235 ml) water
- 1 cup (235 ml) pineapple juice
- 3/4 cup (175 ml) teriyaki sauce
- 3/4 cup (113 g) loosely packed, dark brown sugar
- 3 tablespoons (48 g) tomato paste
- 3 bay leaves (fresh is best)
- 1 1/2 teaspoons (2.9 g) allspice, freshly crushed
- 1/4 cup (60 ml) lemon juice, freshly squeezed
- 1 slice lemon, about 1/4" (4.3 mm) thick
- 1/4 cup (60 ml) lime juice, freshly squeezed
- 2 slices lime, about 1/4" (6.3 mm) thick
- 6 tablespoons (60 g) minced white onion
- 3/4 cup (175 ml) whiskey
- 1/2 cup (120 ml) brandy or cognac
- (1 1/4" [6.3 mm]) slice fresh pineapple, diced finely
- 1/4 teaspoon (0.5 g) cayenne pepper, or more for a spicier sauce

PREP:

Combine water, pineapple juice, teriyaki sauce, brown sugar, tomato paste, bay leaves, and allspice in a medium saucepan over medium-high heat. Stir occasionally until mixture boils, then reduce heat until mixture is just simmering. Simmer for 25 minutes. Place 12 garlic cloves in a small bowl and gently mash. Add to the sauce and whisk to combine.

Add remaining ingredients to the pan and stir. Let mixture simmer for 40 to 50 minutes, or until sauce has reduced by about half and is syrupy; be careful not to allow the sauce to boil over. Adjust seasonings to taste.

Remove from heat; remove and discard bay leaves, lemon slice, and lime slices. Let cool completely before using.

The sauce may be kept refrigerated in an airtight container for up to 4 weeks.

> **To roast garlic**—Cut about 1/2 inch (1.3 cm) off top of garlic. Cut the roots so that the garlic will sit flat. Remove most of the papery skin from the garlic, leaving enough to hold the cloves together. Place the garlic in a small casserole dish or baking pan, drizzle with olive oil, and cover with a lid or foil. Bake in a preheated 325°F (170°C) oven for 1 hour. Remove garlic and let it cool until you can handle it, then gently squeeze the cloves from their skins.

Honey Barbecue Sauce

YIELD: 2 CUPS (475 ML)

- 1 1/2 cups (355 ml) tomato juice or V8
- 1/2 cup (170 g) honey
- 3 tablespoons (45 ml) canola oil
- 2 tablespoons (28 ml) Worcestershire sauce
- 1 tablespoon (20 g) light molasses
- 1 tablespoon (15 ml) lemon juice
- 1/4 teaspoon (0.5 g) cayenne pepper

PREP:

In small saucepan, combine all ingredients and heat to boiling over medium heat. Let simmer for 5 to 7 minutes, or until sauce thickens a bit, stirring frequently.

Mustard Barbecue Sauce

YIELD: 1 2/3 CUPS (400 ML)

- 1 cup (250 g) prepared yellow mustard
- 1/2 cup (120 ml) cider vinegar
- 1/3 cup (75 g) light brown sugar, packed
- 1/4 cup (85 g) honey
- 2 tablespoons (28 ml) water
- 1 1/4 teaspoons (3.1 g) paprika
- 1 teaspoon (6 g) salt
- 3/4 teaspoon (1.4 g) cayenne pepper
- 1/4 teaspoon (0.5 g) white pepper

PREP:

In small heavy-bottomed saucepan, combine all ingredients. Heat over medium heat until mixture is boiling gently, whisking until smooth. Reduce heat to low and simmer gently for 30 minutes, stirring frequently.

This unusual barbecue sauce is good on grilled or barbecued pork or chicken.

Deep South Mustard Barbecue Sauce

YIELD: 2¹/₂ CUPS (570 ML)

- 2 tablespoons (28 g) unsalted (sweet) butter
- I cup (250 g) yellow mustard
- ¹/₂ cup (120 ml) red wine vinegar
- ¹/₂ cup (120 ml) white wine vinegar
- ¹/₂ cup (100 g) sugar
- 2 teaspoons (12 g) salt
- I tablespoon (15 ml) Worcestershire sauce
- I¹/₂ teaspoons (3 g) ground black pepper
- Tabasco sauce (optional)

PREP:

Heat a medium saucepan over medium heat and melt the butter.

Gradually add the rest of the ingredients to the pan, stirring until smooth. Lower the heat when the sauce simmers. Simmer for approximately 20 minutes, and set aside to cool.

Hot Honey-Mustard Glaze

YIELD: ¹/₂ CUP (120 ML)

- ¹/₄ cup (60 g) prepared whole-grain mustard
- ¹/₃ cup (115 g) honey
- 2 tablespoons (20 g) minced onion
- 2 tablespoons (28 ml) cider vinegar
- I teaspoon (5 g) packed brown sugar
- ¹/₄ teaspoon (0.7 g) ground chile pepper, such as chipotle

PREP:

In small saucepan, stir together all ingredients. Simmer over medium heat, stirring occasionally, for about 5 minutes, until slightly thickened. Brush over poultry or pork during the last several minutes of grilling or barbecue cooking.

Tartar Sauce

YIELD: I¹/₂ CUPS (355 G)

Serve with grilled fish such as salmon, tuna, trout, halibut, swordfish, or crab cakes.

- I cup (225 g) mayonnaise
- 2 tablespoons (30 g) Dijon mustard
- 2 tablespoons (18 g) chopped sweet pickles (drained if prechopped)
- I tablespoon (10 g) minced capers
- I tablespoon (2.5 g) finely minced fresh chives
- I tablespoon (4 g) finely chopped fresh parsley
- I teaspoon (5 ml) freshly squeezed lemon juice
- Several dashes hot sauce

PREP:

Combine all ingredients in a medium bowl and mix well. Cover and refrigerate until ready to serve.

Dilled Yogurt and Sour Cream Sauce

YIELD: I CUP (235 G)

- ¹/₂ cup (120 g) low-fat plain yogurt
- ¹/₂ cup (115 g) low-fat sour cream
- I tablespoon (15 ml) red wine vinegar
- I teaspoon (I g) dried dill weed, crushed
- ¹/₂ teaspoon (1.5 g) crushed garlic
- ¹/₈ teaspoon (0.8 g) salt
- Ground black pepper, to taste

PREP:

Place the yogurt and sour cream in a small bowl and whisk in the red wine vinegar, dill, garlic, salt, and black pepper. When well combined, cover and refrigerate until needed. Uncover and serve or transfer to individual dipping bowls.

Dilled Sour Cream Sauce

YIELD: ¹/₂ CUP (120 G)

—☼—

Serve this with simple grilled fish. It also makes a nice dip for cucumbers.

- ¹/₂ cup (115 g) sour cream
- 2 teaspoons (2 g) snipped fresh chives
- 1¹/₂ teaspoons (2 g) snipped fresh dill weed, or ¹/₂ teaspoon (0.5 g) dried

PREP:

Combine all ingredients in small bowl and mix well.

Remoulade Sauce

YIELD: 1¹/₈ CUPS (270 G)

- 1 cup (225 g) mayonnaise
- 1 tablespoon (15 g) Dijon mustard
- 2 tablespoons (30 g) sweet pickle relish
- 2 tablespoons (17 g) minced capers
- 1 tablespoon (4 g) minced fresh tarragon

PREP:

Place the mayonnaise in a small bowl and add the mustard, relish, capers, and tarragon. Stir until well combined. Place in a small jar and refrigerate until needed.

Remoulade Sauce

Black Bean Sauce

Black Bean Sauce

YIELD: ABOUT I CUP (235 ML)

- ¹/₂ cup (85 g) fermented black beans, not rinsed
- ¹/₄ cup (60 ml) mirin (rice wine)
- 2 tablespoons (28 ml) soy sauce
- I tablespoon (15 ml) canola oil
- I tablespoon (14 g) brown sugar
- 3 cloves garlic, minced
- 2 teaspoons (5 g) grated fresh gingerroot
- Pinch dried red chile flakes
- 3 tablespoons (45 ml) water

PREP:

Place the fermented black beans, mirin, soy sauce, canola oil, brown sugar, garlic, gingerroot, and chile flakes in a blender along with 3 tablespoons (45 ml) water. Puree until smooth. Place in a small jar and refrigerate until needed. This sauce will stay fresh in the refrigerator for about 2 weeks.

Creamy Horseradish Sauce

YIELD: I¹/₄ CUPS (300 G)

- I cup (230 g) sour cream
- I tablespoon (15 g) ketchup
- I tablespoon (15 ml) freshly squeezed lemon juice
- I teaspoon (5 ml) vegetarian Worcestershire sauce
- 2 teaspoons (10 g) prepared horseradish
- Pinch salt
- Ground black pepper, to taste

PREP:

Place the sour cream in a bowl and whisk in the ketchup, lemon juice, Worcestershire sauce, horseradish, salt, and black pepper. Set aside in the refrigerator for 1 hour or overnight so the flavors can blend.

Creamy Ponzu Sauce

YIELD: ABOUT ¹/₂ CUP (120 ML)

- ¹/₄ cup (60 ml) ponzu sauce (Japanese dipping sauce)
- ¹/₈ cup (30 g) sour cream
- I tablespoon (15 ml) freshly squeezed lime juice

PREP:

In a small bowl, whisk together the ponzu sauce, sour cream, and lime juice. Serve immediately or refrigerate until needed.

Mustard Cream Sauce

YIELD: ABOUT I CUP (205 G)

- ¹/₂ cup (115 g) sour cream
- ¹/₄ cup (60 g) Dijon mustard
- 2 tablespoons (28 g) mayonnaise
- I tablespoon (3 g) snipped fresh chives
- Kosher salt and freshly ground black pepper, to taste

PREP:

Combine all ingredients in small bowl and mix well before serving with beef, venison, or poultry.

Argentinian Green Sauce (Chimichurri)

YIELD: ²/₃ CUP (160 ML)

- I cup (60 g) tightly packed fresh flat-leaf parsley leaves
- ¹/₄ cup (15 g) tightly packed fresh cilantro leaves
- 4–6 cloves garlic
- 2 bay leaves (optional)
- I jalapeño pepper, stem end removed
- I teaspoon (1.3 g) fresh marjoram leaves, or ¹/₂ teaspoon (0.5 g) dried
- ¹/₄ cup (60 ml) white wine vinegar
- 3 tablespoons (45 ml) extra-virgin olive oil
- ¹/₂ teaspoon (3 g) salt

PREP:

In a food processor, combine parsley, cilantro, garlic, bay leaves, jalapeño, and marjoram; pulse until finely chopped, scraping down as needed. Add vinegar, oil, and salt; pulse until well blended. Serve at room temperature.

Leftover sauce may be refrigerated, tightly covered, for several days.

Remove the seeds and veins from the jalapeño pepper if you prefer a less spicy sauce.

Parsley Sauce

YIELD: ¹/₃ CUP (80 ML)

- ¹/₄ cup (15 g) tightly packed fresh flat-leaf parsley leaves
- ¹/₄ cup (60 ml) extra-virgin olive oil
- 2 cloves garlic, minced
- ¹/₂ teaspoon (0.9 g) finely grated fresh lemon zest
- ¹/₄ teaspoon (1.5 g) salt
- Ground black pepper, to taste

PREP:

In blender, combine all ingredients. Process until parsley is finely chopped, scraping down sides several times. Serve at room temperature.

Leftover sauce may be refrigerated, tightly covered, for several days.

A simple parsley and lemon sauce is *persillade* in France and *gremolata* in Italy.

Peanut Sauce

YIELD: ³/₄ CUP (180 ML)

- 2 tablespoons (32 g) creamy peanut butter
- 2 tablespoons (28 ml) freshly squeezed lemon juice
- I tablespoon (20 g) honey
- I tablespoon (17 g) light-colored miso
- I tablespoon (15 ml) mirin (rice wine)
- I teaspoon (5 ml) soy sauce
- ¹/₂ cup (120 ml) hot water

PREP:

Place the peanut butter, lemon juice, honey, miso, mirin, and soy sauce in a medium bowl, along with ¹/₂ cup (120 ml) hot water, and whisk together until smooth. Set aside until needed.

Peanut Sauce

Spicy Tahini Sauce

YIELD: 1¼ CUPS (300 ML)

- 1 cup (235 ml) Vegetable Stock (page 78)
- 3 tablespoons (45 g) toasted sesame tahini
- 2 tablespoons (28 ml) soy sauce
- 1 tablespoon (15 ml) rice vinegar
- 1 tablespoon (8 g) grated fresh gingerroot
- 1 tablespoon (20 g) honey
- ¼ teaspoon (0.3 g) crushed red chile flakes

PREP:

In a saucepan, whisk together the vegetable stock, tahini, soy sauce, rice vinegar, gingerroot, honey, and chile flakes. Place on the stovetop and bring to a boil. Reduce the heat to medium-low and simmer for about 5 minutes. Set aside until needed.

Lemon-Dill Salmon Sauce

YIELD: ¾ CUP (188 G)

SERVES 6

- ½ cup (115 g) mayonnaise
- ½ teaspoon (1.3 g) paprika
- 1 teaspoon (2 g) ground black pepper
- ¼ cup (60 ml) lemon juice
- 1 teaspoon (1 g) dried dill weed
- 3 tablespoons (18 g) chopped green onion

PREP:

Combine ingredients and serve as a sauce for cooked fish, or use to baste during grilling.

Spicy Tahini Sauce

Spicy Vietnamese Dipping Sauce

YIELD: 1/2 CUP (113 G)

SERVES 2

- 1 clove garlic
- 1/2 fresh red chile pepper, seeds and veins removed
- 1 tablespoon (13 g) sugar
- 2 tablespoons (28 ml) rice vinegar
- 2 tablespoons (28 ml) Vietnamese fish sauce (nuoc mam)
- 2 tablespoons (28 ml) water
- 1 tablespoon (15 ml) freshly squeezed lime juice

PREP:

With mortar and pestle, pound garlic, chile, and sugar to a smooth paste. Transfer to small bowl and add remaining ingredients; stir well to blend.

Fresh Blueberry Sauce

Fresh Blueberry Sauce

YIELD: 1 CUP (235 ML)

- 2 cups (290 g) fresh blueberries
- 1/4 cup (85 g) honey
- 1 tablespoon (15 ml) freshly squeezed lemon juice
- 1/4 teaspoon (1.5 g) salt
- 1/2 teaspoon (2.5 ml) vanilla extract

PREP:

Wash the blueberries and place them in a bowl. Use a masher or slotted spoon to crush them. Stir in the honey, lemon juice, and salt. Place the mixture in a small saucepan on the stovetop and bring to a boil over high heat. Boil for about a minute, stirring to make sure the bottom doesn't scorch. Add the vanilla. Remove the saucepan from the heat and set aside to cool.

Place a sieve over a bowl and pour the sauce into it. Mash the berries with the back of a wooden spoon to press all of the sauce into the bowl. Discard the berry pulp. Transfer the sauce to a jar and refrigerate until needed, for up to 4 weeks.

Boysenberry Sauce

YIELD: 2¹/₂ CUPS (570 ML)

- 7 cups (1 kg) fresh boysenberries
- 1 cup (200 g) sugar

PREP:

Place the boysenberries and sugar in a large pot on the stovetop over medium-high heat and bring to a boil. Reduce to a slow boil and cook, covered, for about 45 minutes. Remove the lid, reduce the heat to medium-low, and continue to cook for about 2 hours, stirring occasionally. (The berries will break up as the sauce thickens.) Remove the pot from the heat and allow to cool.

Place a large sieve over a bowl and pour the sauce into it. Mash the berries with the back of a wooden spoon to press all of the sauce into the bowl. Discard the berry pulp. Transfer the sauce to a jar and refrigerate until needed, for up to 4 weeks. The sauce may also be frozen.

Peach Barbecue Sauce

Try this fruity, tangy sauce with pork or chicken.

YIELD: 1²/₃ CUPS (400 ML)

- 1 (15-ounce [420 g]) can sliced peaches in juice or light syrup, undrained
- ¹/₂ small white onion
- 2 cloves garlic
- 1 teaspoon (2 g) minced fresh gingerroot
- 1 bottle (12 ounces [340 g]) prepared chile sauce
- 2 tablespoons (28 ml) sherry vinegar
- 1 tablespoon (7.5 g) chile powder
- ¹/₂ teaspoon (3 g) salt

PREP:

In blender, combine peaches with juice, onion, garlic, and gingerroot; process on high speed until smooth. Pour into medium heavy-bottomed saucepan. Add chile sauce, vinegar, chile powder, and salt. Heat to boiling over medium-high heat, then reduce heat so mixture bubbles gently and cook for about an hour, stirring frequently.

Cool and store in refrigerator for up to a month.

Wisconsin Cherry Barbecue Sauce

This sauce made from sour pie cherries is particularly good on venison and duck.

YIELD: 1 CUP (235 ML)

- 3 cups (465 g) pitted tart cherries (about 1¹/₄ pounds [560 g] before pitting)
- ¹/₃ cup (80 ml) orange juice
- ¹/₄ cup (40 g) chopped shallots
- 1 tablespoon (8 g) minced fresh gingerroot
- ¹/₂ teaspoon (1.3 g) ground cumin
- 1 small fresh hot pepper, minced (remove seeds before mincing for milder sauce)
- ¹/₂ teaspoon (1 g) freshly ground black pepper
- ¹/₃ cup (75 g) packed brown sugar
- 2 tablespoons (32 g) tomato paste
- 2 tablespoons (28 ml) white wine vinegar
- 1 teaspoon (6 g) salt, or to taste

PREP:

In heavy saucepan, combine cherries, orange juice, shallots, gingerroot, cumin, hot pepper, and black pepper. Heat to gentle boil over medium heat; cook until most liquid has cooked away, about 20 minutes, stirring occasionally. Remove from heat and cool slightly, then puree with food mill (or process until smooth in food processor; sauce will not be as smooth). Return puree to saucepan. Add remaining ingredients. Simmer over low heat for 20 minutes; if sauce is too thin, simmer until thickened to desired consistency.

Mop and Marinade Sauce

Mop and Marinade Sauce

YIELD: 2 CUPS (500 G)

SERVES 6

- ¹/₄ cup (60 g) granulated brown sugar
- ¹/₄ cup (60 ml) red wine vinegar
- ¹/₄ cup (60 ml) olive oil
- ¹/₄ cup (85 g) honey
- ¹/₄ cup (60 ml) real maple syrup
- ¹/₄ cup (60 ml) soy sauce
- ¹/₄ cup (60 g) prepared yellow mustard
- 2 teaspoons (10 ml) Worcestershire sauce
- 2 cloves garlic, chopped
- I teaspoon (2 g) ground black pepper
- I teaspoon (1.4 g) ground thyme
- I teaspoon (1.2 g) ground rosemary

PREP:

Mix all ingredients and pour over meat as marinade, or use as a mopping sauce on ribs or pork tenderloin, basting frequently on the grill.

Soy and Balsamic Fusion Marinade

YIELD: ABOUT ¹/₂ CUP (120 ML)

- ¹/₄ cup (60 ml) dry sake (Japanese rice wine)
- 3 tablespoons (45 ml) soy sauce
- I tablespoon (15 ml) dark sesame oil
- I tablespoon (15 ml) balsamic vinegar
- I tablespoon (15 ml) Worcestershire sauce
- I clove garlic, minced
- ¹/₄ teaspoon (0.4 g) dried tarragon

PREP:

Place the sake, soy sauce, sesame oil, balsamic vinegar, and Worcestershire sauce in a medium bowl and whisk together. Add the garlic and tarragon, and whisk to combine. Use the sauce immediately or refrigerate until needed.

Honey-Ginger Marinade

YIELD: I CUP (235 ML)

- 6 tablespoons (90 ml) freshly squeezed lemon juice
- 3 tablespoons (45 ml) dark sesame oil
- 3 tablespoons (45 ml) soy sauce
- 3 tablespoons (60 g) honey
- I tablespoon (6 g) minced fresh gingerroot
- 3 cloves garlic, minced

PREP:

Prepare the marinade in a medium bowl by whisking together the lemon juice, sesame oil, soy sauce, honey, ginger, and garlic. Use the marinade immediately or refrigerate until needed.

Raspberry Vinegar Marinade

YIELD: 1/3 CUP (80 ML)

- 2 tablespoons (28 ml) raspberry vinegar
- 1 tablespoon (15 ml) dark sesame oil
- 1 tablespoon (15 ml) soy sauce
- 1 tablespoon (15 ml) real maple syrup

PREP:

Put the raspberry vinegar, sesame oil, soy sauce, and maple syrup in a small bowl and whisk to combine. Use the marinade immediately or refrigerate until needed.

Sesame-Ginger Dressing

YIELD: 1 CUP (235 ML)

- 1 tablespoon (15 g) tahini paste
- 1 tablespoon (15 ml) sesame oil
- 1 teaspoon (5 g) packed brown sugar
- 1 tablespoon (6 g) freshly chopped gingerroot
- 1 clove garlic, minced
- 1 tablespoon (15 ml) soy sauce
- 1/4 cup (60 ml) canola oil
- 1 teaspoon (2.7 g) toasted sesame seeds

PREP:

Combine tahini paste, sesame oil, brown sugar, gingerroot, garlic, and soy sauce in a blender or the bowl of a food processor fitted with the blade attachment, then pulse to combine. With motor running, slowly add canola oil in a steady stream to emulsify. Transfer to container, add sesame seeds, and refrigerate for at least 30 minutes.

Raspberry Vinegar Marinade

Raspberry Vinegar Marinade and Garlic-Soy Marinade

YIELD: ³/₄ CUP (175 ML)

- ¹/₂ cup (120 ml) freshly squeezed orange juice
- 3 tablespoons (45 ml) toasted sesame oil
- 2 tablespoons (28 ml) soy sauce
- 3 cloves garlic, minced
- I teaspoon (0.7 g) dried basil, crushed

PREP:

Prepare the marinade in a medium bowl by whisking together the orange juice, sesame oil, soy sauce, garlic, and basil. Use immediately as a marinade or refrigerate until needed.

Spicy Plum Sauce Marinade

YIELD: ¹/₂ CUP (120 ML)

- ¹/₄ cup (75 g) plum sauce
- ¹/₄ cup (60 ml) freshly squeezed lemon juice
- 2 tablespoons (28 ml) soy sauce
- I teaspoon (1.2 g) dried red chile flakes, crushed

PREP:

Place the plum sauce, lemon juice, soy sauce, and chile flakes in a small bowl and whisk to combine. Use immediately or cover and refrigerate for several days.

Raspberry Vinegar Marinade and Garlic-Soy Marinade

Soy-Ginger Marinade

YIELD: I CUP (235 ML)

- ¼ cup (60 ml) chicken broth
- ¼ cup (60 ml) sake (Japanese rice wine)
- ¼ cup (60 ml) soy sauce
- 2 tablespoons (28 ml) teriyaki sauce
- 2 tablespoons (28 g) packed brown sugar
- I tablespoon (8 g) grated fresh gingerroot
- I teaspoon (5 ml) mirin (rice wine)
- 2 cloves garlic, minced

PREP:

Whisk all ingredients together in glass or ceramic bowl; let stand for 5 to 10 minutes before using to marinate beef, venison, or lamb.

Mirin is sweetened Japanese cooking wine. Look for it in the Asian section of large supermarkets, or in Asian specialty stores. A substitute for mirin is cream sherry.

Spicy Fajita Marinade

YIELD: I CUP (235 ML)

- ½ cup (120 ml) soy sauce
- ¼ cup (60 ml) olive oil
- ¼ cup (60 ml) wine vinegar
- 2 cloves garlic, minced
- ¼ teaspoon (0.7 g) grated fresh gingerroot
- I½ teaspoons (1.8 g) hot red pepper flakes
- ½ teaspoon (I g) cayenne pepper
- ½ teaspoon (I g) black pepper

PREP:

Whisk all ingredients together in glass or ceramic bowl; let stand for 5 to 10 minutes before using to marinate beef or chicken for fajitas.

Herb Marinade

YIELD: 1 CUP (235 ML)

- ¹/₂ cup (120 ml) vegetable oil or olive oil
- ¹/₂ cup (80 g) chopped onion
- ¹/₄ cup (60 ml) lemon juice
- ¹/₄ cup (15 g) chopped fresh parsley
- 1 tablespoon (2.5 g) chopped fresh marjoram, or 1 teaspoon (0.6 g) dried
- 1 tablespoon (2.4 g) chopped fresh thyme, or 1 teaspoon (1 g) dried
- 1 teaspoon (6 g) salt
- ¹/₂ teaspoon (1 g) black pepper
- 1 clove garlic, minced

PREP:

Stir all ingredients together in glass or ceramic bowl; use to marinate beef, venison, lamb, pork, or chicken.

White Wine Marinade

YIELD: 1¹/₄ CUPS (295 ML)

- ³/₄ cup (175 ml) vegetable oil
- ¹/₂ cup (120 ml) dry white wine
- 1 tablespoon (15 ml) lemon juice
- 1 clove garlic, minced
- 1 teaspoon (6 g) salt
- ¹/₂ teaspoon (1 g) black pepper

PREP:

Whisk all ingredients together in glass or ceramic bowl; use to marinate lamb, pork, or chicken.

Bourbon Dipping Sauce and Marinade

YIELD: 2³/₄ CUPS (650 ML)

- 1 (12-ounce [340 g]) bottle prepared or homemade chili sauce
- ¹/₄ cup (12 g) finely chopped chives
- ¹/₄ cup (60 ml) olive oil
- 2 tablespoons (28 ml) real maple syrup
- 2 tablespoons (28 ml) bourbon
- 2 tablespoons (28 ml) Worcestershire sauce
- 2 tablespoons (28 ml) low-sodium soy sauce
- 1 teaspoon (5 g) prepared horseradish
- 1 clove garlic, minced finely

PREP:

Whisk all ingredients together in small bowl. Refrigerate and use as a dipping sauce or marinade.

Orange-Lime Marinade

YIELD: ¹/₂ CUP (120 ML)

- ¹/₄ cup (60 ml) frozen orange juice concentrate, thawed
- 2 tablespoons (28 ml) canola oil
- 1 tablespoon (15 ml) lemon juice
- 1 tablespoon (15 ml) lime juice
- 1 teaspoon (1.7 g) finely grated lemon zest
- 1 teaspoon (2.7 g) grated fresh gingerroot
- 1 clove garlic, minced

PREP:

Whisk all ingredients together in glass or ceramic bowl; let stand for 5 to 10 minutes before using to marinate poultry, fish, seafood, or pork.

Honey-Bourbon Marinade

YIELD: I CUP (235 ML)

- $^3/_4$ cup (175 ml) bourbon
- $^1/_2$ cup (115 g) packed brown sugar
- 2 tablespoons (40 g) honey
- I teaspoon (5 ml) soy sauce
- I teaspoon (5 ml) mirin (rice wine)
- I teaspoon (2.7 g) grated fresh gingerroot
- Freshly ground black pepper, to taste

PREP:

Stir all ingredients together in glass or ceramic bowl; use to marinate fish or poultry.

Tomato Coulis

YIELD: 2 CUPS (470 G)

- 3 pounds (1.4 kg) plum tomatoes
- I tablespoon (15 ml) olive oil
- 2 cloves garlic, minced
- I tablespoon (4 g) minced fresh oregano
- $^1/_2$ teaspoon (3 g) salt

PREP:

Put several quarts of water on to boil in a large pot on the stovetop. Place the tomatoes in a blanching basket and put the basket in the water, or simply drop the tomatoes into the boiling water. Within a minute or two, when the tomato skins begin to split and pull away from the flesh, remove the tomatoes with a slotted spoon to bowl of cold water. When the tomatoes are cool enough to handle, peel off the skins and cut out the stem ends. Cut the tomatoes in half crosswise and gently squeeze to remove the seeds. Coarsely chop the tomatoes and place them in a bowl.

Heat the olive oil in a heavy-bottomed skillet on the stovetop. Stir and sauté the garlic for several seconds, then add the tomatoes. Cook over medium-high heat, stirring frequently, for about 5 minutes. Add the oregano and salt. Continue to cook for several minutes until almost all of the liquid has reduced, yielding a thick sauce. Set aside until needed or transfer to a jar and store in the refrigerator for several days.

Tomato Coulis

Basic Dry Rub

YIELD: ABOUT $1/2$ CUP (65 G)

- 2 tablespoons (14 g) sweet paprika
- 1 tablespoon (18 g) salt
- 1 tablespoon (15 g) packed brown sugar
- 1 tablespoon (4 g) dried Italian herb blend
- $1^{1}/_{2}$ teaspoons (3 g) ground black pepper
- $1^{1}/_{2}$ teaspoons (4.5 g) garlic powder
- 1 teaspoon (2.6 g) chili powder
- $1/2$ teaspoon (1.3 g) ground cumin
- $1/2$ teaspoon (1.5 g) dry mustard powder
- $1/2$ teaspoon (0.9 g) cayenne pepper

PREP:

Combine all ingredients in small mixing bowl. Blend well with fork (or your fingertips), making sure that brown sugar is well incorporated. Store at room temperature in tightly sealed glass jar.

Island-Influenced Rub

YIELD: $1/3$ CUP (44 G)

- 1 teaspoon (2.1 g) cumin seeds
- 1 clove garlic
- 10 whole mixed-color peppercorns
- $1/4$ teaspoon (0.5 g) allspice
- 1" x 1" (2.5 x 2.5 cm) piece lime rind (green part only)
- 2 teaspoons (10 ml) olive oil
- 2 teaspoons (10 ml) lime juice

PREP:

With mortar and pestle, pound together cumin seeds, garlic, peppercorns, allspice, and lime rind until the texture is like sand. Add oil and lime juice; mix well with spoon.

Rub mixture evenly to cover all sides of meat. Place in glass dish; cover and refrigerate for 1 to 6 hours.

All-Purpose Seasoning

YIELD: ½ CUP (100 G)

- 1½ teaspoons (1.5 g) dried thyme
- 1½ teaspoons (1.8 g) dried rosemary
- 1½ teaspoons (3 g) fennel seeds
- ¼ cup (72 g) salt
- 1 tablespoon (6 g) freshly ground black pepper
- 1 tablespoon (9 g) onion powder
- 1½ teaspoons (4.5 g) garlic powder
- 1 teaspoon (1.8 g) cayenne pepper
- 1 teaspoon (2 g) ground coriander

PREP:

In spice grinder, process thyme, rosemary, and fennel seeds until very finely chopped, or pound together with mortar and pestle until fine. Place in small jar with remaining ingredients. Cover and shake well to blend. Store at room temperature.

Southwest Rub

YIELD: ¹/₂ CUP (50 G)

- 3 tablespoons (18 g) whole black peppercorns
- I tablespoon (6 g) whole pink peppercorns
- I tablespoon (1.3 g) dried parsley flakes
- I teaspoon (2.5 g) ground cumin
- I teaspoon (3 g) onion powder
- ¹/₂ teaspoon (1.3 g) chile powder
- 3 dried chipotle chile peppers
- I bay leaf, crumbled

PREP:

In spice grinder or blender, process all ingredients until mixture is the texture of coarse meal.

Store at room temperature in tightly sealed glass jar.

Baharat (Spiced Pepper Rub)

YIELD: ¹/₂ CUP (50 G)

- 3 tablespoons (18 g) whole black peppercorns
- I tablespoon (5 g) coriander seeds
- I tablespoon (6 g) cumin seeds
- Seeds from 3 whole cardamom pods
- Small piece of stick cinnamon (about I" [2.5 cm] long)
- 2 teaspoons (3.8 g) ground allspice
- I teaspoon (2.2 g) ground nutmeg

PREP:

In spice grinder or blender, process all ingredients until mixture is the texture of coarse meal.

Store at room temperature in tightly sealed glass jar.

Freshly ground nutmeg and allspice are much more fragrant than preground spices and add extra intensity to flavor. Look for wholenutmeg fruits and whole allspice berries at gourmet shops.

Ancho Chile Rub

Yield: ¹/₂ cup (100 g)

- 3 tablespoons (21 g) paprika
- 2 tablespoons (30 g) packed brown sugar
- 2 tablespoons (15 g) powdered ancho chile
- I tablespoon (18 g) salt
- I tablespoon (6 g) freshly ground black pepper
- I teaspoon (3 g) garlic powder
- I teaspoon (3 g) onion powder
- ¹/₂ teaspoon (1.3 g) ground cumin

PREP:

Combine all ingredients in small mixing bowl. Blend well, making sure the brown sugar is fully incorporated. Store at room temperature in tightly sealed glass jar.

This rub is particularly good with lamb, and also goes well with venison and chicken.

Spanish Paprika Rub

Yield: ¹/₂ cup (70 g)

- ¹/₄ cup (28 g) hot Spanish paprika
- I tablespoon (6 g) freshly ground black pepper
- I tablespoon (18 g) salt
- I tablespoon (13 g) sugar
- 2 teaspoons (6 g) garlic powder
- I teaspoon (0.6 g) finely crumbled dried marjoram

PREP:

Combine all ingredients in small mixing bowl; blend well.

Store at room temperature in tightly sealed glass jar.

Garlic Pepper Rub

YIELD: ¼ CUP (50 G)

- 2 tablespoons (10 g) whole black peppercorns
- 2 tablespoons (10 g) whole white peppercorns
- 1 tablespoon (11 g) mustard seeds
- 1 teaspoon (6 g) kosher salt
- 2 cloves fresh garlic, minced

PREP:

In spice grinder, process peppercorns, mustard seeds, and salt until mixture is the texture of coarse meal, or pound together with mortar and pestle. Place in small bowl with garlic and mix well. Use immediately.

Rosemary Pepper Rub

YIELD: ABOUT ⅓ CUP (40 G)

- 2 tablespoons (12 g) whole black peppercorns
- 2 tablespoons (6.6) dried rosemary leaves
- 1 tablespoon (6 g) whole white peppercorns
- 2 teaspoons (12 g) kosher salt
- 1 teaspoon (1 g) dried oregano
- ½ teaspoon (0.9 g) cayenne pepper

In spice grinder, process all ingredients until mixture is the texture of coarse meal, or pound together with mortar and pestle.

Store at room temperature in tightly sealed glass jar.

Try this fragrant rub on chicken, lamb, pheasant, or quail.

Tunisian Tabil

YIELD: ½ CUP (120 G)

- 2 tablespoons (10 g) coriander seeds
- 1 tablespoon (6.7 g) caraway seeds
- 4 cloves garlic
- 2 dried hot peppers (each about 2″ [5 cm] long)
- ¼ cup (72 g) kosher salt

PREP:

Heat oven to 200°F (93°C). With mortar and pestle, pound together coriander seeds, caraway seeds, garlic, and hot peppers until the texture is like coarse sand. Stir together with salt, mixing well.

Spread mixture on small baking sheet; bake until very dry, about 30 minutes, stirring several times. Cool mixture, then grind to fine powder in spice grinder or blender.

Store at room temperature in tightly sealed glass jar.

Tabil is the Tunisian word for coriander and is recommended for beef or venison steaks, lamb chops, or fish.

Basil Pesto

YIELD: 1 CUP (260 G)

- 2 cups (85 g) fresh basil leaves
- ½ cup (120 ml) extra-virgin olive oil
- ¼ cup (35 g) pine nuts, toasted
- 4 cloves garlic, chopped
- ½ cup (50 g) finely grated Parmesan cheese
- Pinch salt
- Lemon slice

PREP:

In a food processor or blender, puree the basil with ¼ cup (60 ml) of the olive oil, and the pine nuts and garlic. With the machine running, add the remaining olive oil in a thin stream to form a smooth paste. If the paste is too thick, add additional olive oil, a tablespoon (15 ml) at a time. Add the Parmesan cheese and salt, and pulse to combine. Use immediately or transfer to a small jar. Place a lemon slice over the top, cover, and refrigerate or freeze until needed.

Mint Pesto

YIELD: ²/₃ CUP (175 G)

- 2 cups (100 g) loosely packed fresh mint leaves
- ½ cup (30 g) loosely packed fresh flat-leaf parsley
- ½ cup (120 ml) extra-virgin olive oil
- 2 cloves garlic, chopped
- 1 tablespoon (15 ml) freshly squeezed lemon juice
- Pinch salt
- Lemon slice

PREP:

In a food processor or blender, puree the mint and parsley with ¼ cup (60 ml) of the olive oil and the garlic. With the machine running, add the remaining olive oil and the lemon juice in a thin stream to form a smooth paste. Add the salt and pulse to combine. If the paste is too thick, add additional olive oil, a tablespoon (15 ml) at a time. Use immediately or transfer to a small jar. Place a lemon slice over the top, cover, and refrigerate until needed.

Basil Pesto

Peach and Blueberry Salsa

YIELD: 4 CUPS (960 G)

- 2 medium white peaches, peeled, pitted, and diced
- $\frac{1}{3}$ cup (50 g) blueberries, halved
- 2 green onions, minced
- I tablespoon (15 ml) olive oil
- I teaspoon (5 ml) balsamic vinegar
- 2 teaspoons (10 ml) lime juice
- $\frac{1}{2}$ teaspoon (1.5 g) crushed garlic
- I tablespoon (2.5 g) minced fresh sage
- 2 tablespoons (5 g) minced fresh basil

PREP:

Gently combine the peaches, blueberries, and green onions in a medium bowl. In a separate bowl, whisk together the olive oil, balsamic vinegar, lime juice, garlic, sage, and basil. Pour over the peach mixture and toss to combine. Allow the flavors to blend at room temperature for about 1 hour before serving. Use immediately or refrigerate overnight.

Peach and Blueberry Salsa

Peach and Pineapple Salsa with Fresh Tarragon

YIELD: 2 CUPS (500 G)

- 2 peaches, peeled, pitted, and diced
- $\frac{1}{2}$ cup (80 g) diced pineapple
- $\frac{1}{3}$ cup (40 g) diced green bell pepper
- I green onion, minced
- I jalapeño chile, seeded and minced
- 2 teaspoons (10 ml) sherry vinegar
- I teaspoon (0.8 g) minced fresh tarragon

PREP:

Place the peaches, pineapple, bell pepper, green onion, and jalapeño chile in a bowl and gently toss to combine.

In a separate bowl, whisk together the sherry vinegar and tarragon. Pour over the peach mixture and gently toss to combine. Allow the flavors to blend at room temperature for about 1 hour before serving.

Pear-Cantaloupe Salsa

YIELD: 4 CUPS (960 G)

- **2 Bartlett pears, peeled, seeded, and diced**
- **2 cups (310 g) diced cantaloupe**
- **2 tablespoons (28 ml) lemon juice**
- **$^1/_2$ cup (60 g) diced red bell pepper**
- **2 tablespoons (8 g) minced fresh cilantro**
- **2 green onions, minced**
- **$^1/_3$ cup (80 ml) rice vinegar**

PREP:

Place the pears and cantaloupe in a medium bowl and toss with the lemon juice. Add the bell pepper, cilantro, and green onions. Toss to combine. Drizzle the rice vinegar over the pear mixture, then toss to combine. Allow the flavors to blend at room temperature for about 1 hour before serving. Use the salsa immediately or refrigerate overnight.

Mango and Papaya Salsa with Jalapeños

YIELD: 4 CUPS (960 G)

- I firm, ripe mango, peeled, seeded, and diced
- 2 cups (280 g) peeled, seeded, and diced papaya
- I cup (145 g) blueberries, halved
- 4 green onions, minced
- ¼ cup (10 g) minced fresh basil
- 2 tablespoons (28 ml) olive oil
- I teaspoon (5 ml) balsamic vinegar
- I tablespoon (15 ml) lime juice
- 2 cloves garlic, minced
- 2 jalapeño chiles, seeded and minced

PREP:

Gently combine the mango, papaya, blueberries, green onions, and basil in a medium bowl.

In a separate bowl, whisk together the olive oil, balsamic vinegar, lime juice, garlic, and jalapeño chiles. Pour over the mango mixture and toss to combine. Allow the flavors to blend at room temperature for about 1 hour before serving. Use the salsa immediately or refrigerate overnight.

Pear and Avocado Salsa

YIELD: 2 CUPS (500 G)

- I Bartlett pear, peeled, seeded, and diced
- I medium Haas avocado, peeled, pitted, and diced
- I large jalapeño chile, seeded and minced
- I tablespoon (4 g) minced fresh cilantro
- I tablespoon (4 g) minced fresh flat-leaf parsley
- I green onion, minced
- I tablespoon (15 ml) olive oil
- I tablespoon (15 ml) lime juice
- $^{1}/_{8}$ teaspoon (0.4 g) granulated garlic
- Pinch salt

PREP:

Place the pear, avocado, and jalapeño chile in a medium bowl and gently toss to combine. Add the cilantro, parsley, and green onion, tossing to combine.

In a separate bowl, whisk together the olive oil, lime juice, garlic, and salt. Pour over the pear mixture and gently toss to combine. Allow the flavors to blend at room temperature for about 1 hour before serving.

Smooth Tomatillo Salsa

YIELD: 2 CUPS (500 G)

- I pound (455 g) fresh tomatillos, in the husk
- ¼ cup (40 g) minced white onion
- ¼ cup (15 g) minced fresh cilantro
- I tablespoon (15 ml) freshly squeezed lime juice
- I jalapeño chile, seeded and minced
- 2 cloves garlic, minced
- ¼ teaspoon (1.5 g) salt

PREHEAT:

Preheat grill to high with a smoker box in place.

PREP:

Place the tomatillos, still in their husks, in a plastic bag and fill the bag with water. Seal and allow the tomatillos to soak for about 15 minutes.

GRILL:

Remove the tomatillos from the bag and place them on the grill. Grill for 15 to 18 minutes, turning frequently. (The husks will char slightly, but they should not totally blacken.) Remove the tomatillos from the grill and set aside to cool.

SERVE:

When the tomatillos are cool enough to handle, remove and discard the husks and place the tomatillos in a food processor. Pulse to chop and add the onion, cilantro, lime juice, jalapeño chile, garlic, and salt. Puree until smooth. Transfer to a serving bowl.

Salsa Fresca

YIELD: 5 CUPS (1125 G)

- 4 Anaheim chiles
- 2½ pounds (1 kg) pear tomatoes
- ¼ cup (60 ml) freshly squeezed lime juice
- ½ cup (80 g) minced white onion
- ¼ cup (15 g) minced fresh cilantro
- 2 cloves garlic, minced
- ⅛ teaspoon (0.8 g) salt

PREHEAT:

Preheat grill to high.

GRILL:

Place the Anaheim chiles directly on the grill and grill for 8 to 10 minutes, turning frequently. (The skins will blacken.) Remove the chiles from the grill and place in a plastic bag. Seal the bag and set aside to cool. When the chiles are cool enough to handle, peel off the charred skin and place the chiles on a cutting board. Slice the chiles lengthwise, removing the stem ends and seeds. Chop the chiles and set aside.

COOK:

Place several quarts of water in a large stockpot on the stovetop and bring to a boil over high heat. Place the tomatoes in a blanching basket and put the basket in the water, or simply drop the tomatoes into the boiling water. Within a minute or two, when the tomato skins begin to split and pull away from the flesh, remove the tomatoes with a slotted spoon to bowl of cold water.

SERVE:

When the tomatoes are cool enough to handle, peel off the skins and cut out the stem ends. Cut the tomatoes in half crosswise. Gently squeeze the tomatoes over the sink to remove the seeds, then dice the tomatoes and place them in a bowl. Drain off any juice. Add the chopped chiles, lime juice, onion, cilantro, garlic, and salt. Serve immediately or refrigerate until needed.

Jicama and Mango Salsa with Jalapeños

YIELD: 6 CUPS (1500 G)

- 2 cups (260 g) peeled and diced jícama
- I firm, ripe mango, peeled, pitted, and diced
- 2 firm, ripe kiwi fruit, peeled and diced
- ⅓ cup (55 g) diced red onion
- 2 jalapeño chiles, seeded and finely diced
- 5 teaspoons (6.7 g) minced fresh cilantro
- 3 tablespoons (45 ml) freshly squeezed lime juice

PREP:

Place the jícama, mango, kiwi fruit, red onion, and jalapeño chiles in a medium bowl and toss to combine.

Add the cilantro and lime juice, gently toss again, and set aside until needed.

Corn, Black Bean, and Tomato Salsa

YIELD: 4 CUPS (950 G)

- 3 ears fresh corn, husked
- 2 cups (360 g) seeded, diced fresh tomatoes
- 3 tablespoons (12 g) chopped fresh parsley, or 1 tablespoon (1.3 g) dried
- 2 tablespoons (28 ml) freshly squeezed lime juice
- 2 tablespoons (28 ml) extra-virgin olive oil
- 1 tablespoon (4 g) minced fresh cilantro
- ¼ teaspoon (1.5 g) minced canned chipotle pepper in adobo sauce
- ¼ teaspoon (1.3 ml) adobo sauce from pepper
- ¼ teaspoon (1.5 g) salt
- 1 (16-ounce [455 g]) can black beans, drained and rinsed
- 1 green onion, sliced thinly
- 1 clove garlic, minced

PREP:

Boil or microwave corn until cooked and set aside to cool; when cool, cut kernels from cobs. Combine kernels with all remaining ingredients in a medium bowl and stir to blend. Cover and refrigerate for at least 30 minutes before serving with grilled steaks, burgers, pork, or fish.

Mango Chutney

YIELD: 2¹/₂ CUPS (625 G)

- 3 medium green apples, peeled, seeded, and diced
- 2 medium mangoes, peeled, seeded, and diced
- I medium orange, peeled, seeded, and diced
- I Meyer lemon, peeled, seeded, and diced
- I medium yellow onion, diced
- I cup (340 g) honey
- I cup (235 ml) apple cider vinegar
- I cup (235 ml) water
- 2 tablespoons (12 g) finely diced fresh gingerroot
- I teaspoon (1.2 g) dried red chile flakes
- I teaspoon (1.7 g) whole peppercorns
- I teaspoon (1.9 g) ground allspice
- I teaspoon (3.7 g) mustard seeds
- I teaspoon (5 g) whole cloves
- I teaspoon (2 g) celery seeds
- ³/₄ cup (110 g) raisins

PREP:

Combine the apples, mangoes, orange, lemon, and onion in a large stockpot along with the honey, apple cider vinegar, and 1 cup (235 ml) water.

Tie the ginger, chile flakes, peppercorns, allspice, mustard seeds, cloves, and celery seeds in a square of cheesecloth and add to the pot. Bring to a boil over high heat, reduce the heat to medium, and simmer for 20 minutes, stirring occasionally. Add the raisins and continue to cook until thick, 20 to 30 minutes, stirring frequently to prevent scorching. Remove the spice bag. Spoon the mixture into jars and seal tightly. Store in the refrigerator for up to 2 weeks.

Tomato Chutney

YIELD: 2½ CUPS (590 G)

- I small stick cinnamon
- 5 whole allspice berries
- 6 whole cloves
- I teaspoon (2 g) celery seed
- I tablespoon (15 ml) olive oil
- I medium onion, chopped
- 2 cloves garlic, minced
- 3 pounds (1.4 kg) plum tomatoes, peeled and chopped (about 4 cups [720 g])
- ¼ cup (60 g) packed brown sugar
- ¼ cup (60 ml) cider vinegar
- ¾ teaspoon (1.9 g) ground cumin
- ½ teaspoon (3 g) salt
- ¼ teaspoon (0.6 g) nutmeg, preferably freshly grated
- ¼ teaspoon (0.3 g) hot red pepper flakes
- ¼ teaspoon (0.5 g) freshly ground black pepper
- ¼ teaspoon (0.7 g) chile powder
- ⅛ teaspoon (0.2 g) cayenne pepper

PREP:

Create spice bundle from first four ingredients in a small square of cheesecloth (or coffee filter); close and tie with kitchen string. In Dutch oven, heat oil over medium heat until hot. Add onion and cook for 5 minutes, or until golden, stirring frequently. Add garlic and cook for 1 minute longer. Add tomatoes, all other ingredients, and spice bundle. Heat to boiling, then reduce heat and simmer, uncovered, for 25 to 40 minutes, or until most of the liquid evaporates, stirring occasionally.

Crush with a potato masher until chunky and thick. Remove spice bundle and cool before serving.

Refrigerate leftovers for up to several weeks.

Grilled Red Bell Pepper Mayonnaise

YIELD: 2 CUPS (480 G)

- I red bell pepper
- I large egg yolk
- I cup (235 ml) extra-virgin olive oil
- 2 tablespoons (28 ml) freshly squeezed lemon juice
- I teaspoon (3 g) crushed garlic
- Pinch salt
- Ground black pepper, to taste

PREHEAT:

Preheat grill to high.

PREP:

Place the egg yolk in a blender and pulse briefly. With the blender running, add the olive oil in a steady stream. (The egg and oil will emulsify into a thick sauce.) Add the lemon juice, garlic, salt, and black pepper, and pulse to combine.

GRILL:

Place the bell pepper directly on the grill and grill for 10 to 15 minutes, turning frequently. Grill until the skin is charred black. Transfer the pepper to a plastic or paper bag, close the bag, and set aside for about 15 minutes.

SERVE:

When the bell pepper is cool enough to handle, peel off the charred skin and discard the seeds, stem, and white membrane. Coarsely chop the pepper and add to the blender. Pulse to blend for a few seconds to create a smooth mayonnaise. Transfer to a jar and refrigerate for an hour or up to 1 week before serving.

Pineapple-Jalapeño Chutney

YIELD: 1¼ **CUPS (315 G)**

- 1½ teaspoons (5.6 g) mustard seeds
- 1 teaspoon (2.1 g) cumin seeds
- 8 ounces (225 g) canned unsweetened crushed pineapple, drained
- 3 tablespoons (30 g) minced red onion
- 1½ teaspoons (4.5 g) minced pickled jalapeño chiles
- 2 teaspoons (10 ml) freshly squeezed lime juice
- 2 tablespoons (28 g) raw, unsalted pumpkin seeds

PREP:

Place the mustard seeds and cumin seeds in a small skillet and toast them. Place the seeds in a mortar and grind with a pestle to a coarse meal consistency, or use a small food processor.

Place the pineapple in a medium bowl. Add the toasted seed mixture along with the red onion, jalapeño chile, and lime juice and stir to combine. Set aside at room temperature until ready to serve. Before serving, stir in the pumpkin seeds.

Tomato and Green Bell Pepper Chutney

YIELD: 4 CUPS (950 G)

- 2$\frac{1}{2}$ pounds (1.1 kg) plum tomatoes
- 1 large green bell pepper, seeded and diced
- 1 cup (145 g) golden raisins
- 1 cup (60 g) minced fresh parsley
- $\frac{1}{2}$ cup (70 g) pine nuts

PREP:

Place several quarts of water in a large stockpot on the stovetop and bring it to a boil over high heat. Place the tomatoes in a blanching basket and put the basket in the water, or simply drop the tomatoes into the boiling water. Within a minute or two, when the tomato skins begin to split and pull away from the flesh, remove the tomatoes with a slotted spoon to bowl of cold water.

When the tomatoes are cool enough to handle, peel off the skins and cut out the stem ends. Gently squeeze the tomatoes over the sink to remove the seeds. Dice the tomatoes and place in a medium bowl. Add the bell pepper, raisins, and parsley. Pour off any excess liquid, and then add the pine nuts. Refrigerate until needed.

Guacamole

YIELD: 2 CUPS (480 G)

- 2 medium-ripe Haas avocados, peeled, pitted, and diced
- 2 tablespoons (28 ml) freshly squeezed lime juice
- $^1/_3$ cup (55 g) minced white onion
- 1 clove garlic, minced
- 1 medium jalapeño chile, seeded and minced
- $^1/_4$ teaspoon (0.6 g) ground cumin
- $^1/_4$ teaspoon (1.5 g) salt
- $^1/_8$ pound (55 g) cherry tomatoes, diced (about 6 cherry tomatoes)

PREP:

Place the avocados in a bowl. Add the lime juice, onion, garlic, jalapeño chile, cumin, and salt, and mash with a fork until no large chunks remain. Stir in the tomatoes. Serve immediately or set aside at room temperature for up to 1 hour.

Mexican Crema

YIELD: 1 CUP (235 G)

- 1 cup (235 ml) heavy whipping cream
- 1 tablespoon (15 ml) buttermilk

PREP:

Pour the cream into a small saucepan on the stovetop. Heat the cream over low heat to bring it to a lukewarm temperature. (Do not heat it to more than 100°F [38°C].) Stir in the buttermilk and transfer the mixture to a glass jar. Loosely set the lid on the jar, but do not tighten.

Set the jar aside in a warm place—80°F to 90°F (27°C to 32°C)— for 12 to 24 hours. (The crema will culture, becoming somewhat thick.) Stir with a wooden spoon, tighten the lid, and refrigerate for about 4 hours to chill before serving. (The crema will continue to thicken a bit as it chills.) Keep refrigerated and use within 2 weeks of preparation.

Guacamole

Roasted Garlic Aioli

YIELD: 2 CUPS (480 G)

- 3 cloves roasted garlic (see page 37)
- ¹/₂ teaspoon (3 g) salt
- I large egg yolk
- I teaspoon (5 g) Dijon mustard
- I cup (235 ml) extra-virgin olive oil
- I teaspoon (5 ml) lemon juice
- ¹/₂ teaspoon (I g) coarsely ground black pepper

PREP:

Combine roasted garlic with the salt, then mash the two together using the back of a spoon to make a paste. Whisk in egg yolk and Dijon mustard. While whisking, gradually add the olive oil in a steady stream to emulsify. The mixture will become thick, white, and creamy, like mayonnaise. Continue adding the oil until a thick, creamy emulsion forms. Add lemon juice and black pepper, and combine. Cover and refrigerate until ready to use. If adding flavorings or herbs, incorporate them before use.

Garlic-Herb Mayonnaise

YIELD: $^3/_4$ CUP (180 G)

- $^3/_4$ cup (175 g) mayonnaise
- 2 tablespoons (28 ml) freshly squeezed lemon juice
- I tablespoon (2.4 g) minced fresh thyme
- I tablespoon (4 g) minced fresh flat-leaf parsley
- 2 tablespoons (6 g) chopped fresh chives
- $^1/_2$ teaspoon (I.5 g) crushed garlic
- 3–4 drops Tabasco sauce

PREP:

Place the mayonnaise, lemon juice, thyme, parsley, chives, garlic, and hot sauce in a medium bowl and whisk to combine. Transfer to a serving dish and use immediately, or cover and refrigerate for up to 2 days.

Nutty Red Pepper Mayonnaise

SERVES 8

- 2 large red bell peppers
- $^3/_4$ cup (II5 g) walnuts
- 3 cloves garlic, chopped
- 2 cups (450 g) mayonnaise
- $^1/_4$ teaspoon (0.5 g) cayenne, or use more for a spicer blend
- Pinch sugar
- I$^1/_2$ limes, juiced and some pulp
- Salt and freshly ground pepper, to taste

PREP:

Roast the peppers on a charcoal or gas grill until the skins are blackened but the pulp is not burned. Let cool to room temperature in a tightly covered bowl and reserve the oils. Cool an additional 8 hours in the refrigerator.

In a food processor, grind the walnuts and garlic to a coarse powder. Peel the peppers and remove the seeds. Tear red peppers into strips and add to the food processor. Add all of the remaining ingredients, including the reserved pepper oils, and puree until smooth.

Refrigerate for 8 hours. This will keep for up to 4 weeks refrigerated, in a closed container.

Vidalia Onion Marmalade

Serve over beef or venison steaks or burgers.

YIELD: 1½ CUPS (350 G)

- 1 tablespoon (14 g) butter
- 2 tablespoons (28 ml) olive oil
- 2 large Vidalia onions, sliced thinly and separated into rings
- ¾ cup (175 ml) zinfandel wine
- 1 teaspoon (0.7 g) dried basil, crushed
- ½ teaspoon (3 g) salt
- ½ teaspoon pepper

PREP:

In large skillet, melt butter in oil over medium-high heat. Add onions and cook for 5 to 7 minutes, or until tender-crisp, stirring occasionally. Add wine, basil, salt, and pepper. Cook until most of the liquid has evaporated, about 5 minutes longer.

Garlic-Herb Butter

YIELD: ½ CUP (115 G)

- 1 tablespoon (3 g) snipped fresh chives
- 1 teaspoon (0.8 g) minced fresh basil
- 1 teaspoon (1.3 g) minced fresh oregano
- 1 clove garlic, minced
- ½ cup (112 g/1 stick) unsalted butter, room temperature
- Kosher salt, to taste

PREP:

In small bowl, combine chives, basil, oregano and garlic; mix thoroughly. Add pieces of softened butter and mix well with a fork. Once all butter has been added, season with salt. Place in small serving bowl and serve at room temperature. If you want to chill for later use, place on waxed paper and shape into a 1" (2.5 cm) -thick log; slice chilled log into individual servings.

Horseradish-Chive Butter

Use a pat of this zesty butter to top grilled steak or rich fish such as tuna, bluefish, or salmon.

YIELD: ¾ CUP (170 G)

- 3 tablespoons (45 ml) prepared plain horseradish
- 2 tablespoons (6 g) snipped fresh chives
- ½ teaspoon (2.5 ml) white wine vinegar
- ½ teaspoon (3 g) salt
- ½ cup (112 g/1 stick) unsalted butter, room temperature

PREP:

Place paper coffee filter (or two paper towels) in small strainer. Add horseradish; let drain for 5 minutes, then squeeze gently to remove as much moisture as possible. In small bowl, combine drained horseradish, chives, vinegar, and salt; mix thoroughly. Add in pieces of softened butter and mix well with a fork. Place in small serving bowl and serve at room temperature.

To chill for later use, place on waxed paper and shape into a 1" (2.5 cm) -thick log; slice chilled log into individual servings.

Chile-Lime Butter

YIELD: ½ CUP (120 G)

- 1 small shallot, cut into quarters
- ½ teaspoon (3 g) kosher salt
- 1 small hot red pepper, minced finely
- 1 tablespoon (15 ml) freshly squeezed lime juice
- 1 teaspoon (1.7 g) finely grated fresh lime zest (green part only)
- ½ cup (112 g/1 stick) unsalted butter, room temperature

PREP:

With mortar and pestle, pound together shallot and salt until smooth paste forms. Transfer to small bowl; add red pepper, lime juice, and zest, and mix thoroughly. Add pieces of softened butter and mix well with a fork.

Place on waxed paper and shape into a 1" (2.5 cm) -thick log; chill for at least 2 hours or as long as a day. Slice chilled log into individual servings.

Blue Cheese Butter

YIELD: ³/₄ CUP (170 G)

- ¹/₄ cup (30 g) crumbled blue cheese
- I teaspoon (3 g) onion powder
- I teaspoon (2 g) freshly ground black pepper
- ¹/₂ cup (112 g/I stick) unsalted butter, room temperature

PREP:

In small bowl, combine blue cheese, onion powder, and pepper. Mix thoroughly. Add pieces of softened butter and mix well. Once all butter has been added, place in small serving bowl and serve at room temperature. To chill for later use, place on waxed paper and shape into a I" (2.5 cm) -thick log; slice chilled log into individual servings.

Tarragon Mayonnaise

YIELD: ¹/₂ CUP (140 G)

- ¹/₂ cup (115 g) mayonnaise
- I tablespoon (15 g) sour cream
- 2 tablespoons (8 g) chopped fresh tarragon
- ¹/₂ teaspoon (2.5 ml) tarragon vinegar (optional)

PREP:

Place all ingredients in a small mixing bowl and stir to combine. Cover and refrigerate for at least 30 minutes.

Grilled Onion Relish

YIELD: I CUP (235 G)

- I tablespoon (15 ml) red wine vinegar
- ¹/₂ teaspoon (0.7 g) chopped fresh oregano
- I large red onion, sliced thinly
- 2 tablespoons (28 ml) olive oil
- Coarsely ground black pepper

PREHEAT:

Preheat outdoor grill or stovetop grill pan to medium-high.

PREP:

Combine vinegar and oregano in small bowl. Coat onion slices with olive oil and season with pepper. Grill until browned and tender, about 7 minutes per side. Transfer from grill to cutting board and let cool. When cool enough to handle, cut rings in half; combine with vinegar and oregano. Use immediately or cover and refrigerate up to 5 days.

Whole Grain Molasses Mustard

YIELD: I CUP (235 ML)

- ³/₄ cup (180 g) prepared whole-grain mustard
- I tablespoon (14 g) butter, room temperature
- I tablespoon (20 g) honey
- I tablespoon (20 g) light molasses
- I tablespoon (3 g) fresh chopped chives

PREP:

Combine mustard and butter in a small bowl, then blend with a fork until well mixed. Add honey, molasses, and chives, then stir to combine. Set aside or refrigerate until ready for use.

Tomato Topper for Burgers

YIELD: 2 CUPS (500 G)

- I medium red onion, sliced thinly
- 2 tomatoes, sliced

DRESSING:

- 2 tablespoons (28 ml) olive oil
- 2 teaspoons (10 ml) lemon juice
- I tablespoon (3 g) chopped fresh basil, or I teaspoon (0.7 g) dried
- Salt and pepper, to taste

PREP:

Soak onions in ice water for 10 to 15 minutes; drain well. Combine in dish with tomatoes. In small bowl, blend dressing ingredients with wire whisk. Pour over sliced tomatoes and red onions, and toss.

Vegetable Stock

YIELD: 10 CUPS (2.4 L)

- 2 medium unpeeled red potatoes, chopped coarsely
- 2 medium yellow onions, diced
- 1 red or green bell pepper, seeded and diced
- 2 cups (200 g) celery, chopped
- 1/2 pound (225 g) mushrooms, chopped
- 2 cups (200 g) carrots, chopped
- 6 cloves garlic, chopped
- 2 bay leaves
- 2 teaspoons (1.4 g) dried basil
- 1 teaspoon (1 g) dried thyme
- 1 teaspoon (6 g) salt
- 1/2 teaspoon ground pepper

PREP:

Put 3 1/2 gallons (13.2 L) water in a large stock pot on the stovetop over medium-high heat. Add all the ingredients. Bring to a boil. Reduce the heat to low and simmer, uncovered, for about an hour. Turn off the heat and allow the mixture to cool for about 15 minutes before straining into a separate pot. Set aside to use immediately, or transfer to a container and refrigerate for several days, or freeze for several months.

Herbed Feta Spread

YIELD: 3/4 CUP (235 G)

- 1/4 cup (60 g) cream cheese, room temperature
- 1/4 cup (60 g) sour cream
- 4 ounces (115 g) feta cheese, room temperature
- 1 teaspoon (5 ml) fresh lemon juice
- 6 leaves fresh basil, minced
- 1 tablespoon (3 g) chopped, fresh chives
- 1/4 teaspoon (0.3 g) dried oregano
- 1/4 teaspoon (1.5 g) salt
- 1/4 teaspoon (.5 g) coarsely ground black pepper

PREP:

Combine all ingredients in a bowl and mash together using a fork until well mixed. Cover and refrigerate until ready to use.

Using Sauces and Other Enhancements

Each sauce, rub, marinade, and other flavor enhancer can be used in or with a variety of dishes. This list matches these wonderful menu ingredients with some of their typical companions.

RECIPE	PAGE	SUGGESTED USE
Basic Tomato Sauce	page 34	pizza, lasagna
Spicy Tomato Sauce	page 34	spaghetti, pizza
Fresh BBQ Sauce	page 35	tofu, potatoes, scrambled eggs
Quick BBQ Sauce	page 36	ribs, steak, pork chops, chicken breasts, chicken wings
Sumptuous BBQ Rib Sauce	page 36	beef or pork ribs
Lynchburg Special BBQ Sauce	page 37	steak, ribs, pork chops
Honey Barbecue Sauce	page 37	beef, venison, pork, poultry
Mustard Barbecue Sauce	page 37	pork, chicken
Deep South Mustard Barbecue Sauce	page 38	pork, chicken
Hot Honey-Mustard Glaze	page 38	pork, chicken
Tartar Sauce	page 38	grilled fish
Dilled Yogurt and Sour Cream Sauce	page 38	grilled potatoes, vegetables, tofu
Dill Sour Cream Sauce	page 39	grilled fish, cucumber dip
Remoulade Sauce	page 39	shrimp, grilled vegetables, sandwich spread
Black Bean Sauce	page 41	Fish (oriental style)
Creamy Horseradish Sauce	page 41	fish (salmon), potatoes, eggplant, tofu, tempeh
Creamy Ponzu Sauce	page 41	oriental vegetables, chicken, fish
Mustard Cream Sauce	page 42	beef, venison, poultry
Parsley Sauce	page 42	grilled steak, chicken
Argentinian Green Sauce (Chimichurri)	page 42	grilled steak, lamb chops, chicken
Peanut Sauce	page 42	tofu, tempeh, jícama slices, celery sticks, baby carrots
Spicy Tahini Sauce	page 44	pasta, tofu, grilled vegetables (dipping)
Lemon Dill Salmon Sauce	page 44	grilled fish (or baste while cooking)
Spicy Vietnamese Dipping Sauce	page 45	beef tenderloin slices with oriental vegetables
Fresh Blueberry Sauce	page 45	ice cream, grilled fruits
Boysenberry Sauce	page 46	waffles, pancakes, French toast, yogurt, ice cream
Wisconsin Cherry Barbecue Sauce	page 46	venison, duck
Peach Barbecue Sauce	page 46	pork, chicken
Mop and Marinade Sauce	page 47	marinade or to baste ribs, pork tenderloin
Soy and Balsamic Fusion Marinade	page 47	Portobello mushrooms

RECIPE	PAGE	SUGGESTED USE
Honey Ginger Marinade	page 48	tofu
Raspberry Vinegar Marinade	page 49	root vegetables
Garlic-Soy Marinade	page 50	tofu (kebabs), squash
Spicy Plum Sauce Marinade	page 50	tofu
Soy-Ginger Marinade	page 51	beef, venison, lamb
Spicy Fajita Marinade	page 51	beef or chicken fajitas
Herb Marinade	page 52	beef, venison, lamb, pork, chicken
White Wine Marinade	page 52	lamb, pork, chicken
Bourbon Dipping Sauce and Marinade	page 52	shrimp, pork, chicken, beef, venison, doves
Orange-Lime Marinade	page 52	poultry, fish, seafood, pork
Honey-Bourbon Marinade	page 53	fish, poultry
Tomato Coulis	page 53	beef, lamb, pork, chicken
Basic Dry Rub	page 54	pork ribs, pork chops, venison, beef, chicken, turkey
Island-Influenced Rub	page 54	steak, chops, chicken breasts, small roasts
Southwest Rub	page 56	beef, venison, pork, fish, chicken
Baharat (Spiced Pepper Rub)	page 56	lamb, venison, chicken
Ancho Chili Rub	page 56	steak, chicken
Spanish Paprika Rub	page 56	steak, chicken, pork
Garlic Pepper Rub	page 57	beef, pork, venison
Rosemary Pepper Rub	page 57	chicken, lamb, pheasant, quail
Tunisian Tabil	page 57	beef, venison, lamb chops, fish
All Purpose Seasoning	page 57	beef, chicken, pork, fish, game

Mayonnaise, butters, and other spreads are typically used in sandwiches, but can be served with other dishes such as Grilled Red Bell Pepper Mayonnaise with focaccia and Portobello mushrooms.

Pesto can be served with crackers or bread but can also be paired with dishes such as grilled potatoes, vegetables, or steamed rice.

Salsas and chutneys are served as accompaniments to other dishes, as a matter of preference. For instance, you might serve Peach and Blueberry Salsa with fajitas and corn chips, or Mango and Papaya Salsa with Jalapeños with skewers of tempeh, pineapple, and Jalapeño pepper.

CHAPTER FOUR

APPETIZERS

Zesty Pita Crisps, page 91

APPETIZERS, ALSO CALLED STARTERS OR HORS D'OEUVRES,

are foods served before your big meal or at a party or special occasion. By whatever name, appetizers have become one of life's great pleasures. In fact, this whole category should be redefined because it is so extensive. Many people think so highly of appetizers, they prefer to make a meal of these tidbits. Plates of appetizers also provide a wonderful way of feeding children at a feast. Place a platter of starters and some sauces on the children's table at a party and watch their little faces light up.

Grilling has become, perhaps, the preferred way of cooking appetizers, since outdoor patio and deck gatherings have become such an important part of our social lives. And the choice of appetizers has become so international, we can visit many countries in spirit through our choice of starters. Just look at some of the thousands of hors d'oeuvres you can prepare on your grill today. Appetizers range from standbys like bacon-wrapped shrimp or scallops or smoked sausage rounds to seasoned vegetables, Italian bruschetta, Mexican chorizo, or Middle Eastern kabobs.

Indian, Chinese, American, Swedish, Mexican ... you name it, and there will be marvelous appetizers from that nation to satisfy your taste buds until the main course is ready or to keep you fueled and delighted through the entire party. There is no need to go inside when you have the ingredients and a good grill on your deck or patio. You can turn out superb appetizers using the main cooking surface, with help from pots set on side burners to prepare starters like an easy and healthy asparagus wrap, festive and casual warm potato salad with beer, or more upscale-looking char-grilled mushrooms and toast.

If you are looking for something truly exotic to begin your patio party or to surprise and enchant your spouse and children, try an Asian touch or food with a European flair.

The tapas bar has become a relatively common sight in many other countries. If you and your neighbors or relatives get together frequently for patio parties, you might take a leaf from the book on socializing in Spain. Create your own selections of appetizers and go from one home to another, sampling these tantalizing tidbits. In this chapter, you'll find enough recipes to get you off to a good beginning.

Mushrooms Stuffed with Couscous, Mint Pesto, and Walnuts

SERVES 12 (SIDE-DISH SERVINGS)

- ½ cup (60 g) chopped raw, unsalted walnuts
- ⅔ cups (150 ml) water
- ⅓ cup (60 g) uncooked couscous
- 12 large button mushrooms
- 1 tablespoon (15 ml) olive oil
- ½ cup (130 g) Mint Pesto (page 58)
- ⅓ cup (80 g) nonfat plain yogurt
- 2 tablespoons (30 g) low-fat sour cream

PREHEAT:

Preheat grill to medium-high.

PREP:

Brush any dirt from the mushrooms and carefully snap off the stem ends. Reserve the stems for another use. Lightly oil the mushroom tops with the olive oil and set them aside on a platter, gill side up. Stir the mint pesto, yogurt, and sour cream into the couscous. Fill each mushroom cavity with equal amounts of the couscous mixture and top with the toasted walnuts.

COOK:

Place the walnuts in a single layer in a dry, heavy-bottomed skillet over medium-high heat. Shake the pan frequently until the nuts are golden brown and emit a wonderful roasted aroma. Immediately remove the walnuts from the pan and set aside.

Place ⅔ cup (150 ml) water in a small saucepan on the stovetop over high heat and bring to a boil. Add the couscous, stir, cover, and remove from the heat. Set aside for 5 minutes.

GRILL:

Place the mushrooms on a grill rack and transfer to the grill. Grill for 10 minutes, until the mushrooms are moist and tender. Transfer the mushrooms to a platter or individual small plates.

Grilled Spinach Rolls Stuffed with Tofu and Feta

SERVES 6 (SIDE-DISH SERVINGS)

- 12 large leaves spinach or chard
- 5 ounces (140 g) firm-style silken tofu
- ¾ cup (115 g) crumbled feta cheese
- ¼ teaspoon (0.8 g) granulated garlic
- ⅛ teaspoon (0.3 g) freshly grated nutmeg
- Ground black pepper, to taste
- 12 long, thick fresh chives
- ½ teaspoon (2.5 ml) olive oil
- 2 lemons, cut into wedges

PREHEAT:

Preheat grill to medium-high.

PREP:

Wash the spinach and remove the thick stems, taking care not to tear the leaves. Pat them dry with paper towels. Rinse the tofu and pat dry with paper towels. Cut the tofu into cubes and place in a food processor along with the feta cheese, garlic, nutmeg, and black pepper. Pulse to combine. (The resulting mixture should still be a bit lumpy.) Place a spinach leaf on a work surface and spoon one-twelfth of the filling into the center, tuck in the sides, and roll up. Tie one of the chives around the bundle to secure it. Repeat this process to make the rest of the rolls.

GRILL:

Coat your hands with the olive oil and gently rub each roll. Place them on a cold grill tray, and then place the tray on the grill. Grill for about 8 to 10 minutes, turning, to heat through. Serve with lemon wedges.

Basil-Pesto Stuffed Mushrooms

SERVES 12 (SIDE-DISH SERVINGS)

- 12 large button mushrooms
- 1 tablespoon (15 ml) olive oil
- 1/2 cup (55 g) bread crumbs
- 1/4 cup (65 g) Basil Pesto (page 58)
- 1/4 cup (60 g) nonfat plain yogurt
- 2 tablespoons (30 g) low-fat sour cream
- 1 tablespoon (9 g) pine nuts, chopped

PREHEAT:

Preheat grill to medium-high.

PREP:

Brush any dirt from the mushrooms and carefully snap off the stem ends. Reserve the stems for another use. Lightly oil the mushroom tops with the olive oil and set them aside on a platter. Place the bread crumbs, basil pesto, yogurt, and sour cream in a bowl and mix to combine. Spoon equal amounts into the cavity of each mushroom and top with the pine nuts.

GRILL:

Place the mushrooms on a grill rack and transfer to the grill. Grill for 10 minutes, until the mushrooms are moist and tender. Transfer the mushrooms to a platter or individual small plates.

Eggplant with Ricotta and Tomato Coulis

SERVES 8 (SIDE-DISH SERVINGS)

- 2 medium eggplants
- 1/2 cup (120 ml) olive oil
- 2 cups (500 g) ricotta cheese
- 2 tablespoons (8 g) minced fresh oregano
- 1/4 teaspoon (1.5 g) salt
- Ground black pepper, to taste
- 2 cups (470 g) Tomato Coulis (page 53)

PREHEAT:

Preheat grill to medium-high

PREP:

Remove the stem ends of the eggplants. Cut them lengthwise into 1/2" (1.3 cm) slices.

GRILL:

Use a pastry brush to coat one side with some of the olive oil and place oiled side down on the grill. Grill for 4 to 6 minutes, brush the top sides with the remaining oil, turn, and grill for 3 to 5 minutes. (The eggplant should be slightly soft, with grill marks, but not completely blackened.) Transfer the eggplant to a cutting board.

Meanwhile, combine the ricotta cheese with the oregano, salt, and black pepper in a bowl.

COOK:

Place the Tomato Coulis in a small saucepan and heat over medium-low.

SERVE:

Working with one slice of eggplant at a time, place some of the ricotta mixture in the center and roll up. Repeat with the remaining slices. Place the eggplant rolls, seam side down, on a platter or individual serving plates. Pour the warm Tomato Coulis over the top.

Purple Figs Stuffed with Blue Cheese

SERVES 4 (SIDE-DISH SERVINGS)

- 8 large, firm, ripe purple figs
- ¹/₃ cup (40 g) crumbled blue cheese
- 4 thin slices rustic country loaf bread, cut into triangles

PREHEAT:

Preheat grill to medium-high.

PREP:

Cut the stem end from each fig about one-third of the way down and set aside. Hollow out the seedes pulp and place in a small bowl. Add the blue cheese to the pulp and mix to combine. Carefully stuff the cheese mixture back into the hollowed-out figs and put the reserved stem end on top of each fig.

GRILL:

Place the figs upright on the grill rack and place the rack on the grill. Grill for about 5 minutes, until the cheese begins to melt and the caps start to rise.

Meanwhile, place the bread on the grill to toast for 2 to 4 minutes, turning as necessary. Continue to grill the figs for about 2 minutes, then carefully remove using a spatula and tongs. (Do not squeeze the figs too much or you will force the filling out.) Place two figs on each serving plate and arrange grilled bread alongside.

Grilled Kalamata Olives

SERVES 16 (SIDE-DISH SERVINGS)

- 2 cups (200 g) kalamata olives
- 1 tablespoon (15 ml) olive oil
- 1 tablespoon (2.4 g) minced fresh thyme

PREHEAT:

Preheat grill to medium-high with a smoker box in place.

PREP:

Place the olives in a bowl and drizzle with the olive oil. Sprinkle with the thyme and toss to combine. Marinate for about 45 minutes, tossing occasionally.

GRILL:

Put the olives in a grilling basket and grill for 4 to 5 minutes, stirring frequently. (The olives will darken slightly and wrinkle.)

SERVE:

Remove the olives from the grill and place in a serving bowl with a smaller bowl for the pits alongside. Let the olives cool for several minutes before serving because the pits will be very hot.

Crostini with Grilled Zucchini and Eggplant

SERVES 24 (SIDE-DISH SERVINGS)

- 4 medium zucchini
- 2 Japanese eggplants
- 2 tablespoons (28 ml) olive oil
- 4 plum tomatoes
- 2 (1-pound [455 g]) baguettes
- 3 tablespoons (45 ml) extra-virgin olive oil
- 2 tablespoons (28 ml) balsamic vinegar
- 1 tablespoon (4 g) minced fresh oregano
- 1 tablespoon (2.5 g) minced fresh basil
- 1 teaspoon (0.8 g) minced fresh thyme
- ¹/₈ teaspoon (0.8 g) salt
- Several grinds black pepper, to taste

PREHEAT:

Preheat grill to medium-high.

PREP:

Remove the ends from the zucchini and discard. Slice the zucchini lengthwise. Remove the stem ends from the eggplants and discard. Slice the eggplants lengthwise. Place the zucchini and eggplants in a plastic bag and drizzle with the olive oil. Twist the bag to seal, allowing some air to remain in the bag. Toss gently to coat the vegetables evenly.

Meanwhile, remove the cores from the tomatoes and discard. Cut the tomatoes in half and gently squeeze to remove the seeds. Chop the tomatoes and set aside in a large bowl. Add the chopped zucchini and eggplant.

GRILL:

Place the zucchini and eggplant on the grill and grill for 8 to 10 minutes, turning frequently. Remove all of the zucchini and eggplant from the grill and set aside on a cutting board to cool for several minutes. When the zucchini and eggplant are cool enough to handle, chop and set aside.

Cut the baguettes into ¹/₂" (1.3 cm) slices. Arrange the slices on the grill rack in a single layer. Grill for about 2 minutes per side until the bread is lightly browned and crisp on the outside, but still soft and chewy on the inside, creating perfect crostini. Set aside.

SERVE:

In a small bowl, whisk together the extra-virgin olive oil, balsamic vinegar, oregano, basil, thyme, salt, and black pepper. Drizzle over the tomato and grilled vegetable mixture and toss to combine. Place a spoonful of the vegetable mixture on top of each slice of crostini and serve on a platter or allow your guests to serve themselves, mounding the vegetable mixture onto single slices of crostini.

Crostini with Fresh Tomatoes, Basil, and Garlic

SERVES 12 (SIDE-DISH SERVINGS)

- **3 medium tomatoes**
- **I cup (45 g) fresh basil**
- **2 tablespoons (17 g) chopped capers**
- **2 tablespoons (28 ml) extra-virgin olive oil**
- **2 teaspoons (10 ml) freshly squeezed lemon juice**
- **3 cloves garlic, minced**
- **Pinch salt**
- **I (I-pound [455 g]) baguette**

PREHEAT:

Preheat grill to medium.

PREP:

Cut the tomatoes in half crosswise and squeeze out the seeds. Cut out and discard the stem ends. Dice the tomatoes and place in a bowl. Chop the basil or roll up the leaves and cut chiffonade-style into paper-thin shreds. Add the basil to the bowl along with the capers and toss to combine.

In another bowl, whisk together the olive oil, lemon juice, garlic, and salt. Drizzle over the tomato mixture and toss to combine. Set aside at room temperature until ready to serve.

GRILL:

Cut the baguette into ½" (1.3 cm) slices. Arrange the bread on the grill rack in a single layer. Grill for 1 to 2 minutes per side until the bread is lightly browned and crisp on the outside but still soft and chewy on the inside, creating perfect crostini. Set aside.

SERVE:

Place a spoonful of the tomato mixture on top of each slice of crostini and serve on a platter or allow your guests to serve themselves, mounding the tomato mixture onto single slices of crostini.

The Real Bruschetta (Grilled Italian Garlic Bread)

SERVES 4

- ¹/₂ loaf day-old hearty Italian bread
- 4 large cloves garlic
- ¹/₄ cup (60 ml) extra-virgin olive oil
- Kosher salt

PREHEAT:

Preheat grill to medium-high.

PREP:

Slice bread about ¹/₂" (1.3 cm) thick. Peel garlic and cut each clove in half crosswise (not lengthwise), so you have a total of eight short pieces of garlic. Place the oil in a small bowl, and have a pastry brush handy.

GRILL:

Arrange bread on grate over heat. Cook for 2 to 3 minutes per side, turning once or twice and rearranging on grill as necessary so all pieces cook evenly. The bread should be nicely toasted and brown, with perhaps a few lightly charred edges; watch bread carefully as it burns easily. Remove bread from grill and, working quickly, rub each side of each toast with the cut side of a garlic clove. Brush each side of each toast with a little oil, and sprinkle 1 side with a bit of salt.

The correct loaf to use for bruschetta is hearty Italian or French country-style bread, with a dense, chewy texture and a firm crust. Never try to make bruschetta with soft bread; it will fall apart. Loaves typically weigh about 1¹/₂ pounds (680 g). A typical slice will be about 5" (13 cm) across and 3" (7.5 cm) high. The loaf you use should be day-old so it is even more firm; if you like, you can lay the slices out on the counter for a few hours to dry somewhat before cooking.

Grilled Vegetables and Pasta

SERVES 6

- 1 yellow summer squash
- 1 green zucchini squash
- 4 red peppers
- 2 onions
- $1/2$ pound (225 g) mushrooms
- $1/4$ cup (60 ml) olive oil
- 1 (1-pound [455 g]) package small shell pasta
- 4 tomatoes
- 2 tablespoons (5 g) roughly chopped fresh basil
- 1 tablespoon (6 g) chopped green onion or chives
- Salt and pepper, to taste

PREHEAT:

Preheat grill to medium-high.

PREP:

On auxiliary grill burner, bring salted water to boil per pasta package instructions. Cut squash, peppers, onions, and mushrooms into quarters. Brush these vegetables with 2 tablespoons (28 ml) oil. Slice tomatoes.

GRILL:

Grill squash, onions, and peppers for 5 minutes on each side. Grill mushrooms for 5 minutes total. Slice vegetables after cooking to bite-size portions.

COOK:

Boil pasta while vegetables are grilling, as per package instructions. Drain pasta and return to pot.

SERVE:

Add sliced vegetables, remaining olive oil, chopped basil and green onion, and salt and pepper to taste to pasta in the pot. Toss lightly to combine flavors. Remove from pot to serving bowl. Serve warm or at room temperature.

Crusty Grilled Bread with the Works

6 TO 8 SERVINGS

- I large loaf French bread
- ¹/₃ cup (75 g) butter, softened
- ¹/₃ cup (80 ml) olive oil
- 3–4 slices bacon, cooked and crumbled
- 2 cloves garlic, minced
- I cup (115 g) shredded Colby cheese
- I cup (115 g) shredded mozzarella cheese

PREHEAT:

Preheat grill to high.

PREP:

Slice bread about three-quarters of the way through, cutting vertically but angling the cuts somewhat so each slice is wider than if the bread were cut straight across. Place bread on double layer of foil that is a good bit longer than the loaf. In small bowl, blend together butter, oil, bacon, and garlic. Spread slices with butter mixture. Mix together Colby and mozzarella cheeses, and sprinkle between slices. Wrap loaf well with foil.

GRILL:

Place wrapped bread on grate away from heat. Cover and cook for about 8 minutes or until cheeses melt; be careful not to burn the bread.

Black Bean Dip

4 SERVINGS

- 2 tablespoons (20 g) minced garlic
- 2 serrano chiles, seeded and minced
- I (14-ounce [400 g]) can black beans, rinsed and drained
- I tablespoon (15 ml) rice vinegar
- 2 tablespoons (28 ml) olive oil
- 2 tablespoons (8 g) chopped fresh cilantro
- I green onion, chopped
- I tablespoon (7 g) ground cumin
- 3 drops chipotle pepper sauce (Tabasco sauce, or your brand of choice)

PREP:

Add all ingredients to bowl of food processor fitted with blade attachment. Process until all ingredients are chopped and well combined. Cover and chill until ready to serve.

Aussie Chips with Sweet Chile Sauce

SERVES 8 (SIDE-DISH SERVINGS)

- 4 russet potatoes
- ¼ cup (60 ml) canola oil
- 1 teaspoon (3 g) crushed garlic
- ½ teaspoon (3 g) salt
- ¼ cup (60 ml) sweet chile sauce
- ¼ cup (60 g) Mexican Crema (page 71)

PREHEAT:

Preheat grill to medium-high.

PREP:

Scrub the potatoes but do not peel them. Cut the potatoes lengthwise into medium-thick "french-fry" wedges. In a small bowl, whisk together the canola oil, garlic, and salt. Place the potatoes in a plastic bag and drizzle with the oil mixture. Twist the bag to seal, allowing some air to remain in the bag. Toss gently to coat the potatoes evenly. Remove from bag when ready to grill.

GRILL:

Place the potatoes on the grill and grill for 12 to 16 minutes, turning frequently, until they are crisp on the outside and tender and moist on the inside. Transfer the potatoes to a serving platter.

SERVE:

Place the sweet chile sauce and Mexican Crema in small dipping bowls. Pass the potatoes, allowing diners to dip in the sauces as desired.

Zesty Pita Crisps

SERVES 4 TO 6

- 4 whole wheat pita breads
- ³⁄₈ cup (90 ml) olive oil
- 4 cloves garlic, minced
- 1 teaspoon (1 g) dried oregano
- ½ teaspoon (3 g) kosher salt
- ¼ teaspoon (0.5 g) cayenne pepper
- ¼ teaspoon (0.5 g) freshly ground black pepper

PREHEAT:

Preheat grill to medium-high.

PREP:

Carefully break open the pitas. In small bowl, combine remaining ingredients, stirring to blend. Brush both sides of the pita slices with oil mixture. Place on grate over heat. Cook for 1 to 2 minutes per side, or until crisp and nicely toasted. Remove from grill and set aside to cool. Cut into triangle-sized pieces before serving.

Dove Breast Appetizers

SERVES 8 TO 10

- 20 boneless, skinless dove breast halves (about 1 pound [455 g] total)
- 1 cup (235 ml) Italian-style vinaigrette dressing
- 10 slices bacon, cut in half
- 20 toothpicks

PREHEAT:

Preheat grill to high.

PREP:

Soak twenty toothpicks in cold water for 30 minutes.

MARINATE:

In large resealable plastic bag, combine dove breasts and dressing, turning to coat. Refrigerate for at least 4 hours, turning bag occasionally.

COOK:

Meanwhile, precook bacon slices for a few minutes in the microwave; bacon should be about half-cooked but still quite pliable. Refrigerate until needed. Wrap a strip of bacon around each dove breast and secure with a toothpick.

GRILL:

Place dove breasts on grate over heat and cook for 8 to 10 minutes, turning often until the meat is pink inside.

As a variation, insert a jalapeño chile half and onion slice, water chestnut, or piece of pepper cheese before wrapping bacon around dove breasts.

Lettuce Wraps with Grilled Red Peppers and Kalamata Olives

SERVES 6

- 1 large red bell pepper
- 12 large butter lettuce leaves
- 1/2 cup (115 g) crème fraîche
- 4 ounces (115 g) soft goat cheese
- 1/4 cup (25 g) chopped kalamata olives
- 2 tablespoons (8 g) snipped fresh oregano
- Ground black pepper, to taste

PREHEAT:

Preheat grill to high.

PREP:

Wash the lettuce leaves, carefully spin them dry in a salad spinner or shake off the water, and place them on a towel to dry. Set aside.

GRILL:

Place the bell pepper directly on the grill and grill for 10 to 15 minutes, turning frequently. (The skin will be charred black.) Transfer the pepper to a plastic or paper bag, close the bag, and set aside for about 15 minutes. When the bell pepper is cool enough to handle, peel off the charred skin and discard the seeds, stem, and white membrane.

SERVE:

Chop the pepper and place it in medium bowl along with the crème fraîche and goat cheese. Mix with a wooden spoon to combine. Add the olives, oregano, and black pepper and then mix to combine. Place a lettuce leaf, cupped side up, on a work surface. Spoon one-twelfth of the pepper mixture slightly off-center on the leaf. Wrap in the sides of the leaf and place seam side down on a serving plate. Repeat the process with the remaining leaves and pepper mixture. If not serving immediately, you can hold them over in the refrigerator for an hour or so.

Lettuce Wraps with Grilled Red Peppers and Kalamata Olives

CHAPTER FIVE
BEEF, PORK, AND LAMB

Dijon-Style T-Bone Steak, page 96

BEEF IN THE FORM OF STEAKS, BURGERS, ROASTS, AND ALL

other cuts makes for great grilling. Turn the grill on high, oil the beef lightly to sear and prevent sticking, season, and your guests will rave about your culinary skills.

Bone, trim, tie, and flavor the meat before cooking. Leave about ⅛" (0.3 cm) of fat to keep the meat moist. Slash surface fat every inch (2.5 cm) to keep the meat from curling during cooking. Deboned beef may need tying with twine before cooking. Some tougher cuts may be tenderized by pounding or with marinades and rubs.

Steaks and other cuts are usually seared over high heat to help preserve flavor and juiciness. To turn and sear both sides evenly, use tongs or a spatula instead of a fork, which will damage the meat and let juice escape. It's best to cook steaks, after the initial searing, with indirect, reduced heat, with the grill lid closed as much as possible to lock in taste and prevent flare-ups. Adjust the heat after searing, as the recipe instructs, to cook the inside of the steak or other cut. Let the cooked steak "rest" for five minutes on a plate before eating.

For safety, it's best to cook a steak and other beef to a medium-rare stage or 145°F (65°C) at the center, to kill harmful bacteria. This is the recommended safe temperature for whole-muscle meats such as steaks and roasts, as the bacteria that pose a threat exist on the surface of the meat. However, with ground meat, where the potentially contaminated "surface" is mixed into the interior, the safe temperature is considered to be no lower than 160°F (80°C). When transporting meat from the grill, place cooked meat on a clean plate and not on the plate you used to transport raw meat.

> While a grill may heat to 650°F (345°C), beef and other meat will cook at 300°F (150°C) or more.

Lamb and pork provide an alternative to steak or hamburger. The most tender cut of lamb is the chop cut from the loin, with rib chops a close second choice. Prepare lamb for the grill the same way as steak. A rub with black pepper is enough to ready the lamb cut for the grill. A 1" (2.5 cm) -thick lamb chop will take about 4 or 5 minutes to cook to medium-rare when placed 5" or 6" (13 or 15 cm) above hot coals or a hot flame. Using a medium heat setting, a 1" (2.5 cm) chop will need about 6 or 7 minutes on one side and 4 to 5 minutes on the other, if the meat is approximately 8" (20 cm) above the fire.

Pork is just as easy to grill as beef or lamb, using the same techniques. Trim fat as you might with other meats before grilling. It is better to use spices or herbs rather than sauces to enhance the flavor of pork. Lightly oil the meat to avoid sticking, sear the outside, and cook pork to an interior temperature of 160°F (71°C).

When cooking pork sausages, poach them for a few minutes before grilling. Don't puncture the casing, as this may cause the sausage to become dry when cooked.

Flank Steak

SERVES 4

- ¹/₂ cup (120 ml) soy sauce
- 2 tablespoons (28 ml) oil
- 2 tablespoons (40 g) honey, melted
- 1 tablespoon (15 ml) vinegar, wine or white
- 1 teaspoon (2 g) minced gingerroot
- 1 clove garlic, minced
- 1¹/₂ pounds flank steak

PREP:

Place all the ingredients together in a bowl or dish and stir. Let steak marinade for hour or more (but not overnight). Grill steak strips for 5 to 10 minutes a side, using a wire cage if necessary so the strips don't fall into the fire.

Dijon-Style T-Bone Steak

SERVES 6

- 6 T-bone steaks (about 12 ounces [340 g] each), trimmed of excess fat
- ¹/₃ cup (80 g) Dijon mustard
- 2 tablespoons (28 ml) Italian-style vinaigrette dressing
- 1 tablespoon (15 ml) lemon juice
- 1 tablespoon (7 g) chopped green onion
- 1 tablespoon (10 g) minced fresh garlic
- 1 teaspoon (1.8 g) cayenne pepper
- 1 tablespoon (20 g) honey
- Kosher salt to taste

PREHEAT:

Preheat grill to high.

MARINATE:

Score edges of steak to prevent them from curling while cooking; place in shallow, nonmetallic dish or resealable plastic bag. In small bowl, whisk together mustard, dressing, lemon juice, green onion, garlic, pepper, and honey. Pour mustard mixture over steaks, turning to coat. Cover and refrigerate for about 2 hours, turning several times so marinade penetrates steaks evenly.

GRILL:

Remove steaks from marinade, discarding marinade. Place steaks on grate over heat and sear for 2 to 3 minutes per side. Check for doneness; depending on thickness of steaks, they may need only a few minutes, more cooking for medium-rare. When done, remove from grill, season with salt, and let stand for a few minutes before serving.

Blue Cheese Butter Steak

SERVES 6

- ¹/₂ cup (120 ml) red wine vinegar
- ¹/₂ cup (120 ml) olive oil
- 2 teaspoons (2.8 g) ground thyme
- 1 clove garlic, chopped
- 1 teaspoon (2 g) ground pepper
- 6 rib eye steaks
- ¹/₂ cup (112 g [1 stick]) unsalted butter

- ¹/₂ cup (60 g) crumbled Stilton (blue) cheese
- 2 teaspoons (2.7 g) chopped fresh parsley
- 3 tablespoons (24 g) chopped fresh walnuts

PREP:

Mix vinegar, oil, thyme, garlic, and pepper. Pour over steaks and let marinate for 30 minutes on the countertop or 3 hours in the fridge.

Meanwhile, combine butter, cheese, parsley, and walnuts, and set aside.

Grill steaks and top with Stilton butter prior to serving.

Italiano Greek Steaks with Grilled Fresh Salsa

SERVES 6

- 6 (8–10-ounce [225–280 g]) sirloin steaks, 1" (2.5 cm) thick
- $^1/_3$ cup (80 ml) Italian salad dressing
- 2 tablespoons (28 ml) lime juice
- 2 teaspoons (6 g) minced garlic
- 1 tablespoon (1.8 g) Greek seasoning
- 1 cup (180 g) chopped tomato, drained
- $^1/_4$ cup (40 g) finely chopped onion
- 1 teaspoon (3 g) finely chopped seeded jalapeño chile
- $^1/_4$ cup (35 g) chopped peeled, cucumber
- $^1/_4$ cup (60 ml) lime juice
- $^1/_4$ teaspoon (1.5 g) salt
- 4 fresh pineapple slices, $^1/_2$" (1.3 cm) thick
- 6 fresh lemon slices, $^1/_4$" (.6 cm) thick

PREHEAT:

Preheat grill to medium-high.

MARINATE:

Place steaks in a large resealable bag. Stir together next four ingredients in a small bowl. Pour over steaks. Seal, then shake well. Marinate for 2 hours.

PREP:

Stir next six ingredients together in a medium bowl. Cover and chill.

GRILL:

Heat gas grill to medium-high heat. Spray grates with nonstick cooking spray. Grill pineapple and lemon slices for 3 to 4 minutes per side, until grill marks appear. Remove steaks from marinade and discard marinade. Grill steaks 6 to 8 minutes per side, or to desired doneness.

SERVE:

Remove peel from lemon and discard peel. Chop lemon and pineapple. Stir into salsa.

Serve steaks with $^1/_3$ to $^1/_2$ cup (85 to 125 g) salsa on top of each.

Mesquite-Grilled Chuck Eye Steaks

SERVES 6

- 1 cup (235 ml) cider vinegar
- 1/2 cup (120 ml) tomato or vegetable juice
- 1 medium lemon, sliced and seeded
- 1 tablespoon (9 g) sugar
- 2 medium onions, sliced
- 1/4 cup (60 ml) hot pepper sauce, or less or more to taste
- Ground black pepper, to taste
- 1 tablespoon (2 g) dried sage, crushed
- 3 tablespoons (48 g) tomato paste
- 6 boneless chuck eye steaks, 1" (2.5 cm) thick
- 1 cup (225 g) mesquite chips

PREHEAT:

Preheat grill to medium-high.

MARINATE:

In a saucepan, combine vinegar, tomato juice, lemon, sugar, onions, hot pepper sauce, pepper, sage, and tomato paste. Bring to a boil, reduce heat, and simmer for 10 to 15 minutes. Let cool to room temperature. Place steaks in a large nonreactive dish or resealable plastic bag. Pour marinade over them, cover or close, and refrigerate overnight.

Soak 1 cup (225 g) mesquite chips in water to cover.

GRILL:

Meanwhile, light coals in the grill and let them burn down until covered by a film of gray ash. Drain mesquite chips and distribute evenly over hot coals. Place grill rack in place and rub with an oil-soaked cloth. Drain steaks, reserving marinade in a saucepan. Bring marinade to a boil and cook, uncovered, while grilling steaks. Strain and set aside.

Pat steaks with paper towels to remove some of the moisture. Arrange steaks on the grill and cook for 6 to 8 minutes without disturbing. Turn steaks and grill for another 6 to 8 minutes, or until desired doneness.

Serve sauce on the side.

Teriyaki Rib Steaks with Cucumber Sauce

SERVES 4

- 4 rib steaks (about 8 ounces [225 g] each)
- 1 cup (235 ml) bottled teriyaki sauce
- 1 cup (230 g) sour cream
- 1/2 cup (70 g) finely chopped peeled and seeded cucumber
- 1/2 cup (80 g) minced red onion
- 1/4 cup (15 g) chopped fresh mint
- 1 teaspoon (2.5 g) ground cumin
- 1 teaspoon (2 g) ground coriander
- Sea salt, preferably sel gris, and freshly ground black pepper, to taste

PREHEAT:

Preheat grill to 375°F (190°C).

MARINATE:

Marinate steaks in refrigerator for several hours, using your favorite bottled teriyaki sauce.

PREP:

In a bowl, combine sour cream, cucumber. red onion, mint, cumin, and coriander. Mix well, cover, and chill.

GRILL:

Remove steaks from marinade and pat with paper towel to dry. Season steaks on both sides with a little salt and freshly ground pepper to taste. Add steaks to grill and cook for about 10 minutes for medium-rare or 15 minutes for medium-well.

Serve with cucumber sauce.

BBQ Beef Ribs

SERVES 4

- 2 pounds (905 g) beef ribs
- ¼ cup (80 g) peach preserves
- ½ cup (120 ml) water
- Juice of 1 lemon
- 1½ tablespoons (23 g) brown sugar
- 1 tablespoon (15 ml) vinegar
- ½ teaspoon (1.3 g) paprika
- 2 tablespoons (28 ml) Worcestershire sauce
- Freshly ground black pepper

PREHEAT:

Preheat grill to 450°F (230°C).

GRILL:

Place the ribs on a rack in a shallow baking pan and roast in oven for 30 minutes. Remove the ribs and rack from pan and pour off the fat. Reduce oven heat to 350°F.

COOK:

In a small saucepan, combine all other ingredients and cook over medium heat until thickened, stirring constantly. Set sauce aside. Return ribs to the pan, and pour the sauce over them.

GRILL:

Grill uncovered, basting occasionally, until ribs are tender, about 1 hour.

Barbecued Meatloaf

SERVES 6

- ½ cup (55 g) Italian-seasoned or plain bread crumbs
- ¼ cup (65 g) barbecue sauce
- ¼ cup (40 g) finely chopped onion
- 1 egg
- 1 teaspoon (6 g) garlic salt, seasoned salt, or plain salt
- ½ teaspoon (1.5 g) dry mustard
- 1 pound (455 g) lean ground beef, buffalo, or venison
- 8 ounces (225 g) ground pork
- 8 ounces (225 g) ground veal
- 2 tablespoons (30 g) ketchup
- 1 tablespoon (15 ml) real maple syrup or (15 g) packed brown sugar
- ¼ teaspoon (.6 g) chipotle powder or paprika

PREHEAT:

Preheat grill to high.

PREP:

Cover metal baking dish inside and out with foil (make sure the seam is on the outside, so the inside of the pan is protected from burning juices); set aside. In large mixing bowl, combine bread crumbs, barbecue sauce, onion, egg, salt, and mustard powder; mix very well and let stand for 5 minutes. Add beef, pork, and veal; mix gently but thoroughly with your hands. In prepared baking dish, pack meat mixture firmly into a rounded loaf that is about 5" (13 cm) wide and 7" or 8" (17.5 or 20 cm) long.

GRILL:

Place meatloaf on grate away from heat; cover grill and cook for 30 minutes, rotating pan once or twice. Meanwhile, combine ketchup, syrup, and chipotle powder; mix well. When meatloaf has cooked for 30 minutes, brush ketchup mixture on top of meatloaf; re-cover grill and cook for 30 to 40 minutes longer, or until center of meatloaf reaches 160°F (71°C). Use spatula to transfer meatloaf to serving plate; let stand for 10 minutes before slicing.

BBQ Beef Ribs

Basic Grilled Burger

SERVES 4

- 1½ pounds (680 g) ground beef, buffalo, lamb, or venison (85% lean works well)
- 1 teaspoon (6 g) salt, garlic salt, or seasoned salt
- ¼ teaspoon (0.5 g) black pepper or cayenne pepper
- 4 split hamburger rolls, toasted if you like
- Condiments of your choice (ketchup, sliced pickles, mustard, diced onion, etc.)

PREHEAT:

Preheat grill to medium-high.

PREP:

In mixing bowl, combine ground meat, salt, and pepper; mix gently but thoroughly with your hands. Divide into four equal portions; shape each portion into ¾" (1.9 cm) -thick patty, patting meat just enough to hold together (for rare burgers, shape into 1" [2.5 cm] -thick patties).

GRILL:

Place burgers on grate over heat. Cook to desired doneness, 4 to 5 minutes per side for medium-rare; a covered grill helps reduce flare-ups and helps cook the meat more evenly. Serve with buns and condiments.

Variations

DIETER'S BURGERS

Follow basic recipe, substituting 1 pound (455 g) extra-lean ground meat (90 to 92% lean) for the 1½ pounds (680 g) ground meat; reduce salt to ¾ teaspoon (4.5 g). Shape into four patties that are ½" (1.3 cm) thick. Grill as directed; cooking time will be reduced slightly.

TURKEY OR POULTRY BURGERS

Follow basic recipe, substituting 1¼ pounds (560 g) ground turkey or other poultry (85 percent lean) for the ground beef; add ¼ cup (55 g) small-curd cottage cheese for additional juiciness if the ground poultry is very lean. Shape into four patties that are just under ¾" (1.9 cm) thick. Grill as directed, cooking to 165°F (74°C), well-done.

BARBECUE-ONION BURGERS

Follow basic recipe, adding ¼ cup (40 g) finely diced onion to meat mixture before shaping patties. Grill first side as directed, then turn and brush 1 teaspoon (5 g) barbecue sauce over the browned side of each burger. Just before burgers are done, gently turn burgers and brush second side of each burger with an additional teaspoon (5 g) of barbecue sauce; cook for 1 minute longer or until done.

CHEESE-STUFFED BURGERS

Follow basic recipe, but divide seasoned meat into eight equal portions. Shape each portion into a patty that is about ⅜" (1 cm) thick or a bit thinner. Top half of the patties with a generous tablespoon (8 g) of blue cheese crumbles or with a thin slice of Cheddar or American cheese (use a 1-ounce [28 g] slice of sandwich cheese, trimming the corners); keep the edges of the patty free of cheese. Top each patty with a second patty, then seal edges very well. Grill as directed; cooking time may need to be increased slightly.

PIZZA BURGERS

Follow basic recipe, adding ½ teaspoon (0.5 g) dried oregano, ½ teaspoon (0.3 g) dried marjoram, and 1 minced garlic clove to meat mixture before shaping patties. Grill as directed. When burgers are almost done, top each with 1 tablespoon (15 g) prepared marinara sauce and one slice (1 ounce [28 g]) mozzarella cheese. Cook for 1 to 2 minutes longer, until sauce is hot and cheese melts.

THAI-STYLE BURGERS

Follow basic recipe, adding 3 tablespoons (12 g) finely chopped fresh cilantro, 2 tablespoons (5 g) finely chopped basil leaves, 1 tablespoon (15 ml) lime juice, ¼ teaspoon (0.3 g) hot red pepper flakes, and 1 minced clove garlic to meat mixture before shaping patties. Grill as directed, brushing patties with Asian fish sauce or soy sauce after turning (use about 2 tablespoons [28 ml] fish sauce total).

In a medium bowl mix all the hamburger ingredients together until well blended. In a separate bowl, mix the Pico de Gallo ingredients together and set aside.

Divide the hamburger mixture into six equal portions and shape into flat patties.

Grill hamburgers according to your preference, approximately 15 to 30 minutes. Top with Pico de Gallo.

Spicy Summertime Burgers with Pico de Gallo

SERVES 6

Burgers:

- 1½ pounds [680 g] lean ground beef
- 1½ tablespoons (23 g) Dijon mustard
- ¼ cup (60 ml) Worchestershire sauce
- ½ cup (60 g) bread crumbs
- ¼ teaspoon (0.5 g) pepper
- ½ teaspoons (3 g) salt
- 2 teaspoons (5 g) ground cumin
- 2 teaspoons (4 g) ground coriander
- 1 tablespoon (4 g) chopped fresh parsley
- 1 tablespoon (1.7 g) chopped fresh rosemary
- 1 tablespoon (2.4 g) chopped fresh thyme
- 1 tablespoon (2.5 g) chopped fresh basil
- 3 cloves garlic, crushed
- Dash Tabasco or other hot sauce

Pico de Gallo:

- 3–4 tomatoes, diced finely
- ¼ cup (15 g) fresh cilantro, chopped
- ½ white onion, diced
- 2 cloves garlic, chopped finely
- 1 tablespoon (15 ml) white wine vinegar
- 1 tablespoon (15 ml) lime juice
- Salt and pepper, to taste

Dawn's Dream Burgers

SERVES 8

Sauce:

- 1 cup (240 g) ketchup
- ½ cup (120 g) dark brown sugar
- ¼ cup (85 g) honey
- ¼ cup (85 g) molasses
- 2 teaspoons (6 g) dry mustard
- 2 teaspoons (3.7 g) ground, dried ginger
- 2 teaspoons (10 ml) Worchestshire sauce
- 2 teaspoons (10 ml) Tabasco or other hot sauce
- Dash salt and pepper

Burgers:

- 1 egg, beaten
- ½ cup (40 g) quick oats
- ⅓ cup (55 g) chopped onion
- 1 tablespoon (9 g) garlic powder
- ¼ pound (115 g) bacon, cooked crisp
- 1 (8-ounce [225 g]) package shredded Cheddar cheese
- 2 pounds (905 g) lean hamburger
- ½ cup (120 ml) reserved sauce

PREHEAT:

Preheat grill to medium.

PREP:

Combine all the sauce ingredients in a pan and bring to a boil; set aside and reserve 1 cup (235 ml) of sauce. In a bowl, mix all of the burger ingredients together, including ½ cup (120 ml) or a bit more of the reserved sauce, to moisten meat.

GRILL:

Make eight patties and grill until cooked to your liking. During the last 5 minutes of cooking, baste burgers with the remaining sauce. Serve with your favorite topping, such as lettuce and tomato.

Jamaican Triple Burgers with Jerk Sauce and Orange-Chipotle Mayonnaise

SERVES 6

Orange-Chipotle Mayonnaise:

- I cup (225 g) mayonnaise
- 3 tablespoons (54 g) frozen orange juice concentrate
- I tablespoon (15 ml) minced canned chipotles

Jerk Sauce:

- I bunch green onions, coarsely chopped (about 1½ cups)
- I tablespoon (2.4 g) fresh thyme, chopped
- 2 medium jalapeño chiles, seeded and chopped
- I clove garlic, peeled
- ½ cup (115 g) packed light brown sugar
- ½ cup (120 ml) light vegetable oil
- ½ cup (120 ml) soy sauce
- I teaspoon (1.9 g) ground allspice

Burgers:

- 2 pounds (905 g) ground beef chuck (80% lean)
- 6 large, crisp sesame-seed hamburger rolls
- I sweet Vidalia onion, sliced thinly
- 3 firm ripe tomatoes, sliced
- 6 romaine lettuce leaves

FOR ORANGE-CHIPOTLE MAYONNAISE:

Mix all ingredients in small bowl. Season to taste with salt and pepper and set aside.

PREHEAT:

Preheat grill to medium-high.

PREP:

By hand or in a mini food processor, finely chop the green onions, thyme, chiles, and garlic. Add brown sugar, oil, soy sauce, and allspice; process until almost smooth. Season to taste with a little salt and pepper.

GRILL:

Set aside ³/₄ cup (175 ml) of the jerk sauce and mix the remaining sauce into the ground beef. Shape into six burgers the approximate size of the rolls. Make a deep indentation in the center of each burger and sprinkle lightly with salt and pepper. Grill burgers for 4 to 5 minutes on each side for medium-rare, 1 or 2 minutes longer for well-done. Brush burgers occasionally on both sides with remaining sauce. Slice the rolls into three layers. Place, cut side down, on the cooler side of grill, and toast lightly.

SERVE:

Spread Orange-Chipotle Mayonnaise over all of the cut surfaces of rolls.

Place the burgers on bottom layer of rolls, top with the middle slice of rolls, and add onion, tomato, and lettuce. Put top of roll in place and serve, passing reserved ³/₄ cup (175 ml) Jerk Sauce separately.

Chipotle-Spiked Burgers with Spicy Salsa

SERVES 6

Spicy Salsa:

- 2 cups (360 g) diced tomatoes
- 1 red onion, diced finely
- 1 clove garlic, diced finely
- 1 jalapeño chile, seeds removed and diced finely
- $\frac{1}{2}$ teaspoon (3 g) salt
- Juice of 1 lime
- 1 tablespoon (4 g) finely chopped cilantro

Burgers:

- 2.5 pounds (1 kg) ground chuck
- 1 tablespoon (15 ml) chipotle-flavored Tabasco sauce
- 1 tablespoon (15 ml) Worcestershire sauce
- 1 teaspoon (6 g) onion salt
- $\frac{1}{2}$ teaspoon (1 g) ground pepper
- Oil to brush grill rack
- 9 ounces (255 g) white Cheddar cheese
- 6 bolillo rolls (Mexican-style rolls) or kaiser rolls, lightly toasted

PREHEAT:

Preheat grill to medium-high.

PREP:

To prepare the salsa: in a medium bowl combine the diced tomatoes, onion, garlic, jalapeño, salt, lime juice, and cilantro. Stir until well mixed and set aside. To make the patties, in a large bowl combine the ground chuck, chipotle Tabasco, Worcestershire sauce, onion salt, and pepper. Using your hands, mix to combine all ingredients, being careful not to overwork the meat. Form the mixture into six equal-size patties shaped to fit the buns.

GRILL:

Lightly brush the grill rack with oil. Arrange the patties on the grill rack and cook in a closed grill, turning once, until desired doneness (about 4 to 6 minutes per side for medium-rare). During the last few minutes of cooking, top each patty with $1\frac{1}{2}$ ounces (42 g) of the cheese; close the grill to allow the cheese to melt.

SERVE:

To assemble the burgers, arrange the patties on roll bottoms and top with a generous portion of the salsa. Arrange roll tops over salsa.

Rick's Tequila Lime Kabobs

Rick's Tequila Lime Kabobs

SERVES 4

- Bamboo skewers

Marinade:

- ¹/₂ cup (120 ml) tequila
- 2 teaspoons (10 ml) canola oil
- Juice of 2 limes
- ¹/₄ cup (60 ml) hoisin sauce
- 4 cloves garlic, minced
- Juice from 1 (20-ounce [560 g]) can pineapple chunks

Steak:

- 2 pounds (905 g) steak, cut into 1" (2.5 cm) cubes (top round works well)

Vegetables:

- 1 each red and green bell pepper, cut into 1" (2.5 cm) chunks
- 1 onion, cut into 1" (2.5 cm) cubes
- 1 (20-ounce [560 g]) can pineapple chunks, drained (save juice for marinade)
- 2 limes, sliced into ¹/₄" (.6 cm) slices

PREHEAT:

Preheat grill to medium.

PREP:

Soak bamboo skewers in water for 30 minutes to prevent burning.

MARINATE:

Place all marinade ingredients in a bowl or resealable plastic bag and blend well. Add steak cubes and marinate for at least 1 hour.

GRILL:

Thread your choice of peppers, onion, pineapple, and meat onto the skewers. Place a slice of lime on one or both sides of each cube of meat. A slice of pineapple on the opposite side of the meat adds a nice flavor. Grill for 5 minutes per side, turning once. Drizzle marinade over the kabobs after turning. Discard the lime slices.

Beef and Button Mushroom Skewers

SERVES 4 TO 6

- 1¹/₂ pounds (680 g) beef tenderloin, cut into 1" (2.5 cm) cubes
- 1¹/₂ cups (350 ml) Italian-style vinaigrette dressing
- 10 ounces (280 g) large button mushrooms, washed, stems removed
- 2 red onions, peeled, cut into quarters

PREHEAT:

Preheat grill to medium-high.

MARINATE:

Place beef in nonreactive bowl or large resealable plastic bag. Pour dressing over beef, tossing to coat thoroughly. Cover and refrigerate for 1 to 2 hours, stirring occasionally.

PREP:

If using bamboo skewers, soak them in cold water for at least 30 minutes prior to grilling. With slotted spoon, transfer beef to another bowl. Add mushrooms to remaining marinade; stir to coat evenly. Thread beef, mushrooms, and onions alternately on metal or bamboo skewers.

GRILL:

Place skewers on grate over heat. Cook to desired doneness, 8 to 10 minutes for medium-rare, turning to cook all sides evenly.

Grill-Roasted Rosemary Pork Loin

SERVES 8

- 2 pounds (905 g) boneless pork loin, trimmed of excess fat
- 3 fresh rosemary sprigs
- 4 cloves garlic
- Freshly ground pepper
- 4–6 tablespoons (55–85 g) unsalted butter, softened
- Piece of heavy kitchen string (about 3 feet [90 cm] long), soaked in water

PREHEAT:

Preheat grill to high.

PREP:

Slice loin down the middle vertically, about three-quarters of the way through. Open loin up. Remove leaves from rosemary sprigs and mince them with the garlic. Mix together well. Season rosemary mixture with pepper to taste. Sprinkle about half of the rosemary mixture inside the loin. Dot with 2 to 3 tablespoons (28 to 45 g)

butter. Close loin, then tie together in several places with wet kitchen string. Rub outside of loin with an additional 2 to 3 tablespoons (28 to 45 g) butter, and then with remaining rosemary mixture.

GRILL:

Position drip pan between coal banks or away from heated area of gas grill. Place loin on grate directly over heat. Grill until seared on all sides, about 3 minutes per side; watch for flare-ups and squirt with water as necessary. Move loin to grate over drip pan. Cover grill and cook until internal temperature reaches 155°F (68°C), about 45 minutes. Transfer loin to serving platter; tent lightly with foil and let stand for 10 minutes before slicing. The internal temperature of the loin will rise during this time; final temperature should be 160°F (71°C).

Soak the string you use to tie up roasts and poultry for the rotisserie spit to protect it from burning. Also, soak the wooden skewers that you intend to use for kebabs for thirty minutes before using them for cooking.

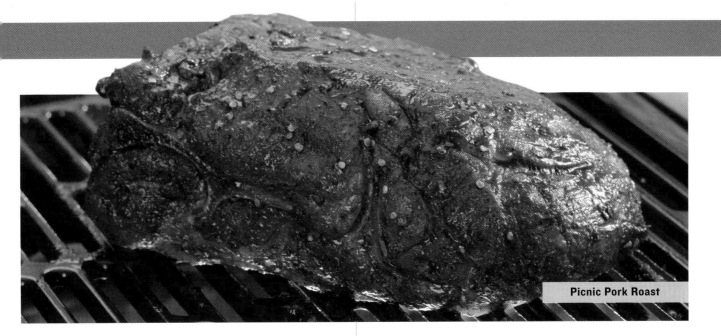

Picnic Pork Roast

Picnic Pork Roast

SERVES 8

Rub:

- I cup (225 g) brown sugar
- I tablespoon (3.6 g) red pepper flakes
- I tablespoon (9 grams) dry mustard
- 2 teaspoons (6 g) garlic powder
- 2 teaspoons (6 g) onion powder
- 2 teaspoons (5 g) paprika
- I teaspoon (0.6 g) marjoram
- I tablespoon (6 g) lemon pepper

Roast:

- 8 pounds (3.6 kg) picnic pork shoulder
- 4 sprigs rosemary
- I cup (235 ml) white wine

PREHEAT:

Preheat grill, using indirect heat by leaving the heat off under the drip pan and putting the far burner on 220°F (104°C), or medium heat.

MARINATE:

Mix the rub ingredients together in a medium-size bowl. Rub evenly all over pork shoulder. Place pork in a large resealable plastic bag and refrigerate overnight or up to 24 hours. Remove the pork from the bag and set it aside so that it may come to room temperature.

GRILL:

Place a drip pan underneath the grill grate on one side of the grill; add rosemary and wine to drip pan. Place pork on cool side of the grill over the drip pan.

Close grill lid and let pork grill slowly for 5½ hours.

Use a disposable aluminum tray filled with water, fruit juice, wine, or a marinade to add extra flavor and moisture to slow-cooked foods like roasts, whole chickens, turkeys, or ducks. Place the tray on top of the sear plates below the grill surface and immediately under the foods being cooked. This will buffer the heat from below, thereby slowing the cooking process and protecting the bottom of the food from overcooking. Check the tray periodically during cooking and keep it filled with liquid.

Crown Roast

SERVES 6

- I crown roast of pork, with 12 bones
- 14 ounces (425 ml) pineapple juice
- I teaspoon (2 g) black pepper
- ½ teaspoon (1.5 g) garlic powder
- I teaspoon (0.7 g) dried basil

PREHEAT:

Preheat grill to 300°F (150°C).

PREP:

Rinse roast with water and pat dry, then brush with pineapple juice. Mix dry ingredients together and apply all over the roast.

GRILL:

Turn on right side of grill place a pan with the remaining pineapple juice over the heated side. Place crown roast on the left-hand side.

Check meat after 1 hour for inside temperature, and every 20 minutes after. Cook till desired doneness is reached. Remove from grill and tent with aluminum foil. Let stand 10 minutes. Cut between bones and serve.

Roasted Pork Boston Butt

SERVES 8 TO 10

- Garlic powder
- Salt and freshly ground pepper
- 1 fresh pork Boston butt roast (8–10 pounds [3.6–4.5 kg])

PREHEAT:

Preheat grill to medium-low.

PREP:

Prepare a dry rub using garlic powder, salt, and freshly ground pepper. The amount of each depends on your preferences; however, don't be too heavy with any one because you want the flavor of the meat to come through. Season roast liberally with mixture, rubbing in with your fingers. Place rubbed roast in resealable plastic bag and refrigerate for 24 to 48 hours.

GRILL:

Place roast on grate over heat. Cook for 6 hours, adding coals as necessary to maintain 225°F to 250°F (105°C to 120°C) temperature, or until roast is so tender it almost falls off the bones. Turn roast every 30 minutes during cooking. Remove from heat and let it cool enough to handle. Pull or separate pork with 2 forks. This is delicious served plain, or you may serve with sauces on the side.

Barbecued Smoked Ribs

SERVES 4

- 2–3 racks of ribs
- 6 tablespoons (42 g) paprika
- 2 tablespoons (12 g) black pepper
- 2 tablespoons (36 g) kosher salt
- 1 tablespoon (7.5 g) chile powder
- 2 tablespoons (30 g) brown sugar
- 2 pinches cayenne pepper
- Prepared barbecue sauce, if desired

Remove membrane from underside of ribs. Combine remaining ingredients and coat ribs. Cook, meaty side down, at low temperature for 2 hours.

Baste ribs periodically with prepared barbecue sauce, if desired. Let stand for 15 minutes.

Barbecued Smoked Ribs

Spiced Pork Loin Stuffed with Mosaic of Oven Dried Fruits

SERVES 8

Spice Marinade:

- I clove garlic, chopped
- I medium onion, chopped
- 2 tablespoons (10 g) soft pink peppercorns
- 2 tablespoons (10 g) soft green peppercorn
- I tablespoon (6 g) freshly ground black pepper
- I teaspoon (1.2 g) chile flakes
- I teaspoon (2.5 g) paprika
- I teaspoon (6 g) kosher salt
- 6 ounces (175 ml) mushroom soy sauce
- 6 ounces (175 ml) balsamic vinegar

Stuffing:

- 6 ounces (170 g) chicken meat and pork trimming without fat
- I shallot, chopped
- 2 ounces (55 g) garlic, chopped
- 3 ounces (85 g) dried prunes, chopped
- 3 ounces (85 g) dried apricots, chopped
- 2 ounces (55 g) raisins
- 2 ounces (55 g) dried banana, chopped
- 2 ounces (55 g) dried apple
- 2 ounces (55 g) pistachios, blanched and chopped (optional)
- 2 ounces (55 g) dried pumpkin seeds

Pork Loin:

- 2–4 pounds (0.9–1.9 kg) boneless pork loin, fat trimmed

PREHEAT:

Preheat grill to medium.

PREP:

Place all ingredients in a food processor and blend to a paste.

To make stuffing: combine chopped chicken meat and pork trimming with shallot, garlic, dried fruits, pistachios, and pumpkin seeds. Refrigerate both mixtures in different bowls.

With a boning knife, put a 4" (10 cm) incision in center of pork loin from end to end. Stuff pork with filling. Tie with string at about 1" (2.5 cm) intervals.

MARINATE:

Rub marinade over pork (be careful not to press pork too hard—this will push stuffing out). Place in glass or ceramic dish, cover, and marinate overnight in refrigerator.

GRILL:

Place pork on lightly oiled grill and cook, turning frequently and carefully, for 2 to 2½ hours or until tender and cooked through.

Let stand for 15 minutes before carving and serving.

Succulent Pork Spareribs

SERVES 3 OR 4

- I rack pork spareribs (about 3¹/₂ pounds [1.6 kg])
- ¹/₄ cup (60 ml) peanut oil
- I teaspoon (3 g) dry mustard
- I teaspoon (2.5 g) paprika
- ¹/₂ teaspoon (0.9 g) cayenne pepper
- ¹/₂ teaspoon (0.5 g) dried oregano
- ¹/₂ teaspoon (1.3 g) ground cumin
- I cup (240 g) ketchup
- ¹/₃ cup (90 g) tomato paste
- ¹/₄ cup (85 g) honey
- 2 tablespoons (28 ml) Worcestershire sauce
- I tablespoon (15 ml) cider vinegar
- 2 cloves garlic, chopped

PREHEAT:

Preheat grill to medium.

MARINATE:

In nonreactive dish or large resealable plastic bag, combine ribs and about half of the sauce (or enough to coat), turning to coat; reserve remaining sauce. Refrigerate ribs and remaining sauce for at least 6 hours, or as long as overnight.

COOK:

Begin heating a stockpot full of water to boiling. Peel membrane from back side of ribs and cut rack as necessary to fit into stockpot. When water is boiling, add ribs; return to boiling and cook for 3 or 4 minutes. Remove ribs and set aside until cool. Meanwhile, combine oil, mustard powder, paprika, cayenne pepper, oregano, and cumin in saucepan; mix well. Cook over medium heat until hot, stirring several times. Add ketchup, tomato paste, honey, Worcestershire sauce, vinegar, and garlic; stir to blend. Cook for 5 to 10 minutes longer, stirring occasionally. Remove from heat; set aside until cool.

GRILL:

Remove ribs from marinade; discard marinade. Place ribs on grate directly over heat; sear on both sides. Move ribs to area away from heat. Baste with reserved sauce. Cook until well-done throughout, about 20 minutes, turning and basting with sauce several times. Cut into individual ribs and serve with remaining sauce for dipping.

Spicy Roasted Pork Ribs

SERVES 2

- I rack pork back ribs (about 2 pounds [905 g])

Dry Spice Rub:

- I tablespoon (7.5 g) chile powder
- I¹/₂ teaspoons (.2 g) dried cilantro
- I¹/₂ teaspoons (3.8 g) paprika
- I¹/₂ teaspoons (7.5 g) packed dark brown sugar
- I teaspoon (2.5 g) ground cumin
- I teaspoon (18 g) kosher salt
- ¹/₂ teaspoon (1 g) freshly ground pepper
- Prepared barbecue sauce, as needed (about I cup [250 g], plus additional for serving)

PREHEAT:

Preheat grill to medium.

BAKE:

Heat oven to 300°F (150°C). Line bottom of broiler pan with foil; spray broiler-pan rack with nonstick spray. Peel membrane from back side of ribs and cut rack in half to fit broiler pan if necessary. In small bowl, stir together all rub ingredients. Sprinkle and press all of the rub into both sides of rib rack. Place ribs on broiler-pan rack, meaty-side up. Bake until tender, 2 to 2¹/₂ hours, rotating pan after the first hour and every 30 minutes thereafter. If ribs are prepared in advance, cool, wrap, and refrigerate until ready for final cooking.

GRILL:

Place ribs on grate over heat. Baste with barbecue sauce until ribs are well coated; grill until nicely glazed and heated through, 10 to 15 minutes, turning ribs frequently and brushing with sauce. Cut into individual ribs and serve with additional barbecue sauce for dipping.

Cathy's Kick in the Pants BBQ Ribs

SERVES 6

- I (25-ounce [700 g]) jar applesauce
- I (7-ounce [200 g]) can chipotle peppers in adobo sauce
- 6 slabs pork ribs
- 3 tablespoons (54 g) kosher or sea salt
- I¹/₂ tablespoons (7.5 g) black peppercorns
- I¹/₂ apples, halved
- 2 onions, quartered
- 3 cloves garlic, peeled
- 15–16 fresh thyme sprigs
- I cup (235 ml) olive oil
- Barbecue sauce

Rub:

- 3 tablespoons (8 g) dried thyme
- I tablespoon (3 g) dried oregano
- I tablespoon (9 g) garlic powder
- 3 tablespoons (54 g) kosher or sea salt
- 3 tablespoons (18 g) freshly ground pepper

PREHEAT:

Preheat grill to 300°F (150°C).

COOK:

Pour applesauce into medium-size saucepan and place over medium heat on a side burner of your grill. Add the chipotle peppers to the applesauce and stir to combine. Cook over medium heat for 15 to 20 minutes. Remove from heat and let cool. After cooled, place in your food processor and pulse 8 to 10 times, until the mixture is semismooth, with small pieces of the pepper still in the sauce. Set aside until ready to baste the ribs. Cut each slab of ribs in half. Fill a large stockpot with enough water to cover the ribs and place on a side burner of your grill. First, add to the water the salt, peppercorns, apples, onions, garlic cloves, and fresh thyme, and stir to dissolve the salt. Next, place the ribs into the water and bring to a boil. Turn down your heat to low, and simmer the ribs for 1 hour. When done, remove the ribs from the water and set aside to cool to the touch, approximately 15 to 20 minutes.

GRILL:

Make dry rub by mixing together the dried thyme, oregano, garlic powder, salt, and freshly ground pepper. Coat both sides of ribs with olive oil. Sprinkle the rub onto both sides of the ribs, pressing in with your fingers. Place the ribs onto the preheated grill and grill both sides with just the rub for 5 minutes on each side. Next, take the apple-chipotle sauce and brush on the top side of the ribs. Grill for 5 minutes, turn, and baste the other side. Repeat this step one more time. Last, baste the ribs with barbecue sauce, and continue cooking and turning 2 to 3 times, for approximately 15 to 20 minutes. Serve with barbecue sauce on the side.

Blackberry Barbecued Ribs

SERVES 4

- 1½ cups (480 g) blackberry jam
- ½ cup (120 g) ketchup
- ½ cup (115 g) brown sugar
- 1-2 teaspoons (2-4 g) minced fresh gingerroot
- 1-2 teaspoons (5-10 ml) hot sauce
- ½ teaspoon (1 g) freshly ground black pepper
- 1 rack pork spareribs (4-5 pounds [1.9-2.3 kg])

PREHEAT:

Preheat grill to 350°F (180°C).

PREP:

In food processor or blender, place blackberry jam, ketchup, brown sugar, gingerroot, hot sauce, and pepper; whirl until ingredients are pureed.

COOK:

In a medium saucepan over medium-high heat, add blackberry mixture and bring to a boil; boil for 2 to 3 minutes, stirring constantly. Remove from heat and set aside.

GRILL:

Rinse ribs and pat dry. Trim and disgard any excess fat. Place on grill away from heat source for 40 minutes, turning every 20 minutes. Baste one side of ribs with one-third of prepared sauce; turn ribs sauce side down and cook 10 minutes, or until sauce browns and forms a thick, sticky glaze. Repeat and cook for an additional 10 minutes.

Cut between bones into individual serving potions and serve with remaining sauce.

BBQ Pork Chops

SERVES 6

- 6-8 pork chops (cuts, still with the bone)
- ⅓ cup (80 ml) reduced-sodium (light) soy sauce
- 2 cloves garlic
- 1 (12-ounce [355 ml]) can diet 7-Up
- 2 tablespoons (12 g) dehydrated fat-free chicken stock
- 1 tablespoon (4 g) dried oregano
- 1 teaspoon (2 g) celery seeds
- 1 small onion, chopped finely
- ½ cup (120 ml) white wine, or 2 tablespoons (28 ml) white wine vinegar

Place all ingredients in a large resealable plastic bag and seal (remember to let the air out). Mix the ingredients by rubbing the sides of the bag together.

Marinate in the fridge for a minimum of 2 hours.

Grill for approximately 4 minutes on each side or to preference. Do not overcook.

Barbecued Pork Tenderloin

SERVES 4 TO 6

Barbecue Marinade

- ¹/₄ cup (55 g [¹/₂ stick]) unsalted butter
- I small rib celery, minced
- I cup (160 g) finely chopped onion
- 3 cloves garlic, minced
- I cup (235 ml) red wine vinegar
- I cup (235 ml) Worcestershire sauce
- 2 tablespoons (18 g) dry mustard
- 2 tablespoons (14 g) paprika
- I tablespoon (15 g) packed brown sugar
- I tablespoon (20 g) light molasses
- 2 teaspoons (3.6 g) cayenne pepper
- I¹/₂ pounds (680 g) pork tenderloin
- I tablespoon (15 ml) dark sesame oil

PREHEAT:

Preheat grill to high.

MARINATE:

In small saucepan, melt butter over medium-high heat. When butter is foamy, add celery, onion, and garlic; sauté until soft. Stir in remaining marinade ingredients and heat to boiling, stirring occasionally. Remove from heat and let cool. This can be done a day ahead of time. You should get about 3 cups (710 ml). Place pork in glass baking dish or resealable plastic bag. Add cooled marinade, turning pork to coat. Cover and refrigerate for 8 to 12 hours, or overnight.

GRILL:

Drain pork, transferring marinade to small saucepan. Heat marinade to boiling. Cook until marinade is thick and syrupy, 5 to 8 minutes. Pat pork dry with paper towels and brush with sesame oil. Place pork on grate directly over heat. Grill until seared on all sides, about 3 minutes per side. Move pork to area away from heat. After a few minutes, begin basting pork with reduced marinade. Continue cooking, basting frequently, until center of pork reaches 155°F (68°C). Transfer pork to serving platter and let stand for 5 minutes. Slice pork on the diagonal and serve hot.

Always trim excess fat from your foods to reduce the occurrence of flare-ups during cooking.

Grilled Pork Chops

SERVES 2

Brine:

- ¹/₃ cup (75 g) packed light brown sugar
- ¹/₄ cup (72 g) kosher salt
- 3 cups (710 ml) water
- 4 whole cloves garlic, plus 2 crushed
- 2 bay leaves, crumbled
- 1 teaspoon (1.7 g) whole black peppercorns, crushed

Chops:

- 2 pork loin chops, 1–1¹/₂" (2.5–3.8 cm) thick (6–8 ounces [170–225 g] each)
- 1 tablespoon (15 ml) olive oil
- Freshly ground pepper

PREHEAT:

Preheat grill for high heat; you'll also need an area of the grill that is cooler, so bank the coals appropriately if using charcoal.

MARINATE:

In nonmetallic mixing bowl, dissolve brown sugar and salt in 1 cup (235 ml) hot water. Add garlic, bay leaves, peppercorns, and 2 cups (475 ml) cold water. Add pork chops and weight down with plate (or combine brine and chops in large resealable plastic bag; press to remove as much air as possible and seal). Refrigerate for 1 hour.

GRILL:

Remove chops from brine, discarding brine. Rinse chops briefly and pat dry with paper towels. Rub chops with oil; sprinkle with pepper to taste. Place chops on grate directly over high heat and cook for about 3 minutes per side or until nicely browned. Move chops to cooler area of grill or reduce heat if using gas grill. Cook until center of chops reaches 155°F (68°C), 8 to 10 minutes longer. Transfer chops to platter and cover with foil; let stand for 5 minutes. The internal temperature of the chops will rise during this time; final temperature should be 160°F (71°C).

— ☼ —

Brush chops with your favorite barbecue sauce during the last 5 minutes to add juiciness and flavor.

Paprika Pork Cutlets

SERVES 3 TO 4

- 1 pound (455 g) pork tenderloin

Spice Rub:

- 1 tablespoon (15 ml) olive oil
- 2 teaspoons (5 g) sweet Hungarian paprika
- 1 teaspoon (1.8 g) dried Italian herb blend, well crushed
- ¹/₂ teaspoon (3 g) salt
- ¹/₂ teaspoon (1.5 g) garlic powder
- ¹/₂ teaspoon (1.5 g) dry mustard
- ¹/₂ teaspoon (1 g) freshly ground pepper

PREHEAT:

Preheat grill to medium.

PREP:

Trim fat from pork. Cut crosswise into eight slices. Place pork slices between two sheets of heavy-duty plastic wrap, and flatten each slice to ¹/₄" (.6 cm) thickness using a meat mallet or rolling pin. In small bowl, combine Spice Rub ingredients and mix well. Rub spice mixture evenly over both sides of pork slices.

GRILL:

Place pork slices on grate over heat. Cook for 3 to 4 minutes per side, or until just done. Let stand for 5 minutes before serving.

BBQ Thai Strips

SERVES 4

- 1 green onion, chopped finely
- 1 large clove garlic, chopped
- 2 tablespoons (28 ml) canola oil
- 2 teaspoons (10 ml) hot sauce
- 1 tablespoon (16 g) chunky peanut butter
- 1 tablespoon (15 g) brown sugar
- 1/2 teaspoon (0.6 g) crushed chiles
- 3/4 pound (340 g) pork scaloppine or schnitzel
- 1 lime or lemon, cut into eighths
- Fresh lime wedges, for garnish

PREHEAT:

Heat grill to medium-high.

MARINATE:

Combine green onion, garlic, oil, hot sauce, peanut butter, brown sugar, and crushed chiles; stir and add to meat. Marinate at least 20 minutes or overnight for stronger flavor.

PREP:

Cut pork into long strips, about 1" (2.5 cm) wide. Place pork strips in a shallow dish. Insert fork into lime wedges and squeeze juice over meat. Lay squeezed lime wedges over meat. Thread meat onto wooden bamboo skewers (that have been soaked for 30 minutes in water); place a lime wedge garnish on tip of skewer.

GRILL:

Grill 4" to 6" (10 to 15 cm) from heat for 3 to 4 minutes. Brush with extra marinade. Turn skewers over and cook 3 to 4 minutes more. Serve hot over a bed of shredded lettuce and shredded carrots. Garnish with green onion curls and thinly sliced cucumber. Serve with hot dipping sauce.

Ribs in Beer

SERVES 4 TO 5

- 4–5 pounds (1.9–2.3 kg) beef, venison, or pork ribs
- 2 large onions, quartered
- 3–4 (12-ounce [355 ml]) cans beer, or enough to cover ribs
- 1 tablespoon (6 g) pepper, or to taste
- Salt
- Prepared barbecue sauce, as needed (about 1 cup [250 g])

PREHEAT:

Preheat grill to medium.

COOK:

Peel membrane from back side of ribs if you like; cut rack as necessary to fit into Dutch oven. In Dutch oven, combine ribs and onions. Add beer to cover; add pepper and salt to taste. Simmer over medium heat until tender, 1 to 1½ hours. Remove from Dutch oven and drain well.

GRILL:

Place ribs on grate over heat. Baste with barbecue sauce until ribs are well coated; grill until nicely glazed and heated through, 10 to 15 minutes, turning ribs frequently and brushing with sauce. Cut into individual ribs and serve with additional barbecue sauce for dipping.

Barbecued Holiday Ham

SERVES 6

- 1 cup (225 g) smoking chips
- ½ cup (120 ml) brandy
- 1 cooked ham
- Whole cloves
- ¼ cup (60 g) brown sugar
- 2 teaspoons (4.6 g) ground cinnamon
- 1 (16-ounce [455 g]) jar applesauce

PREHEAT:

Preheat grill to medium.

PREP:

Soak smoking chips in brandy in a nonreactive metal dish for 1 hour. Prepare the ham by scoring the skin in diamond patterns with a sharp knife, placing the clove stems in the intersections. Mix the brown sugar, cinnamon, and applesauce in a bowl and baste the ham thoroughly.

GRILL:

Place the ham on a roasting tray so that there is a surface between the grill and the ham to catch any excess drippings. Place dish with smoking chips on grill, cover grill with lid, and heat for 5 to 10 minutes, or until liquid is hot. Place the tray over the grill, cover grill with lid, and smoke, basting ham frequently and adding brandy to dish if necessary, for 2½ to 3 hours, or until ham is cooked.

Ribs in Beer

Ham Steak with Peach-Mustard Glaze

SERVES 2 OR 3

- 2 tablespoons (40 g) peach preserves
- I tablespoon (15 ml) bourbon or dark rum (optional)
- I teaspoon (3 g) dry mustard
- I teaspoon (5 ml) canola oil
- A good pinch of ground dried ginger
- I ham steak (1–1½ pounds [455–680 g])

PREHEAT:

Preheat grill to medium-high.

PREP:

In small bowl, combine preserves, bourbon, mustard powder, oil, and ginger; stir to blend. Pat ham steak dry with paper towels. Make small cuts at 1" (2.5 cm) intervals around edges of ham; this prevents curling during cooking.

GRILL:

Place ham on grate over heat; cook for about 4 minutes. Turn ham and brush half of the preserve mixture over the ham. Cook for about 4 minutes longer. Turn ham and brush with remaining preserve mixture. Cook for about 3 minutes, then turn and cook for about 3 minutes longer, or until ham is heated through and nicely glazed.

BBQ Vermont Rack of Lamb

Apple-Butter Lamb

SERVES 6

- 1 (28-ounce [785 g]) jar apple butter
- 2 tablespoons (28 ml) apple cider vinegar
- 2 firm, ripe mangoes, peeled and quartered
- 3 firm, ripe peaches, peeled and quartered
- 1/2 ripe pineapple, cut into chunks (optional)
- 6–8 center-cut baby lamb chops (pork or chicken will work as well; cubed meat portions can also be used, alternated on skewers with fruit, before grilling)
- 2 large cloves garlic, minced
- Fresh rosemary, to taste
- Oil for brushing
- Salt and pepper, to taste

PREHEAT:

Preheat grill to medium-high.

MARINATE:

In a medium bowl, whisk together the apple butter and cider vinegar. Add mangoes, peaches, and pineapple (if desired) to mixture. Score the meat and insert minced garlic and rosemary. Marinate meat and fruit in apple butter/vinegar for 2 hours or overnight.

GRILL:

Brush meat with oil, season with salt and pepper, and put on grill. Over direct heat, brown meat on all sides, brushing with glaze. Cook 2 minutes on each side, then move to indirect heat to keep warm, turning every 5 to 6 minutes to keep glaze from scorching. Cooking time will vary based on type and thickness of meat and individual taste. Brush occasionally with additional glaze. Skewer mangoes, peaches, and pineapple, and grill to taste, brushing with glaze. Simultaneously bring remainder of marinade to boil in small pot on grill; let boil gently for approximately 3 to 5 minutes.

SERVE:

When meat is cooked to taste, remove from grill, arrange individual servings on plates along with fruit, either on or off the skewer. Pour remainder of warm marinade on portions.

BBQ Vermont Rack of Lamb

SERVES 6

- 1/4 cup (60 ml) orange juice (preferrably fresh and pulpy)
- 1/2 cup (120 ml) dry white wine
- 2 tablespoons (10 g) orange rind
- 1/4 cup (60 ml) soy sauce
- 1 teaspoon (3 g) dried mustard
- 1 tablespoon (8 g) grated fresh gingerroot
- 1 teaspoon (1 g) dried thyme leaves
- Salt and pepper, to taste
- 1 rack of lamb, bone in

PREHEAT:

Heat grill to medium-high.

MARINATE:

Combine all ingredients except lamb. Pour over the rack of lamb. Cover and refrigerate overnight, basting and turning occasionally. Drain and reserve marinade.

GRILL:

Place rack of lamb on low—watch carefully as it will burn easily. Baste occasionally with marinade, turning over frequently. Cook for about 1 hour, until pink inside (or desired doneness). Remove from grill and slice along each rib.

Grilled Lamb with Port Glaze

SERVES 6

- ¼ cup (60 g) raspberry-honey mustard
- 4 teaspoons (6.8 g) orange zest
- 4 teaspoons (8.8 g) freshly grated nutmeg
- 2½ cups (590 ml) port wine
- ¼ cup (85 g) honey
- 2 tablespoons (28 ml) balsamic vinegar
- 4–5 pounds (1.9–2.3 g) boneless leg of lamb
- 1½ cups (355 ml) water
- 1 cinnamon stick

PREHEAT:

Preheat grill to medium-high (about 400°F [200°C]).

COOK:

To make the glaze, combine the mustard, orange zest, nutmeg, 1 cup (235 ml) port wine, honey, and balsamic vinegar in a saucepan. Bring to a simmer and cook until the mixture thickens and reduces slightly. Place the lamb on a wire rack set in a roasting pan. (We use a deep cast-iron pot with lid, and 2 steel skewers to hold the roast above the bottom of the pot.) Brush generously with the glaze. Pour the remaining 1½ cups (355 ml) port wine and the water into the pot. Add the cinnamon stick.

GRILL:

Place on the grill, cover with a lid, and cook for about 2 hours or until cooked to your liking, brushing with the glaze about every 20 minutes. For the last 10 minutes, remove the lid from the pot and finish the lamb roast. Remove from heat and brush one last time with the glaze. Let rest before slicing. Serve with roasted red potatoes and asparagus.

Grilled Lamb Chops with Mint Cream Sauce

SERVES 2

Marinade:

- ¹/₂ cup (120 ml) olive oil

- 3 tablespoons (45 ml) lemon juice

- 1 teaspoon (1.2 g) dried rosemary, or 1 tablespoon (1.7 g) chopped fresh

- 1 teaspoon (1 g) dried oregano, or 1 tablespoon (5 g) chopped fresh

- 1 teaspoon (1 g) dried thyme, or 1 tablespoon (2.5 g) chopped fresh

- ¹/₂ teaspoon (3 g) salt

- ¹/₂ teaspoon (1 g) freshly ground pepper

- ¹/₄ teaspoon (0.5 g) finely grated fresh lemon zest

Chops:

- 4 lamb chops, 1" (2.5 cm) thick (about 1¹/₄ pounds [560 g] total)

Mint Cream Sauce:

- ¹/₃ cup (80 g) sour cream

- 2 tablespoons (8 g) finely chopped fresh mint leaves

- ¹/₄ teaspoon (0.8 g) finely minced garlic

PREHEAT:

Preheat grill for high heat.

MARINATE:

In nonreactive dish, whisk together all marinade ingredients. Add lamb chops, turning to coat. Cover and marinate at room temperature for about 1 hour, turning chops in marinade once or twice.

PREP:

Meanwhile, combine all sauce ingredients in small bowl; stir together. Cover and refrigerate until needed.

GRILL:

Drain chops, discarding marinade. Place chops on grate over heat and cook for about 3 minutes per side (medium-rare) or until desired doneness. Serve with Mint Cream Sauce.

Mint is a perennial herb that is easy to grow in your home garden. And there are a number of varieties, so you can plant the ones you like best.

All-Day Beef Brisket

Season the meat the night before you want to serve it, then start the actual cooking in the morning. The meat cooks slowly most of the day and has a final resting time before it's ready to serve.

SERVES 8 TO 10

Brisket Spice Mixture:

- 3 tablespoons (45 g) packed brown sugar
- 2 tablespoons (36 g) kosher salt
- 2 tablespoons (14 g) paprika
- 2 tablespoons (13 g) freshly ground black pepper
- 1 tablespoon (9 g) garlic powder
- 1 teaspoon (3.7 g) mustard seeds
- 1 teaspoon (1.8 g) cayenne pepper

Brisket:

- 1 choice beef brisket (about 6 pounds [2.7 kg])
- Buns, barbecue sauce, mustard, and sliced onion, for serving

PREHEAT:

Preheat grill to low.

MARINATE:

Combine spice-mixture ingredients in mixing bowl; stir with fork until well mixed. Set aside 2 tablespoons (20 g) of the mixture; rub remaining mixture into both sides of brisket. Place in resealable plastic bag and refrigerate overnight or for 8 to 12 hours.

GRILL:

Position filled water pan between coal banks or away from heated area of gas grill. Rub reserved 2 tablespoons (20 g) spice mixture over brisket. Place brisket, fat side up, on grate over water pan. Cover grill and cook until brisket reaches at least 165°F (74°C), 6 to 8 hours; replenish coals (and water in pan) as necessary to maintain a temperature of 200°F to 225°F (95°C to 110°C). When brisket is at least 165°F (74°C), remove from grill and wrap well in heavy-duty foil. Wrap a thick layer of newspaper or towels around foil-wrapped brisket; set aside at room temperature for an hour or a bit longer. This allows the juices to equalize and also helps finish tenderizing the meat.

SERVE:

When ready to serve, unwrap brisket carefully, pouring any juices into small bowl. Slice brisket across the grain and arrange in serving dish; pour accumulated juices over brisket and serve with buns and condiments.

Leg-o-Lamb on a Spit

SERVES 8 TO 10

- 1 butterflied, boneless leg of lamb (3–4 pounds [1.4–1.9 kg])
- Kosher salt and freshly ground pepper
- 1/2 cup (112 g [1 stick]) unsalted butter
- 2 teaspoons (6 g) garlic powder
- A piece of heavy kitchen string (about 4 feet [1.2 m] long), soaked in water

PREHEAT:

Preheat grill to high.

PREP:

Set up rotisserie and, if possible, position drip pan in area under center of rotisserie. Season butterflied leg of lamb with salt and pepper to taste, then tie into a round roast with wet kitchen string (or have the butcher tie the roast for you, then season the outside just before roasting).

COOK:

Melt butter in small saucepan over medium heat; stir in garlic powder. After lamb has cooked for about 15 minutes, baste with garlic butter.

GRILL:

Place roast on rotisserie spit and secure with provided prongs. Turn motor on to begin roasting the lamb. Continue cooking, basting frequently, for 1 1/4 to 1 1/2 hours, or until temperature is 160°F (71°C) in the thickest part of the roast. Remove the spit from the grill, then slide roast off the spit onto serving platter. Let stand for 5 minutes before carving.

Lamb Chops with Maple Mustard

SERVES 8

Marinade:

- 2 tablespoons (30 g) Dijon mustard
- 2 tablespoons (28 ml) real maple syrup
- 2 tablespoons (28 ml) balsamic vinegar
- I tablespoon (1.7 g) fresh rosemary or I½ (1.8 g) teaspoons dried
- 2 cloves garlic, minced
- Freshly ground pepper, to taste

Chops:

- 8 lamb chops (about I″ [2.5 cm] thick)

PREHEAT:

Preheat grill to medium-high.

MARINATE:

In a shallow glass dish, combine all marinade ingredients. Add the lamb chops and turn to coat. Marinate at room temp for 30 minutes or cover and refrigerate for up to 8 hours.

GRILL:

Reserve the marinade and place chops on a greased grill for 5 to 7 minutes, or until desired doneness, basting with reserved marinade.

Grilled Lamb Loin

SERVES 4

Marinade:

- I cup (235 ml) olive oil
- ½ cup (80 g) finely chopped onion
- ½ cup (50 g) chopped green onions (white and green parts)
- 2 tablespoons (8 g) minced fresh parsley
- 2 tablespoons (28 ml) fresh lemon juice
- I tablespoon (10 g) minced shallots
- I teaspoon (6 g) kosher salt
- I teaspoon (2 g) freshly ground pepper

Lamb:

- 2 boneless lamb loins (8 ounces [225 g] each), trimmed

PREHEAT:

Preheat grill to high.

MARINATE:

In nonreactive dish, whisk together all marinade ingredients. Add lamb, turning to coat. Cover and let marinate at room temperature for 1 to 2 hours, turning lamb in marinade several times.

GRILL:

Drain lamb, discarding marinade. Place lamb on grate over heat and sear all sides, 1 to 2 minutes per side. At this stage the lamb should be rare to medium-rare. If you want the meat more well-done, continue to cook to desired doneness, turning as needed. Remove from heat and let stand for 5 minutes before slicing.

Lamb Chops with Maple Mustard

Fabulous Fajitas

SERVES 4

Marinade:

- 2 tablespoons (28 ml) fresh orange juice
- I tablespoon (15 ml) white vinegar
- I teaspoon (4 g) sugar
- ¹/₂ teaspoon (1.3 g) ground cumin
- ¹/₂ teaspoon (0.5 g) dried oregano
- I large clove garlic, chopped
- Salt and pepper, to taste

Fajitas:

- I pound (455 g) beef, venison, or buffalo steak, cut into thin strips
- I green bell pepper, cored and cut into strips
- I red bell pepper, cored and cut into strips
- I onion, sliced thinly
- 8 flour tortillas

Condiments:

- I cup (115 g) shredded Cheddar or Monterey Jack cheese
- I cup (235 g) salsa
- I cup (235 g) guacamole or sliced avocado
- I cup (240 g) refried beans
- I cup (180 g) chopped tomato
- I cup (55 g) shredded lettuce

PREHEAT:

Preheat grill to medium.

MARINATE:

Combine marinade ingredients and pour over steak in resealable plastic bag. Refrigerate for 6 to 8 hours, turning occasionally.

GRILL:

Place grill wok on grate over heat for about a minute, then add green and red peppers and onion. Stir-fry until vegetables are tender-crisp. Transfer vegetables to a dish; set aside. Drain steak, discarding marinade. Add steak to wok; stir-fry for 2 to 4 minutes. Return vegetables to wok and toss to combine. Serve on warmed tortillas with desired condiments.

The Everything Grill

SERVES 6

Shrimp Marinade and Basting Sauce:

- ¹/₄ cup (60 ml) olive oil
- ¹/₂ teaspoon (1 g) ground black pepper
- ¹/₂ teaspoon (1.5 g) garlic powder
- 2 tablespoons (28 ml) lemon juice
- 18 Louisiana shrimp
- 3 baking potatoes
- Two commercial or homemade BBQ sauces

Chicken and Rib Dry Rub:

- 2 teaspoons (5 g) ground cumin
- 2 teaspoons (4 g) ground black pepper
- 2 teaspoons (6 g) garlic powder
- 2 teaspoons (6 g) onion powder

Add Subhead:

- 24 chicken wing sections
- 2 racks baby back ribs

Rib-Basting Sauce:

- ¹/₄ cup (60 ml) olive oil
- ¹/₄ cup (60 ml) red wine vinegar
- ¹/₄ cup (60 g) prepared mustard
- ¹/₄ cup (85 g) honey
- ¹/₄ cup (60 g) ketchup
- ¹/₄ cup (60 ml) soy sauce

Baked Potato Filling:

- ¹/₃ cup (38 g) American Cheddar, shredded
- ¹/₄ cup (30 g) bacon bits
- ¹/₂ cup (60 g) sour cream
- 2 teaspoons (2.7 g) chopped parsley
- ¹/₄ cup (25 g) chopped green onion

PREHEAT:

Preheat grill to 375°F (190°C).

MARINATE:

Mix ingredients for shrimp marinade and basting sauce. Marinate shrimp in resealable plastic bag with half of marinade for 30 minutes, reserve remaining half.

PREP:

Mix ingredients for chicken and rib dry rub, coat wings and ribs, and allow to dry; set aside. Mix ingredients for rib-basting sauce; set aside.

GRILL:

Remove shrimp from marinade bag and skewer; refrigerate. Wash potatoes and cut in half lengthwise. Wrap individually in foil and place on upper rack of grill. After 20 minutes, place wings and ribs on grill and move partially cooked potatoes to lower grill. Frequently baste ribs while turning. Turn and rotate chicken wings frequently.

After an additional 20 minutes, open potatoes and scoop out middle with spoon. Return potatoes to grill with foil loosely opened. Continue basting ribs and rotating chicken.

After an additional 15 minutes, coat ribs and wings with your two favorite BBQ sauces. Place shrimp on grill and baste with remaining shrimp marinade for 3 to 5 minutes while turning. Continue turning chicken and ribs while coating with additional sauce. Meanwhile, place cheese and bacon in potato boats, loosely close foil, and move to upper rack of grill.

SERVE:

Place wings and shrimp on a large platter. Cut ribs into two-bone portions and place on platter. Remove potatoes from foil and scoop sour cream in potato boats, sprinkle with parsley and green onion, and place on platter.

Easy Rack of Lamb

SERVES 4

- **2 racks of lamb, frenched (8-bone racks, about 1½ pounds [680 g] each)**
- **1 tablespoon (15 ml) olive oil**
- **2 teaspoons (1.4 g) ground sage**
- **Kosher salt and freshly ground pepper**
- **Freshly grated Parmesan cheese, for serving**

PREHEAT:

Preheat grill to high.

PREP:

Cut each rack of lamb in half so you end up with four sections containing four bones each. Cut off the first bone from each section, cutting close to the bone and leaving the meat attached to the section; discard cut-off bones. You will now have four sections with three rib bones in each. Wrap the tips of each bone with foil to prevent them from burning over the fire. Rub oil and sage over each section; season with salt and pepper to taste.

GRILL:

Place lamb on grate over heat and sear each side, turning once; the outside should be crisp. Remove lamb from grill and let stand for 5 minutes. Cut sections into three chops each. Return individual chops to grill and cook for about 1 minute on each side (for medium-rare). Remove from grill; remove and discard foil from the bone tips. Serve with Parmesan cheese.

The Everything Grill

CHAPTER SIX
POULTRY

Rolled and Stuffed Turkey Breast, page 134

CHICKEN, TURKEY, DUCK, AND OTHER POULTRY CAN BE

grilled and served in a variety of ways, including sandwiches, tacos, pizza toppings, and dozens of salads and appetizers. Look for the freshest poultry, and make sure you cook the whole bird or parts well without drying them out.

Grilling poultry is as easy as cooking meat and seafood and follows the same general rules. In other words, there is no mystery to creating a superb meal around a platter of grilled chicken breasts or wings, rotisserie turkey or duck, or pasta with grilled chicken.

Sear poultry as you would a steak, using direct heat and a medium setting. Do not move or turn the poultry until it releases from the grate, and cook it on the other side for about 40 percent of the total cooking time. Once the poultry is nicely browned, move it to indirect heat to finish cooking. The lid of the grill should be closed as much as possible to avoid flare-ups and to give the poultry the smokiness that is the hallmark of great grilling. Closing the lid of the grill will also speed cooking time. Be sure to avoid continuous flipping of the poultry with a fork, which not only slows down the cooking process but also punctures the skin, letting out all the juices.

The internal temperature of a properly cooked chicken will be about 175°F (79°C) at the thigh. You can test the doneness of poultry by puncturing the skin at the drumstick joint and pressing; if the juice is clear, not pink, the bird is likely cooked properly.

Golden Glazed Grilled Chicken Breasts

SERVES 6

- ½ cup (170 g) honey
- ¼ cup (60 ml) lemon juice
- ¼ teaspoon (0.5 g) curry powder
- I clove garlic, crushed
- I tablespoon (11 g) mustard seeds
- I tablespoon (15 g) Dijon mustard
- 3 tablespoons (42 g) butter
- I tablespoon (6 g) minced green onion
- 6 boneless, skinless split chicken breasts (about 1½ pounds [680 g] total)
- ½ teaspoon (3 g) salt
- ½ teaspoon (1 g) ground pepper
- Shredded spinach leaves and chopped pistachio nuts, for garnish

PREHEAT:

Preheat grill to medium-high.

PREP:

Place the honey and next four ingredients in a small saucepan, heating on a grill rack till hot and well blended, stirring frequently. Whisk in the mustard, butter, and onion, and keep warm.

GRILL:

Lightly coat the grill rack with oil. Season the chicken with salt and pepper and place on the rack, 4 to 6 inches (10.2 to 15.2 cm) from the heat source, cooking for 7 minutes per side or till the chicken tests done, basting with the warm sauce frequently.

Place each chicken breast on a bed of spinach and drizzle sauce over top, sprinkling on the nuts.

Caribbean Chicken with Pineapple-Cantaloupe Salsa

SERVES 4

- 1 teaspoon (1.9 g) ground allspice
- 1 teaspoon (2.3 g) ground cinnamon
- 1 teaspoon (2.5 g) ground cumin
- 1 teaspoon (1.8 g) cayenne pepper
- 1¼ teaspoon (7.5 g) salt
- 2 tablespoons (28 ml) olive oil
- 4 boneless chicken breasts
- 14 ounces (400 g) cantaloupe cubes
- 14 ounces (400 g) pineapple chunks
- 2 tablespoons (28 ml) fresh lime juice
- 3 tablespoons (12 g) finely chopped fresh mint

PREHEAT:

Preheat grill to medium.

PREP:

In a small bowl, combine first four ingredients and 1 teaspoon (6 g) of the salt and stir until evenly mixed. Stir in oil to make a paste. Brush mixture on both sides of chicken. Place cantaloupe cubes in medium bowl along with pineapple, lime juice, mint, and remaining salt.

GRILL:

Grill chicken for 7 to 8 minutes on each side. Serve right away topped with salsa or refrigerate overnight. Mint will darken as it stands, so if making ahead of time, add mint just before serving.

Grilled Chicken with Chile-Lime Marinade

SERVES 6

- 6 small boneless chicken breasts, skin on
- 6 boneless chicken thighs, skin on
- 1 cup (235 ml) orange juice
- ¼ cup (60 ml) lime juice
- ¼ cup (60 ml) light olive oil
- 1 jalapeño chile, veined, seeded, and chopped
- 2 teaspoons (10 ml) canned chipotles in adobo sauce, minced
- 2 tablespoons (28 ml) Worcestershire sauce
- 2 teaspoons (3.4 g) finely grated orange zest
- 2 teaspoons (3.4) finely grated lime zest
- 2 teaspoons (6 g) minced garlic
- 2 teaspoons (5.2 g) chile powder
- 2 teaspoons (12 g) kosher salt
- 1 teaspoon (2 g) freshly ground pepper

PREHEAT:

Preheat grill to medium.

MARINATE:

Rinse chicken pieces well in cold water and pat dry on paper towels. Arrange in one or two layers in a wide shallow refrigerator dish. In a small bowl, combine the remaining ingredients, mix well, and pour evenly over the chicken. Cover with plastic wrap and refrigerate for 1 hour.

GRILL:

Start the coals in a chimney starter, empty into grill, and spread the hot coals out. Wipe the rack well with oil and set over the hot coals. Heat for 10 minutes. Lift chicken out of the marinade and place, skin side down, over medium-hot coals. Cook, brushing with marinade every 1 or 2 minutes, for 5 minutes. Turn the chicken, brush generously with marinade again, and cook another 5 minutes or until chicken no longer exudes pink juices. Brush once more with the marinade.

Huli-Huli Chicken

SERVES 4

- 1 (3-pound [1.4 kg]) chicken
- Salt and pepper
- 4 sprigs fresh thyme
- 2 cloves garlic, chopped
- 1 cup (340 g) honey
- 1 cup (235 ml) good-quality dark soy sauce
- 1 cup (235 ml) lime juice
- 1 tablespoon (15 g) light brown sugar

PREHEAT:

Preheat grill to medium.

PREP:

Season the inside of the chicken with salt and pepper. Place the thyme and garlic under the skin on the breast. Combine the honey, soy sauce, lime juice, and brown sugar, stirring until the brown sugar dissolves.

GRILL:

Place the chicken on the spit and brush with the glaze every few minutes until the glaze starts to stick to the chicken. Continue to roast until done, about 1 hour. Remove the chicken from the spit and let rest for 10 minutes before carving.

Grilled Artichoke-Stuffed Chicken Breasts

SERVES 4

- 2 tablespoons (28 ml) extra-virgin olive oil
- I teaspoon (I g) dried thyme
- ¼ teaspoon (0.3 g) crushed red pepper flakes
- I (7-ounce [200 g]) jar artichoke hearts, drained, rinsed, and chopped
- 2 teaspoons (6 g) minced garlic
- ¼ teaspoon (1.5 g) salt
- ¼ teaspoon (0.5 g) black pepper
- 3 ounces (85 g) fresh goat cheese with herbs, crumbled
- 3 tablespoons (21 g) oil-packed sun-dried tomatoes, minced (drain before mincing)
- 2 tablespoons (5 g) finely chopped fresh basil
- 4 large (8-ounce [225 g]) boneless chicken breast halves, skin on
- Extra-virgin olive oil, as needed
- Garlic salt and black pepper, to taste

PREHEAT:

Preheat grill to medium.

PREP:

Rinse the chicken breasts under cold water and pat dry with paper towels. Place each breast between two sheets of plastic wrap and use a meat mallet or the back of a small pan to gently pound and flatten the breasts to a thickness of about ¼" (.6 cm).

COOK:

Warm the olive oil, thyme, and red pepper flakes in a medium-size sauté pan over medium-high heat for 1 to 2 minutes, then add the artichoke hearts, garlic, salt, and pepper. Cook for 3 to 4 minutes, stirring occasionally. Remove pan from the heat. Add the goat cheese, sun-dried tomatoes, and basil, then mix to evenly distribute the ingredients and allow the stuffing to cool. Place the breasts skin side down, and spread each one with one-fourth of the stuffing. Fold the breasts in half over the stuffing and use toothpicks to skewer the sides closed.

GRILL:

Brush or spray both sides with olive oil and season with garlic salt and pepper. Grill the breasts over direct medium heat until the meat juices run clear and the cheese is melted, 8 to 12 minutes, turning once halfway through grilling time. Remove from the grill and carefully remove the toothpicks.

Jerk Marinated Chicken Breast Stuffed with Okra, Spinach, and Bell Pepper

SERVES 6

- 6–8 chicken breasts
- 10 ounces (280 g) Grace jerk seasoning diluted with 4 ounces (120 ml) mushroom soy sauce

Filling for Chicken:

- 6 medium okra, sliced
- 2 ounces (55 g) shallots, chopped
- 2 ounces (55 g) garlic, chopped
- 8 ounces (225 g) spinach, blanched and chopped
- 1 medium bell pepper, seeded and diced (yellow or red)
- 6 ounces (170 g) ground chicken meat
- 2–3 ounces (60–90 ml) olive oil

PREHEAT:

Preheat grill to medium-high.

MARINATE:

Marinate the chicken breasts in jerk marinade to cover for 10 minutes; reserve additional marinade.

PREP:

Combine all filling ingredients except for the ground chicken and sauté for 2 to 3 minutes in olive oil. Refrigerate filling (okra, spinach, bell pepper). Once cooled, mix with ground chicken. Create a 2" (5 cm) incision pocket in the neck of each chicken breast with a knife. Use your finger to open the pocket. Use a medium-size pastry bag with a medium-size tube to stuff filling into chicken. Let chicken sit for 5 minutes.

GRILL:

Grill chicken, basting frequently with reserved marinade, for 10 minutes on each side or until done. Place any remaining marinade that hasn't touched the raw chicken in a saucepan and heat over low heat. Serve with chicken.

Yam and Cashew-Stuffed Chicken

SERVES 4

- I small yam or sweet potato (canned yam is acceptable)
- ½ cup (75 g) roasted cashews
- I clove garlic, chopped finely
- I tablespoon (15 ml) olive oil
- Salt and pepper, to taste
- 4 boneless, chicken breasts skinless or skin on

Glaze:

- 2 cups (475 ml) 100% cranberry juice
- 4 ounces (120 ml) good quality red wine
- 2 ounces (60 ml) balsamic vinegar
- 2 tablespoons (40 g) honey
- 2 tablespoons (16 g) cornstarch

PREHEAT:

Preheat grill to medium-high.

ROAST:

Roast yam for 30 minutes or until tender. Set aside and let cool. When cooked, Mash yam with cashews in a bowl; add chopped garlic, olive oil, salt, and pepper and mix well.

PREP:

Place chicken on cutting board. Starting with thickest point of the breast, cut a 1½" x 3" (3.8 x 7.5 cm) -wide "pocket" into the chicken (be careful not to cut through bottom or sides of breast). Stuff as much yam mixture into chicken as possible. Meanwhile, add cranberry juice, red wine, and balsamic vinegar to a medium-size saucepan and bring to a boil. Reduce by half. Add honey and cornstarch (mix with ½ ounce [14 ml] water); remove from heat. This should have a syrupy consistency.

GRILL:

Place on very hot grill for 4 to 5 minutes a side, or until stuffing reads 170°F (80°C).

SERVE:

Pour glaze over chicken right before plating. Serve with grilled veggies and roast potatoes.

South Pacific Chicken Skewers

SERVES 4

Marinade for Chicken:

- ½ cup (120 ml) soy sauce
- ¾ cup (175 ml) vegetable oil
- 2 tablespoons (28 ml) distilled white vinegar
- 3 tablespoons (60 g) honey
- 1½ teaspoons (4.5 g) garlic powder
- 2½ teaspoons (4.6 g) ground ginger
- I teaspoon (2 g) coursely ground black pepper
- ½ teaspoon (0.6 g) crushed red pepper flakes
- 3 whole green onions, split lengthwise and chopped
- 20 2" (5 cm) -wide chicken tenders
- 40 (I" [2.5 cm]) pineapple chunks

PREHEAT:

Preheat grill to medium-high.

MARINATE:

Put all marinade ingredients in a blender and pulse until thoroughly blended. Makes about ¾ cup (175 ml). Place chicken tenders and marinade in resealable bag and let marinate for 12 to 24 hours.

PREP:

Drain chicken. Thread one chunk of pineapple on an 8" (20 cm) skewer all the way down to the end of skewer, then thread chicken on, and finish with another chunk of pineapple.

GRILL:

Grill over hot coals until done (3 to 5 minutes per side).

Rolled and Stuffed Turkey Breast

SERVES 6 TO 8

- ³/₄ cup (120 g) diced onion
- ¹/₂ cup (60 g) thinly sliced celery
- ¹/₂ cup (65 g) coarsely chopped carrots
- I tablespoon (14 g) butter
- ¹/₂ cup (25 g) fresh bread crumbs
- 2 tablespoons (28 ml) white wine or water
- I teaspoon (2 g) mixed dried herb blend of your choice
- I boneless turkey breast half (about 2¹/₂ pounds [I kg]), skin on or skinless
- Salt and freshly ground pepper
- ¹/₂ cup (120 ml) chicken broth
- I tablespoon (15 ml) olive oil or canola oil
- 6 pieces heavy kitchen string (each about 18" [45 cm] long), soaked in water

PREHEAT:

Preheat grill to high.

PREP:

Butterfly turkey breast by slicing horizontally through the breast (parallel to the cutting board), almost but not quite all the way through. Open up turkey breast like a book. Cover with a sheet of plastic wrap, then pound thicker areas to even out thickness as much as possible. Remove plastic wrap; sprinkle turkey with salt and pepper to taste. Place turkey on work surface with the seam parallel to you; if the turkey has the skin on, place the half with the skin farthest from you (skin side down).

COOK:

In medium skillet, sauté onion, celery, and carrots in butter over medium heat until tender, about 7 minutes. Remove from heat. Stir in bread crumbs, wine, and herbs; set aside. Spread vegetable mixture over turkey, leaving the last 2" (5 cm) at the edge away from you clear of stuffing. Starting with the edge closest to you, roll breast up, tucking edges in as much as possible. Tie the roll with kitchen string at I" (2.5 cm) intervals, keeping skin stretched and smooth underneath string if using skin-on breast. Some filling will fall out of the ends during rolling and tying, and this is unavoidable.

GRILL:

Combine chicken broth and oil in measuring cup. Position filled water pan between coal banks, or away from heated area of gas grill. Place turkey roll on grate over water pan, skin side up. Brush with broth mixture. Cover grill and cook until center of turkey roll reaches 170°F (77°C), brushing every 15 minutes with broth mixture and rotating roll once or twice (don't turn the roll, just rotate it, keeping the skin side up). Total cooking time will be about an hour. Transfer to serving platter; tent loosely with foil and let stand for 10 minutes before slicing.

For fresh bread crumbs, remove crusts from day-old French- or Italian-style bread and cut into pieces. Process the bread in a blender until it is chopped into uniform crumbs.

Orange-Glazed Cornish Game Hens

SERVES 4

- 2 fresh Cornish game hens, washed and cut in half
- Poultry seasonings (celery salt, onion powder, sage, salt and pepper)
- ¹/₂ (8-ounce [225 g]) jar orange marmalade
- 2 tablespoons (28 g) margarine or butter

PREHEAT:

Preheat grill to medium.

PREP:

In a small glass or ceramic bowl, mix the orange marmalade and the margarine or butter. Cover and microwave about 25 seconds, until the margarine melts; stir mixture.

Season hens with poultry seasonings.

GRILL:

Brush glaze all over Cornish hens on the grill. Keep checking hens so the sauce does not burn—turn down heat if it starts to burn. Brush glaze 2 to 3 times before removing from grill.

Chicken Under a Brick (Pollo al Mattone)

SERVES 4 TO 5

- 1 whole chicken skin-on (3–4 pounds [1.4–1.9 kg])
- Salt and freshly ground black pepper
- $^{3}/_{4}$ cup (175 ml) olive oil
- 2 tablespoons (3.4 g) fresh rosemary leaves, or 1 tablespoon (3.3 g) dried
- $^{1}/_{2}$ teaspoon (0.6 g) hot red pepper flakes (optional)
- Juice from 1 lemon
- 4–6 cloves garlic, minced

PREHEAT:

Preheat grill to medium-high.

MARINATE:

Split chicken by cutting along the backbone with kitchen shears or knife. Open up chicken flat, like a book; with the split chicken skin side up, press over the breastbone firmly with your hands to flatten as much as possible (if you like, you may cut the chicken along the breastbone also so it is in two halves); salt and pepper to taste. Place in large nonreactive dish. In small bowl, combine oil, rosemary, pepper flakes, lemon juice, and garlic; stir to mix. Pour mixture over chicken, turning to coat. Cover and refrigerate for at least 1 hour and as long as 8 hours (turn several times if marinating over an hour).

GRILL:

Wrap a brick completely in foil (if you've cut chicken in half, wrap two bricks). Position filled water pan between coal banks, or away from heated area of gas grill. Drain chicken, discarding marinade. Place chicken, skin side down, on grate over water pan. Place foil-wrapped brick on top of chicken, turning brick sideways to weight down both halves (for halved chicken, place one brick on each half). Cover grill and cook for 20 minutes. Remove brick(s), then flip chicken and replace brick(s). Continue cooking for about 20 minutes longer, or until juices run clear and thigh reaches 170°F (77°C). Transfer chicken to platter; tent loosely with foil and let stand for 5 to 10 minutes before cutting into serving pieces.

Crab-Stuffed Chicken Breast

SERVES 4

- ¼ cup (40 g) finely diced onion
- 3 tablespoons (42 g) butter
- 3 ounces (85 g) mushrooms, chopped fairly finely (about 1 cup after chopping)
- 4 boneless, skinless chicken breast halves (about 6 ounces [170 g] each)
- Salt and pepper
- 4 ounces (115 g [about ¾ cup]) shredded crabmeat
- ¼ cup (60 g) mayonnaise
- ¼ cup (30 g) bread crumbs
- 1 tablespoon (4 g) chopped fresh herbs (a mix of parsley, marjoram, and thyme works well)
- 4 pieces heavy kitchen string (each about 18" [45 cm] long)

PREHEAT:

Preheat grill to medium-high.

COOK:

In medium-size skillet, sauté onion in 1 tablespoon (14 g) of the butter over medium heat for about 5 minutes. Add mushrooms; cook, stirring frequently, until liquid released by mushrooms has been reabsorbed, about 7 minutes. Remove from heat; set aside to cool completely.

PREP:

Place each chicken breast half between two sheets of plastic wrap. Pound with meat mallet until a uniform ¼" (.6 cm) thick; it will be about 6" x 7" inches (15 x 17.5 cm). Sprinkle one side with salt and pepper to taste. In mixing bowl, combine cooled mushroom mixture with crabmeat, mayonnaise, and bread crumbs; mix gently but thoroughly. Divide mixture evenly among four breast halves, mounding in the center of each breast half. Fold ends over filling, tucking edges up as much as possible. Tie each bundle with a cross of kitchen string (as though putting a cross of ribbon on a gift-wrapped box). Wrap each tied breast half tightly in plastic wrap to make a smooth bundle. If possible, refrigerate for an hour or longer, to allow the bundles to firm up; if you like, the chicken can be prepared earlier in the day and refrigerated until you're ready to cook it.

GRILL:

In small saucepan or microwave-safe dish, melt remaining 2 tablespoons (28 g) butter. Mix in herbs. Unwrap chicken bundles; place on grate away from heat. Brush with herb butter; turn and brush second side. Cover grill; cook for 25 minutes or until internal temperature reaches 160°F (71°C), turning twice and brushing with herb butter. Cut strings and remove before serving.

Oriental Chicken Breasts

SERVES 4

- 2 tablespoons (28 ml) mirin (rice wine)
- 2 tablespoons (28 ml) sake (Japanese rice wine)
- 2 tablespoons (13 g) chopped fresh green onion
- 1 tablespoon (15 ml) dark sesame oil
- 1 tablespoon (6 g) minced fresh gingerroot
- 4 boneless, chicken breast halves, skin-on (about 6 ounces [170 g] each)

PREHEAT:

Preheat grill to high.

MARINATE:

In small bowl, combine mirin, sake, green onion, sesame oil, and gingerroot; mix well. Place chicken breasts in shallow dish and pour marinade over chicken, turning to coat. Let stand at room temperature for 30 minutes.

GRILL:

Remove breasts from marinade, reserving marinade; place chicken on grate over heat. Cook for 4 to 6 minutes per side, or until internal temperature reaches 160°F (71°C) and juices run clear. While chicken is cooking, boil remaining marinade in small pan for 5 to 7 minutes. Drizzle cooked marinade over chicken before serving.

Oven-Roasted and Grilled Chicken

SERVES 6 TO 8

- 6–8 bone-in chicken breast halves, skin on or skinless (about 10 ounces [280 g] each)
- $^1/_4$ cup (55 g [$^1/_2$ stick]) butter, melted
- Garlic salt
- Dried parsley flakes
- Freshly ground pepper
- Prepared barbecue sauce as needed (about 1$^1/_4$ cups [315 g])

PREHEAT:

Preheat grill to medium.

BAKE:

Heat oven to 325°F (170°C). Place chicken breasts in baking dish large enough to hold them without overlapping. Drizzle melted butter over each breast and sprinkle breasts with garlic salt, parsley, and pepper to taste. Cover dish with foil. Bake for 1$^1/_2$ hours or until chicken is tender and cooked through.

GRILL:

Place chicken on grate over heat. Baste with barbecue sauce until chicken is well coated; grill until nicely glazed and heated through, 8 to 10 minutes, turning chicken frequently and brushing with sauce.

Grilled Balsamic Chicken and Salad

SERVES 2

Dressing and Marinade:

- $^1/_3$ cup (80 ml) balsamic vinegar
- $^1/_3$ cup (80 ml) olive oil
- 1 tablespoon (15 g) Dijon mustard
- $^1/_4$ teaspoon (1.5 g) seasoned salt
- $^1/_4$ teaspoon (1 g) sugar
- $^1/_8$ teaspoon (0.3 g) pepper

Chicken:

- 2 boneless, skinless chicken breast halves (about 6 ounces [170 g] each)
- 1 medium Vidalia onion, cut into slices and placed on skewers
- 1 medium zucchini or yellow summer squash, cut in half

Salad:

- 4 cups (80 g) mixed young greens
- 2 tablespoons (5 g) chopped fresh basil
- $^1/_2$ cup (75 g) halved grape tomatoes
- $^1/_4$ cup (25 g) raw cauliflower, broken into small flowerets before measuring
- $^1/_4$ cup (25 g) sliced olives
- $^1/_4$ cup (30 g) sliced celery
- $^1/_4$ cup (40 g) crumbled feta cheese
- $^1/_4$ cup (10 g) croutons
- 4 small, fresh, water-packed mozzarella cheese balls
- $^1/_2$ medium cucumber, sliced

PREHEAT:

Preheat grill to medium.

MARINATE:

In small bowl, blend together all dressing ingredients. Pour 3 to 4 tablespoons (45 to 60 ml) dressing into small bowl and brush over chicken, onion, and squash; reserve remaining dressing. Let chicken stand for 10 to 15 minutes, before grilling. Combine all salad ingredients in large bowl.

GRILL:

Place chicken, onion, and squash on grate over heat. Cook, turning several times, for 12 to 15 minutes, or until vegetables are tender and chicken is done (internal temperature should be 160°F (71°C), and juices should run clear).

SERVE:

Toss salad with desired amount of dressing. Separate onion into rings and chop squash; add to salad and toss gently. Slice chicken $^1/_4$" (.6 cm) thick and arrange over tossed salad.

Lemon-Herb Chicken

SERVES 4

- 4 boneless, skinless chicken breast halves (about 6 ounces [170 g] each)

Marinade:

- $^1/_3$ cup (80 ml) lemon juice
- $^1/_3$ cup (80 ml) canola oil
- 1 teaspoon (5 ml) Worcestershire sauce
- $^3/_4$ teaspoon (4.5 g) onion salt
- $^1/_2$ teaspoon (0.5 g) dried thyme
- $^1/_2$ teaspoon (1 g) pepper
- 1–2 cloves garlic, minced

PREHEAT:

Preheat grill to medium.

MARINATE:

Place chicken breasts in a resealable plastic bag. In small bowl, whisk marinade ingredients together; pour over chicken breasts. Marinate in refrigerator for 8 hours, turning occasionally.

GRILL:

Place drained chicken breasts on grate over heat. Cook for 6 to 7 minutes per side, or until internal temperature reaches 160°F (71°C) and juices run clear. Let chicken stand for 5 minutes before serving.

Grilled Chicken Salad with Chutney

SERVES 4

- 4 boneless, skinless chicken breast halves (about 6 ounces [170 g] each)
- 4 teaspoons (8 g) lemon pepper
- 2 teaspoons (12 g) garlic salt
- 1 large Vidalia onion, sliced
- 1 tablespoon (15 ml) olive oil
- 8 cups (200 g) mesclun greens or spinach
- 1 (10-ounce [280 g]) package frozen asparagus, cooked and chilled
- 1 cup (40 g) croutons
- Vinaigrette dressing (about $^1/_2$ cup [120 ml])
- $^1/_3$ cup (85 g) chutney

PREHEAT:

Preheat grill to medium.

PREP:

Sprinkle chicken breasts with lemon pepper and garlic salt.

GRILL:

Place chicken on grate over heat and cook for 6 to 7 minutes per side, or until internal temperature reaches 160°F (71°C) and juices run clear. Let chicken stand for 5 minutes, then slice diagonally across the grain. Brush onion slices with olive oil and grill until tender.

SERVE:

Divide greens among four plates. Top each with asparagus, onions, croutons, and chicken. Drizzle with vinaigrette. Top with scattered dollops of chutney (about 4 teaspoons [20 g] per salad).

Teriyaki Chicken with Mustard Dipping Sauce

SERVES 6 TO 8

- 8 boneless, skinless chicken breast halves (about 6 ounces [170 g] each)

Marinade:

- ¹/₂ cup (120 ml) dry sherry
- ¹/₂ cup (120 ml) soy sauce
- ¹/₄ cup (60 ml) canola oil
- ¹/₄ cup (50 g) loosely packed brown sugar
- ¹/₄ teaspoon (0.5 g) freshly ground pepper

Mustard Dipping Sauce

- ¹/₂ cup (115 g) mayonnaise
- ¹/₃ cup (80 g) Dijon mustard
- 1 teaspoon (5 ml) Worcestershire sauce
- ¹/₄–¹/₂ teaspoon (1.25–2.5 ml) hot sauce

PREHEAT:

Preheat grill to medium.

MARINATE:

Place chicken breasts in resealable plastic bag. Mix marinade ingredients well and pour over chicken, turning to coat. Refrigerate for 1 to 2 hours, turning several times.

PREP:

Blend together all dipping sauce ingredients in small bowl; cover and refrigerate.

GRILL:

Drain chicken breasts, discarding marinade; place on grate over heat. Cook for 6 to 7 minutes per side, or until internal temperature reaches 160°F (71°C) and juices run clear. Let chicken stand for 5 minutes before serving with prepared Mustard Dipping Sauce.

Apricot-Glazed Grilled Chicken Breasts

SERVES 4

Brine:

- I quart (9464 ml) water
- 1/2 cup (144 g) kosher salt
- 1/2 cup (100 g) sugar

Chicken:

- 4 boneless, skinless chicken breast halves (about 6 ounces [170 g] each)

Apricot Glaze:

- 2 tablespoons (28 g) butter
- I tablespoon (15 ml) olive oil
- 2 tablespoons (40 g) apricot preserves
- I tablespoon (20 g) orange marmalade
- 1/8–1/4 teaspoon (0.3–0.6 g) ground nutmeg
- I tablespoon (15 ml) olive oil
- Freshly ground pepper

PREHEAT:

Preheat grill to high.

MARINATE:

In large nonreactive bowl or pot, combine water, salt, and sugar; stir until salt and sugar dissolve completely. Add chicken breast halves; weight down with small plate or bowl to submerge completely. Refrigerate for 20 to 30 minutes.

COOK:

Prepare Apricot Glaze. In small saucepan, melt butter in oil over medium heat. Add preserves, marmalade, and nutmeg. Stir until preserves have melted. Set aside.

GRILL:

Rinse chicken and pat dry with paper towels. Drizzle oil over chicken and sprinkle with freshly ground pepper to taste. Place chicken on grate over heat; cover grill and cook for 5 minutes. Turn breasts; re-cover grill and cook for 5 to 6 minutes longer, or until internal temperature reaches 160°F (71°C) and juices run clear; brush glaze on chicken during the last 3 or 4 minutes of cooking.

Chicken on a Can

SERVES 4 TO 6

- I large whole chicken, skin-on
- 2 tablespoons (28 ml) olive oil
- I tablespoon (18 g) salt
- I teaspoon (2 g) pepper
- 2 tablespoons (30 g) dry rub, or Greek or Italian seasoning blend
- I (12-ounce [355 ml]) can beer
- A few dashes of Worcestershire sauce

PREHEAT:

Preheat grill to medium.

PREP:

Remove neck and giblets from chicken and set aside for another use. Remove and discard fat inside body cavity. Rinse chicken inside and out, and pat dry with paper towels. Rub chicken lightly with oil, then rub inside and out with salt, pepper, and dry rub.

GRILL:

Position drip pan between coal banks or away from heated area of gas grill. Open beer can; drink or pour off about half of the beer. Add Worcestershire sauce to beer remaining in can. Use a pointed can opener to pierce 2 additional holes in the top of the can (this step is optional, but it does provide better steam). Holding the chicken upright, with the body cavity opening down, insert the beer can into the cavity. Prop the chicken on its legs and the beer can to form a tripod on the grate over drip pan. Be careful and precise when setting up the tripod, to prevent spills. Cover grill and cook chicken until the internal temperature registers 170°F (77°C) in the thigh, generally 1 1/4 to 2 hours. The juices should run clear when thigh is stabbed with a sharp knife.

Carefully remove chicken from grill with tongs and a large metal spatula held underneath the beer can for support. The shorter the move, the better, so have a platter right next to the grill or as close as possible. Be careful not to spill hot beer on yourself. Let chicken rest for 10 minutes before carving.

Twice-Grilled Chicken Burritos

SERVES 4

- 1 pound (455 g) boneless, skinless chicken breasts or thighs
- ¹/₂ red bell pepper, cored and cut into ¹/₂″ (1.3 cm) strips
- ¹/₂ green bell pepper, cored and cut into ¹/₂″ (1.3 cm) strips
- 1 small onion, sliced vertically into ¹/₂″ (1.3 cm) slivers
- ¹/₄ cup (60 ml) canola oil
- 2 tablespoons (28 ml) freshly squeezed lime juice
- 2 cloves garlic, minced
- 1 teaspoon (2.6 g) chile powder blend
- 4 burrito-size flour tortillas
- 1 cup (115 g) shredded Monterey Jack cheese
- Salsa and sour cream for garnish (optional)

PREHEAT:

Preheat grill to medium-high.

MARINATE:

Place chicken in 11″ x 7″ (27.5 x 17.5 cm) glass baking dish. Scatter bell peppers and onion slices over chicken. In small glass jar, combine 3 tablespoons (45 ml) of the oil, the lime juice, garlic, and chile powder blend; cover tightly and shake to blend. Pour mixture over chicken and vegetables, stirring to coat. Cover and refrigerate for 1 to 2 hours.

GRILL:

Place a 12″ x 18″ (30 x 45 cm) sheet of heavy-duty foil on work surface, shiny side up; transfer peppers and onion to foil, letting excess marinade drip back into dish with chicken. Place packet on grate over heat and cook for 10 minutes, turning once (be careful not to pierce foil when turning). Move foil packet to side of grate, turning it as you move it. Drain chicken and place on grate over heat. Cover and cook for 6 to 7 minutes per side, or until internal temperature reaches 160°F (71°C) for breasts or 170°F (77°C) for thighs and juices run clear, turning chicken and vegetable packet once. Remove chicken and vegetables from grill, but keep grill going for final cooking.

SERVE:

Slice chicken across the grain into thin strips. Place one-quarter of the strips at the base of a flour tortilla. Add about one-quarter of the vegetables (but don't overfill the burrito); top with ¹/₄ cup (29 g) cheese. Fold up the bottom of the tortilla over the filling. Fold in the sides, then roll tortilla up tightly. Repeat with remaining ingredients. Brush rolled burritos with remaining 1 tablespoon (15 ml) oil. Place on grate over heat, seam side down. Cook for about 2 minutes or until burritos are firm and lightly browned. Carefully turn burritos and cook for about 2 minutes longer. Serve with salsa and sour cream on the side.

Lemonade-Glazed Wings

SERVES 4 AS MAIN DISH OR 8 AS APPETIZER

Lemonade Marinade:

- ¼ cup (60 ml) frozen lemonade concentrate, thawed
- ¼ cup (60 ml) soy sauce
- 3 tablespoons (45 ml) vegetable oil
- 2 tablespoons (40 g) honey
- 2 teaspoons (10 g) Dijon mustard
- ½ teaspoon (1.5 g) finely minced garlic
- ½ teaspoon (0.4 g) chopped fresh thyme leaves, or ¼ teaspoon (0.3 g) dried

Wings:

- 2–3 pounds (905 g–1.4 kg) chicken wings or drumettes

PREHEAT:

Preheat grill to medium-high.

MARINATE:

In small saucepan, combine all marinade ingredients. Heat just to boiling over medium heat, stirring occasionally. Remove from heat and set aside until completely cool. Place wings in large resealable plastic bag. Add half of the cooled marinade, turning to coat. Refrigerate for 3 to 5 hours, turning bag occasionally. Refrigerate remaining marinade also.

GRILL:

Drain wings, discarding marinade. Place on grate over heat. Cover grill and cook for 20 to 25 minutes, turning wings and brushing with reserved marinade every 5 to 10 minutes. Wings are done when they are nicely browned and cooked through. If wings are getting too browned before they are cooked through, move to cooler area of grill to finish cooking.

Basic Grilled Chicken

SERVES 4 TO 5

- 1 whole chicken, skin-on (4–5 pounds [1.9–2.3 kg]), or about 4 pounds (1.9 kg) skin-on parts
- Garlic salt, seasoned salt, or plain salt
- Lemon pepper, other seasoned pepper, or plain pepper

PREHEAT:

Preheat grill to high.

PREP:

Cut chicken into serving pieces. Sprinkle generously with salt and pepper of your choice, rubbing seasonings in with your fingertips.

GRILL:

Position filled water pan between coal banks or away from heated area of gas grill. Place chicken on grate over water pan. Cover grill and cook for 35 minutes, turning chicken about every 10 minutes. Now transfer chicken to the grate over heat. Re-cover and cook for 10 to 15 minutes longer, turning chicken every 5 minutes, until chicken is crispy and cooked through; internal temperature of the thigh should read 170°F (77°C) and juices should run clear.

Italian Turkey Burgers

SERVES 4

- I pound (455 g) ground turkey
- $^1/_2$ cup (125 g) tomato-and-basil pasta sauce
- $^1/_3$ cup (55 g) finely chopped onion
- $^1/_4$ cup (30 g) Italian-seasoned bread crumbs
- $^1/_4$ cup (25 g) freshly grated Parmesan cheese
- I tablespoon (0.4 g) dried parsley flakes
- $^1/_2$ teaspoon (3 g) onion salt
- $^1/_4$ teaspoon (0.8 g) finely minced garlic
- 4 (I-ounce [28 g]) slices mozzarella cheese
- 4 onion rolls or buns
- I clove *garlic*, halved
- Lettuce and tomato for serving (optional) or additional pasta sauce

PREHEAT:

Preheat grill to medium.

PREP:

In mixing bowl, combine ground turkey, sauce, onion, bread crumbs, Parmesan cheese, parsley, onion salt, and garlic; mix gently but thoroughly with your hands. Divide into four equal portions; shape each portion into a $^3/_4$" (1.9 cm) -thick patty, patting meat just enough to hold together.

GRILL:

Place burgers on grate over heat. Cook until center reaches 165°F (74°C), 6 to 7 minutes per side. Top with cheese slices; cover grill to melt cheese. Rub rolls with garlic clove and toast on grill. Serve burgers on buns with lettuce and tomato, or with additional pasta sauce.

Thai BBQ Chicken

SERVES 4

- I small bunch fresh cilantro, preferably with the stems, washed and dried
- 2 cloves garlic, smashed
- 3 tablespoons (45 ml) fish sauce
- I teaspoon (2 g) coarsely ground black pepper
- 6 boneless chicken breast halves, or 8 boneless thighs
- I head leaf or butter lettuce, washed and dried
- $^1/_2$ English cucumber, cut into thin half-moons
- I small bunch mint, washed and dried
- I jar sweet and sour dipping sauce
- $^1/_4$ cup (35 g) chopped roasted peanuts

PREHEAT:

Preheat grill to medium-high.

MARINATE:

Divide the bunch of cilantro in half and coarsely chop one of the halves. Cut off the stems of the other half. Combine the chopped half with the garlic, fish sauce, and black pepper in a blender or food processor, and process to a paste. Pour over the chicken and toss well to coat. Marinate for at least 2 hours or, ideally, overnight

GRILL:

Cook the chicken 4 to 5 minutes on each side, until the chicken is cooked all the way through.

SERVE:

Arrange the lettuce, cucumber, mint, and remaining half of the cilantro on a large platter. Place $^1/_4$ cup of the sauce into each of four individual dipping bowls and sprinkle with the peanuts. Cut the chicken into $^3/_4$" (1.9 cm) slices and place on the platter.

Turkey on the Grill

SERVES 8 TO 10

- I medium-size whole turkey, skin-on (8–I0 pounds [3.6–4.5 kg])
- ¼ cup (55 g [½ stick]) butter, softened
- I teaspoon (0.6 g) dried marjoram
- ½ teaspoon (0.5 g) dried thyme
- I clove garlic, minced finely (optional)
- 2 tablespoons (28 ml) olive oil or canola oil
- Salt and freshly ground pepper
- I cup (235 ml) chicken broth
- I cup (235 ml) white wine or apple juice
- ¼ cup (60 ml) soy sauce
- I tablespoon (7 g) paprika

PREHEAT:

Preheat grill to medium.

PREP:

Remove neck and giblets from turkey and set aside for another use. Remove and discard fat inside body cavity. Rinse turkey inside and out, and pat dry with paper towels. Loosen skin over breast by working your fingertips underneath the skin, starting above the cavity. In small bowl, blend together the butter, marjoram, thyme, and garlic. Spread butter mixture between skin and breast meat, using your fingertips to pack butter under the skin and smoothing from the outside. Rub outside of turkey with oil; season inside and out with salt and pepper to taste. Let turkey stand at room temperature for about an hour while you prepare grill. Also combine broth, wine, soy sauce, and paprika in measuring cup or bowl.

GRILL:

Position filled water pan between coal banks or away from heated area of gas grill. Place turkey, breast side up, on grate over water pan. Cover grill and begin cooking. After about 30 minutes, baste turkey with broth mixture. Re-cover grill and continue cooking, basting every 15 minutes and replenishing coals as necessary, until turkey thigh reaches 170°F (77°C) and juices run clear; cooking time should be 3½ to 4½ hours. Transfer turkey to serving platter; tent loosely with foil and let stand for 15 to 20 minutes before carving.

Herbed Turkey Strips

SERVES 4 TO 5

- I½ pounds (680 g) boneless, skinless turkey breast meat (from wild or domestic turkey)
- ½ cup (120 ml) canola oil
- ½ cup (120 ml) lemon juice
- I teaspoon (6 g) seasoned salt
- I teaspoon (2.5 g) paprika
- I teaspoon (0.7 g) dried basil
- ½ teaspoon (0.5 g) dried thyme
- ½ teaspoon (I g) black pepper
- ¼ teaspoon (0.3 g) hot red pepper flakes
- 2 green onions, minced
- I clove garlic, minced

PREHEAT:

Preheat grill to medium.

MARINATE:

Cut turkey meat into lengthwise strips, about I" (2.5 cm) wide. In mixing bowl, whisk together remaining ingredients. Pour over turkey and marinate in refrigerator for 2 hours.

GRILL:

Drain turkey, discarding marinade. Place on grate over heat and cook until no longer pink in the center, 10 to 15 minutes, turning occasionally.

Barbecued Turkey Legs

SERVES 4

Brine:

- 4 cups (940 ml) cold water
- $^{1}/_{4}$ cup (72 g) canning/pickling salt
- $^{1}/_{4}$ cup (60 g) packed brown sugar
- I tablespoon (8 g) pickling spice

Turkey:

- 4 turkey legs, skin-on (about I2 ounces [340 g] each)
- $^{3}/_{4}$ cup (I90 g) barbecue sauce

PREHEAT:

Preheat grill to medium.

MARINATE:

In nonreactive container, combine brine ingredients, stirring until salt and sugar dissolve. Add turkey legs; weight with small ceramic plate to keep submerged. Refrigerate for about 2 hours.

GRILL:

Position filled water pan between coal banks or away from heated area of gas grill. Drain turkey legs, discarding brine; pat dry with paper towels. Brush legs on all sides with barbecue sauce. Place legs on grate over water pan. Cover grill and cook until turkey legs are tender and reach an internal temperature of 170°F (77°C), 2 to 3 hours; replenish coals (and water in pan) as necessary to maintain a temperature of 250°F to 300°F (120°C to 150°C). Remove legs from grill; brush again with barbecue sauce. Wrap well in heavy-duty foil. Wrap a thick layer of newspaper or towels around foil-wrapped turkey legs; set aside at room temperature for 45 minutes to an hour. This allows the juices to equalize and also helps finish tenderizing the legs.

Grilled Chicken Wings with Sweet Mustard Grilling Sauce

SERVES 4

Sauce:

- I2 whole chicken wings
- 1/3 cup (33 g) Basic Dry Rub
- 2 large carrots, peeled and cut into sticks
- 2 large stalks celery, cut into sticks

PREHEAT:

Preheat grill to high.

PREP:

Wash chicken wings thoroughly, then drain and pat them dry.

MARINATE:

Toss chicken wings with either of the dry rubs in a large mixing bowl, coating evenly. For hotter wings, coat even heavier with dry rub. Cover and refrigerate for 24 hours.

GRILL:

Remove from refrigerator. Spray pan or grill with nonstick cooking spray. Place wings on grill and cook until brown and crisp on all sides, about 15 minutes, turning a few times

SERVE:

Remove and serve with dipping sauce and carrot and celery sticks.

GRILL:

To vary the flavor for this chicken wing recipe, combine 2 or more other dry rubs in this book (See pages 54-57). For a cool dipping sauce, serve with prepared honey Dijon dressing or blue cheese dressing.

Hot and Spicy Turkey Burgers

SERVES 4

Sauce:

- $^{1}/_{2}$ cup (120 g) ketchup
- I tablespoon (15 ml) vinegar
- I tablespoon (15 ml) Worcestershire sauce
- 2 cloves garlic, minced
- $^{1}/_{4}$–$^{1}/_{2}$ teaspoon (0.3–0.6 g) crushed chiles
- $^{1}/_{4}$ teaspoon (1.3 ml) Tabasco sauce
- $^{1}/_{4}$ teaspoon (0.5 g) ground pepper

Burgers:

- I pound (455 g) ground turkey
- $^{1}/_{3}$ cup (27 g) quick-cooking oats

PREHEAT:

Preheat grill to medium-high.

PREP:

In a small bowl, mix all sauce ingredients together. Set aside. Combine turkey and oats in a large bowl. Add one-half the sauce and mix thoroughly. Form mixture into four patties.

GRILL:

Grill for 5 to 7 minutes per side. Baste with remaining sauce after burgers have been turned.

Hot and Spicy Turkey Burgers

CHAPTER SEVEN
GAME

Greek Pheasant Skewers, page 156

GAME INCLUDES MEATS LIKE VENISON FROM DEER, ELK, AND

buffalo meat. It includes birds like pheasant and quail. Game can extend to truly exotic dishes like boar or antelope. Today, most game meats can be found at specialty grocery stores. And preparation of game is so similar to traditional fare, it's not difficult for an outdoor chef to draw raves for his or her skewered venison with tropical fruits or Spiced Boar Burgers (page 159). Most game meats like venison or elk are lean, so a chef has to take a bit more care not to overcook this kind of meat. Choose a tender cut and avoid cooking beyond a medium-rare state. As with beef, coat game meat lightly with cooking oil and use a medium direct heat. Unlike beef or domestic poultry, game should be served immediately and not allowed to rest after cooking because it will lose tenderness.

Rubs and marinades will improve the flavor and tenderness of game, and game meat can be left for a longer time in a marinade than domestic beef or other meats can.

Game can be served in as many variations as other meats and poultry can. For instance, the grill can be used to cook dishes like Mustard-Pepper Grilled Venison Tenderloin (page 152), Chile Venison Burgers (page 154), Honey-Grilled Pheasant (page 158), Apple-Ginger Quail (page 159), or Blue Cheese Venison Steak (page 152). That open campfire just went upscale with your new grill and some of these outstanding recipes.

Stir-Fry Alligator and Snow Peas

SERVES 4

- 1 pound (455 g) alligator meat, trimmed and cut into $^1/_8$" (.3 cm) slices
- 2 tablespoons (16 g) cornstarch
- $^1/_2$ teaspoon (3 g) salt
- $^1/_2$ cup (120 ml) plus 2 tablespoons (30 ml) peanut oil
- 3 egg whites, lightly beaten
- 1$^1/_2$ cups (150 g) green onion bulbs (white part only), cut into 1" (2.5 cm) pieces before measuring
- 1 cup (150 g) cut-up bok choy (1" [2.5 cm] pieces)
- 1 tablespoon (10 g) minced garlic
- $^1/_2$ cup (125 g) miso
- 1 pound (455 g) snow peas
- 1 cup (235 ml) unsalted chicken broth
- 2 tablespoons (28 ml) soy sauce
- 2 teaspoons (10 ml) sesame oil
- 1 teaspoon (2 g) minced fresh gingerroot

PREHEAT:

Preheat grill to high.

PREP:

Place alligator meat in nonreactive bowl. Sprinkle cornstarch over meat, tossing to coat. Add salt and 2 tablespoons (28 ml) peanut oil; mix well. Mix in egg whites; let stand at room temperature for 20 minutes.

GRILL:

Place wok on grate and let it get very hot. Pour remaining $^1/_2$ cup (120 ml) peanut oil into wok and let it heat up. Add alligator meat and cook, stirring constantly, for about 4 minutes. Remove alligator meat with slotted spoon and set aside.

COOK:

Carefully pour off all but $^1/_4$ cup (60 ml) oil from the wok. Add green onions, bok choy, and garlic; stir-fry for about 1 minute. Add miso and alligator meat to the wok. Cover and let cook for 2 minutes. Add snow peas, chicken broth, soy sauce, and sesame oil; stir-fry for about 1 minute. Add gingerroot; stir-fry for about 1 minute longer.

Miso is fermented soybean paste that may be carried at natural-foods stores, health-food stores, and in the refrigerator case at large supermarkets.

Elk Tenderloin Grilled with Asian Spices

SERVES 3

- 1 elk tenderloin or venison loin portion (about 12 ounces [340 g])
- 4 cloves garlic
- 2 shallots, quartered
- 1 fresh red chile pepper, seeds and veins removed
- 1" x 1" (2.5 x 2.5 cm) piece of lemon zest
- 1 tablespoon (13 g) sugar
- $^1/_2$ teaspoon (3 g) coarse salt
- 2 tablespoons (16 g) sesame seeds
- 1 tablespoon (15 ml) dark sesame oil
- 1 tablespoon (15 ml) canola oil
- 2 teaspoons (10 ml) soy sauce
- Spicy Vietnamese Dipping Sauce, optional (page 45)

PREHEAT:

Preheat grill to medium-high.

MARINATE:

Pat tenderloin dry. With sharp knife, score in a diamond pattern on all sides, cutting about $^1/_8$" (.3 cm) deep and $^1/_2$" (1.3 cm) apart. Place in glass baking dish; set aside. With mortar and pestle, pound garlic, shallots, pepper, lemon zest, sugar, and salt to a smooth paste. Stir in sesame seeds, sesame oil, canola oil, and soy sauce. Pour mixture over tenderloin, turning to coat all sides. Cover and refrigerate for 2 to 4 hours, turning once or twice.

Thirty minutes before you're ready to cook, remove tenderloin from refrigerator and allow to stand at room temperature.

GRILL:

Place tenderloin on grate over heat. Cook to medium-rare or medium doneness, about 15 minutes, turning several times.

SERVE:

Slice thinly before serving. Serve with dipping sauce, with or without Vietnamese serving accompaniments.

Vietnamese Serving Accompaniments

To serve Vietnamese-style, present the tenderloin—very thinly sliced—with the following accompaniments, arranged attractively on a platter. Each diner places a few pieces of meat on a lettuce leaf, along with green onions, fresh cilantro, bean sprouts, and a few cooked noodles. The parcel is rolled up and dipped into the Spicy Vietnamese Dipping Sauce (page 45), then eaten out of hand with the cucumber and carrots on the side.

- $1/2$ head Boston lettuce with large leaves, leaves separated
- 3 green onions, sliced $1/4$" (.6 cm) thick
- A handful of fresh cilantro leaves
- 4 ounces (115 g) fresh bean sprouts
- 4 ounces (115 g) thin rice vermicelli, cooked according to package directions and drained
- 1 cucumber, peel scored and seeds removed, cut into wedges about 2" (5 cm) long
- 1 cup (130 g) baby carrots

Mustard-Pepper Grilled Venison Tenderloin

SERVES 3 TO 4

- I tablespoon (6 g) whole mixed-color peppercorns
- I cup (235 ml) chicken broth
- I teaspoon (0.7 g) coarsely chopped fresh rosemary, or ½ teaspoon (0.6 g) coarsely crushed dried
- ¼ cup (60 g) Dijon mustard
- I tablespoon (15 ml) olive oil
- 2 teaspoons (10 ml) balsamic or red-wine vinegar
- I teaspoon (3.7 g) mustard seeds
- 2 whole venison tenderloins (8–12 ounces [225–340 g] each) or 1½ pounds (680 g) elk, moose, or beef tenderloin, trimmed as necessary

PREHEAT:

Preheat grill to medium-high.

PREP:

Crush peppercorns coarsely with mortar and pestle (or place peppercorns on work surface and place a heavy skillet on top, then press and twist the skillet to crush the peppercorns).

MARINATE:

Combine crushed peppercorns, chicken broth, and rosemary in small saucepan. Heat to boiling over high heat, and cook until reduced to ⅓ cup (80 ml), about 15 minutes. Remove from heat. Add mustard, oil, vinegar, and mustard seeds; stir well and set aside to cool to room temperature. Place tenderloins in nonreactive dish and pour about 3 tablespoons (45 ml) of the mustard sauce over the tenderloins; brush evenly on all sides of tenderloins. Let stand at room temperature for 20 or 30 minutes. Set remaining sauce aside until serving time.

GRILL:

Place tenderloins on grate over heat. Grill for about 5 minutes per side or to desired doneness. Slice tenderloins across the grain into 1" (2.5 cm) –thick pieces and serve with mustard-pepper sauce.

Blue Cheese Venison Steak

SERVES 4

- 4 venison steaks (about 6 ounces [170 g] each), trimmed of all fat and connective tissue
- Freshly ground pepper
- 5 ounces (140 g) blue cheese, crumbled
- ½ cup (50 g) minced green onions (white and green parts)

PREHEAT:

Preheat grill to medium.

PREP:

Season steaks with pepper. In a small bowl, combine blue cheese and green onions. Mix with a fork and set aside.

GRILL:

Place steaks on grate directly over heat and sear each side quickly. Move steaks to area away from heat; cook until almost desired doneness. Keep a close eye on the steaks; venison cooks quickly and must not be overcooked. When steaks are almost done, top each steak with some of the blue cheese mixture and cook until done to taste.

Blue Cheese Venison Steak

Rubbed-Hot Venison Steaks

SERVES 4

- 2 tablespoons (14 g) paprika
- 2 teaspoons (12 g) kosher salt
- 2 teaspoons (10 g) packed brown sugar
- 2 teaspoons (4 g) freshly ground black pepper
- 1 teaspoon (2.6 g) ground dried chile pepper, such as ancho or chipotle
- ½ teaspoon (1.3 g) ground cumin
- ¼ teaspoon (0.5 g) cayenne pepper
- 4 elk or venison steaks (about 6 ounces [170 g] each), trimmed of all fat and connective tissue
- 2 tablespoons (28 ml) olive oil

PREHEAT:

Preheat grill to high.

PREP:

In small bowl, combine paprika, salt, brown sugar, black pepper, chile pepper, cumin, and cayenne pepper; mix very well. Sprinkle spice mixture over both sides of steaks, rubbing in gently with your fingertips. Let steaks stand at room temperature for up to 30 minutes while the grill heats up.

GRILL:

Drizzle oil over steaks, then place on grate over heat. Cook for 3 to 5 minutes per side, depending upon the thickness of the steaks (do not cook beyond medium-rare). Remove from grill and let stand for about 5 minutes before serving.

Chile Venison Burgers

Turn all your burgers at once using a hinged grilling basket.

SERVES 8 TO 10

- 2 pounds (905 g) ground venison (substitute beef or buffalo if you like)
- 4 small onions, minced
- 1 cup (115 g) seasoned bread crumbs
- ¼ cup (15 g) finely chopped fresh parsley
- 2 tablespoons (28 ml) soy sauce
- 1 tablespoon (3 g) dried oregano
- 1 tablespoon (16 g) tomato paste
- 1 tablespoon (15 ml) rice vinegar
- 2 teaspoons (5 g) ground cumin
- 1 teaspoon (3 g) garlic powder
- 1 egg, lightly beaten
- 1 tablespoon (20 g) chile sauce, such as Heinz
- 8–10 split hamburger rolls, toasted if you like
- Garlic-Herb Butter, optional (page 74)

PREHEAT:

Preheat grill to medium.

PREP:

In mixing bowl, combine all ingredients except hamburger rolls and herb butter; mix gently but thoroughly with your hands. Cover with plastic wrap and refrigerate for about 2 hours; this allows the flavors to blend.

Shape into patties that are sized the way you like them; as a starting point, divide the mixture into eight portions and shape each portion into a ¾" (1.9 cm) -thick patty, patting meat just enough to hold together (for rare burgers, shape into 1" [2.5 cm] -thick patties). Let stand at room temperature while you prepare grill.

GRILL:

Place burgers on grate over heat. Cook to desired doneness, 4 to 5 minutes per side for medium-rare; a covered grill helps reduce flare-ups, and helps cook the meat more evenly. Serve with buns and Garlic Herb Butter.

Spiced Boar or Pork Burgers

SERVES 3

- 1¼ teaspoons (2.5 g) fennel seeds
- ¾ teaspoon (2.8 g) mustard seeds
- 3 tablespoons (45 ml) broth (any kind), wine, or water
- 1½ teaspoons (4.5 g) finely chopped garlic
- ½ teaspoon (3 g) salt
- ½ teaspoon (1.3 g) paprika
- ¼ teaspoon (0.5 g) freshly ground black pepper
- ¼ teaspoon (0.3 g) hot red pepper flakes (optional)
- 1 pound (455 g) ground boar (substitute ground pork, if you like)
- 3 rye or whole wheat hamburger buns
- Condiments of your choice (ketchup, sliced pickles, mustard, diced onion etc.; caramelized onions are particularly good with these burgers)

PREHEAT:

Preheat grill to medium-high.

COOK:

With mortar and pestle, crush fennel and mustard seeds coarsely (or crush the seeds in a small bowl using a spoon). Combine crushed seeds with broth in small microwave-safe bowl and microwave until just boiling, or heat broth to boiling in a small saucepan on stovetop and combine with seeds in small bowl. Cool broth completely, then combine with garlic, salt, paprika, black pepper, and red pepper flakes; mix well. Add to ground boar; mix gently but thoroughly with your hands. Cover and refrigerate for at least 1 hour or as long as 8 hours.

PREP:

Divide into three equal portions; shape each portion into a ¾" (1.9 cm) -thick patty, patting meat just enough to hold together.

GRILL:

Place burgers on grate over heat. Cook until internal temperature reaches 160°F (71°C), 5 to 7 minutes per side; a covered grill helps reduce flare-ups and helps cook the meat more evenly. Serve with buns and condiments.

Steak with Moroccan Marinade

SERVES 2

- 2 choice elk, moose, venison, or beef steaks, 1" (2.5 cm) thick (6–8 ounces [170–225 g] each)
- ¾ teaspoon (1.4 g) coriander seeds
- ¼ teaspoon (0.5 g) fennel seeds
- ¼ teaspoon (0.4 g) whole black peppercorns
- ¼ teaspoon (0.3 g) hot red pepper flakes
- ½ small onion, cut into 1" (2.5 cm) chunks
- ¾ cup (45 g) tightly packed fresh parsley leaves
- ¼ cup (15 g) loosely packed fresh cilantro leaves
- ¼ preserved lemon rinsed and cut into 1" (2.5 cm) cubes
- 2 cloves garlic
- 2 tablespoons (28 ml) fresh lemon juice
- 2 tablespoons (28 ml) olive oil
- ½ teaspoon (3 g) kosher salt
- About 10 saffron threads, crushed, or a good pinch of powdered saffron

PREHEAT:

Preheat grill to medium-high.

MARINATE:

Poke steaks with fork at ½" (1.3 cm) intervals on both sides; set aside. In small cast-iron or other heavy skillet, combine coriander seeds, fennel seeds, peppercorns, and pepper flakes. Toast over medium-high heat, stirring constantly, until fragrant; be careful to prevent burning. Grind with mortar and pestle or electric spice grinder (or crush with the bottom of a heavy pan); set aside. In food processor, combine onion, parsley, cilantro, preserved lemon, and garlic. Pulse until finely chopped. Add lemon juice, oil, salt, saffron, and reserved ground spices and pulse to combine. Pour half the mixture into nonreactive dish that will hold steaks comfortably. Top with steaks, then spoon remaining parsley mixture over steaks, pressing gently. Cover and refrigerate for 2 to 4 hours.

GRILL:

Place steaks on grate over heat. Grill for about 5 minutes per side, or to desired doneness.

Greek Pheasant Skewers

SERVES 4

Greek Marinade

- $^1/_3$ cup (80 ml) freshly squeezed lemon juice
- 2 tablespoons (28 ml) dry vermouth or water
- 2 tablespoons (28 ml) olive oil
- I clove garlic, pressed or finely minced
- $^1/_2$ teaspoon (0.5 g) dried oregano
- $^1/_4$ teaspoon (0.3 g) dried thyme
- $^1/_8$ teaspoon (0.3 g) coarsely ground pepper
- $1^1/_4$ pounds (560 g) boneless, skinless pheasant meat, cut into 1" (2.5cm) chunks

Skewers:

- 2 medium carrots
- $^1/_2$ red bell pepper, cored and cut into 1" (2.5 cm) chunks
- $^1/_2$ green bell pepper, cored and cut into 1" (2.5 cm) chunks
- $^1/_2$ medium red onion, cut into 1" (2.5 cm) chunks
- Hot cooked orzo or rosamarina pasta (optional)

PREHEAT:

Preheat grill to medium.

MARINATE:

In nonreactive mixing bowl, whisk together all marinade ingredients. Spoon about half the mixture into a small bowl and set aside. Add pheasant to mixing bowl with marinade, stirring to coat. Cover and refrigerate for 30 minutes to 1 hour, stirring occasionally.

COOK:

Meanwhile, peel carrots and cut into 1" (2.5 cm) lengths. Microwave, steam, or boil just until tender-crisp. Refresh under cold running water; drain and set aside.

GRILL:

Drain pheasant, discarding marinade. Arrange pheasant, carrots, peppers, and onion on skewers which have been water-soaked for 30 minutes; fold over thinner or irregularly shaped pheasant pieces to form a thicker chunk. Place skewers on grate over heat.

Cook until pheasant is cooked through and vegetables are tender-crisp, 12 to 15 minutes, turning and brushing occasionally with reserved marinade. Serve over a bed of orzo, if you like.

Orzo is rice-shaped pasta. Rosamarina is thicker and wider pasta.

Honey-Grilled Pheasant

SERVES 4 TO 5

- 2 whole, dressed pheasants, skin on (1 1/2–2 1/4 pounds [680 g–1 kg] each)
- 1/2 teaspoon (1 g) freshly ground pepper
- Kosher salt
- 1 whole head garlic, loose papery skin rubbed off
- 2 small bunches of fresh rosemary
- 4–6 baby carrots, peeled

Honey Baste

- 1/4 cup (55 g [1/2 stick]) unsalted butter
- 2 tablespoons (28 ml) canola oil
- 2 teaspoons (13 g) honey
- 1 teaspoon (6 g) kosher salt

PREHEAT:

Preheat grill to high.

PREP:

Wipe pheasants dry, inside and out, with paper towels. Season cavities with pepper, and salt to taste. Cut off the top of the garlic head, then split the head in half from top to bottom. Place half into the cavity of each pheasant, along with a bunch of rosemary and 2 or 3 baby carrots. Close cavities with small skewers.

GRILL:

Position drip pan between coal banks, or away from heated area of gas grill. To make the baste: Melt butter in small saucepan over low heat. Stir in oil, honey, and salt. Brush the outside of the pheasants with some of the baste. Place pheasants on grate over drip pan. Cover grill and cook for 45 minutes to 1 hour, brushing occasionally with honey baste. To check for doneness, pierce thigh of pheasants; juices should run clear. Transfer pheasants to plate and let stand for 5 to 10 minutes before carving; remove vegetables and herbs from cavities as you carve. Serve carrots and garlic with pheasant.

Grilled Quail Salad

SERVES 4

- 4 whole, dressed quail, cut in half lengthwise through breast (4–6 ounces [115–170 g] each)
- 1 cup (235 ml) Italian-style vinaigrette dressing

Garlic Vinaigrette:

- 1/4 cup (60 ml) heavy cream
- 1 clove garlic, minced
- 1 teaspoon (5 g) Dijon mustard
- 1 tablespoon (15 ml) rice vinegar
- 1/4 cup (60 ml) extra-virgin olive oil
- Salt and freshly ground pepper

Salad:

- 8 cups (200 g) mesclun mix, Boston lettuce, or your preferred salad mixture
- 2 cups (240 g) grated carrots
- 1 cup (70 g) sliced white mushrooms
- 1 red bell pepper, cored, seeded, and sliced
- 20 cherry tomatoes
- 1 cucumber, sliced
- 1 purple onion, sliced

PREHEAT:

Preheat grill to medium.

MARINATE:

Place quail in nonreactive dish; add dressing, turning to coat. Cover and refrigerate for at least 2 hours. Meanwhile, prepare garlic vinaigrette: Place cream, garlic, mustard, and vinegar in a small bowl. Slowly add oil while beating with a wire whisk until emulsified; season with salt and pepper to taste. Cover and refrigerate until needed.

GRILL:

Drain quail; place on grate over heat. Cook until skin is browned and quail is cooked through, 10 to 15 minutes, turning several times. While quail is cooking, arrange salad ingredients in an attractive manner on individual serving plates or large platter. Arrange cooked quail on salad; drizzle with a little garlic vinaigrette. Serve remaining vinaigrette on the side.

Apple-Ginger Quail

SERVES 2

- 4 whole, dressed quail, skin on (4–6 ounces [115–170 g] each)
- ¼ cup (60 g) applesauce
- 1 tablespoon (15 ml) soy sauce
- 1 teaspoon (2 g) finely minced fresh gingerroot
- ½ teaspoon (1.5 g) dry mustard

PREHEAT:

Preheat grill to medium.

MARINATE:

Rinse quail; pat dry. Arrange in glass baking dish. In small bowl, combine remaining ingredients, stirring to blend. Pour over quail, then brush the applesauce mixture over all sides of the quail with a pastry brush. Cover dish and set aside to marinate at room temperature for 30 minutes or up to 1 hour, refrigerated.

GRILL:

Drain quail, reserving applesauce mixture. Place quail on their sides on grate over heat and cook for 3 to 4 minutes. Turn so the other side faces the heat; brush reserved applesauce mixture over the grilled side. Turn and brush again after 3 or 4 minutes, then continue cooking with no additional brushing, turning several times, until the quail are just cooked through; total cooking time will be about 15 minutes.

Barbecued Quail

SERVES 4

- 8 whole, dressed quail, skin on (4–6 ounces [115–170 g] each)
  ¼ cup (60 ml) peanut oil
- ¼ cup (60 ml) lemon juice
- ¼ cup (60 ml) Worcestershire sauce
- ¼ cup (60 ml) beer
- Kosher salt and freshly ground pepper
- Honey Barbecue Sauce (page 37)

PREHEAT:

Preheat grill to medium.

MARINATE:

Rinse quail and pat dry with paper towels; transfer to large glass or ceramic bowl. In smaller bowl, whisk together oil, lemon juice, Worcestershire sauce, beer, and salt and pepper to taste. Pour mixture over the quail, turning to coat. Cover and refrigerate for about 2 hours, turning quail occasionally.

GRILL:

Drain quail, discarding marinade. Place quail on grate over high heat and sear on both sides, 2 to 3 minutes per side. Move quail to area away from heat. Brush with Honey Barbecue Sauce and cook until juices run clear and temperature is 160°F (71°C), turning and brushing frequently with sauce.

Semiboned quail from your supermarket are fine for this recipe.

Grilled Goose Breast Filets

SERVES 6 AS MAIN DISH OR 10 TO 12 AS APPETIZER

- 2¹/₂–3 pounds (1.1–1.4 kg) boneless, skinless Canada Goose breast meat
- 2–3 cups (475–710 ml) merlot, burgundy, or other hearty red wine
- 1 clove garlic, minced
- ¹/₂ cup (112 g [1 stick]) butter, melted
- Poultry seasoning, to taste
- Salt and pepper, to taste

PREHEAT:

Preheat grill to medium.

MARINATE:

Place goose breasts in nonreactive bowl or deep dish. Add enough wine to barely cover goose; sprinkle garlic over. Refrigerate for 4 to 24 hours, turning several times.

GRILL:

Drain goose, discarding wine. Place goose on grate over heat; brush with butter and sprinkle with poultry seasoning and salt and pepper to taste. Cook for 8 to 10 minutes per side, basting with butter and sprinkling several times. Transfer goose to serving platter; tent loosely with foil and let stand for 5 minutes. Slice breasts on diagonal and drizzle with remaining melted butter.

Backstrap in Bacon

SERVES 4 TO 6

- ¹/₂ cup (85 g) steak seasoning
- ¹/₂ cup (120 ml) water
- 1 pound (455 g) venison loin, cut into 1" (2.5 cm) chunks
- About ¹/₂ pound (225 g) bacon slices, cut in half

PREHEAT:

Preheat grill to medium.

MARINATE:

In mixing bowl, blend together seasoning and water. Add venison, stirring to coat. Cover and refrigerate for 6 to 8 hours, stirring occasionally.

PREP:

Near the end of the marinating time, soak a handful of wooden toothpicks (one for each venison chunk) in water for 30 minutes. Drain venison, discarding marinade. Wrap each chunk in bacon and secure with a toothpick.

GRILL:

Place bacon-wrapped chunks on grate over heat and cook for 8 to 10 minutes, or until desired doneness is reached. Do not overcook; the center should still be pink.

Wright Sweet Venison Kabobs

SERVES 4

Marinade

- ¹/₂ cup (120 ml) soy sauce
- ¹/₂ cup (115 g) packed brown sugar
- ¹/₄ cup (60 ml) olive oil
- 2–2¹/₂ pounds (905 g–1.1 kg) venison loin (substitute lean beef if you like)
- 1¹/₂ (8-ounce [225 g]) jars button mushrooms, drained
- 1 pint (300 g) cherry tomatoes
- 1 (20-ounce [560 g]) can pineapple chunks

PREHEAT:

Preheat grill to medium.

MARINATE:

In saucepan, combine marinade ingredients; heat over medium heat, stirring constantly, until brown sugar dissolves. Set aside to cool. Cut venison into 2" (5 cm) cubes; transfer to nonmetallic bowl. Pour cooled marinade over venison, tossing to coat. Cover and refrigerate for 4 to 6 hours, stirring several times.

GRILL:

Thread venison, mushrooms, tomatoes, and pineapple alternately on skewers. Place skewers on grate over heat and cook for 20 to 30 minutes, or until meat has reached desired doneness, turning several times.

CHAPTER EIGHT
FISH AND SEAFOOD

Cedar Planked Fish, page 182

MEATY FISH LIKE TUNA, BLUEFISH, SWORDFISH, AND OTHERS

are easy to grill because they stay together on the grate and are done to perfection quickly. Shellfish like shrimp, oysters, and lobster tails also are a cinch to grill. More tender fish will take a bit more care but there is nothing to prevent the outdoor chef from grilling and enjoying any of the bounty of the oceans, lakes, and rivers. Just make sure fish and other seafood are as fresh as they can be from the local store.

The grill should be really hot to grill fish properly, and this means about ten minutes of preheating. Ensure the grate is as clean as possible and lightly oil the fish, not the grate. Trim any thin parts of the fish fillet away to allow for even cooking of the whole piece. Leave the fish alone on the grill, with the lid down, until it cooks for about 60 percent of the total time recommended in the recipe. By this time, the fish will likely release from the grate easily. Cook the other side in the same way; serve the fish with the first cooked side up to display its grill marks. Try your best not to overcook any fish; take it off the grill when the flesh just begins to separate (flake) into layers.

Shellfish that is large enough can be grilled on the grate. To test for doneness, cut into a scallop, shrimp, or other goodie to see if it is white at its core. If the seafood is too small to place on the grate without slipping through, place it in a wire basket and grill it. Either way, the results will be phenomenal if the chef takes that extra bit of care when grilling food from the sea.

Glazed Grilled Salmon Fillet

SERVES 6

- 1½ cups (340 g) packed brown sugar
- 6 tablespoons (85 g) butter, melted
- 4–6 tablespoons (60–90 ml) fresh lemon juice
- 2¼ teaspoons (2.9 g) fresh dill weed
- ½–¾ teaspoon (0.5–1.4 g) cayenne pepper
- 1 salmon fillet (about 2 pounds [905 g])
- Lemon pepper seasoning

COOK:

In small bowl, combine first five ingredients; mix well. Remove ½ to ¾ cup (120 to 175 ml) to a saucepan; simmer until heated through. Set aside remaining mixture for basting during grilling. Sprinkle salmon with lemon pepper seasoning.

GRILL:

Place salmon on grill with skin side down. Grill covered over medium heat for 5 minutes. Brush with the reserved brown sugar mixture. Grill 10 to 12 minutes longer, basting occasionally. Serve with the warmed sauce drizzled over the fillet.

Grilled Salmon with Sweet Maple Glaze

SERVES 6

Maple-Soy Glaze:

- ¹/₄ cup (60 ml) soy sauce
- ¹/₂ cup (120 ml) real maple syrup, preferably Grade B

Salmon:

- ¹/₃ cup (80 ml) soy sauce
- ¹/₃ cup (80 ml) real maple syrup
- 4 (8-ounce [225 g]) salmon fillets, about 1¹/₂" (3.8 cm) in thickest part
- Freshly ground black pepper
- Vegetable oil
- Lemon wedges

Glazed Vegetables:

- 3 tablespoons (45 ml) vegetable oil
- 3 cloves garlic, minced
- Salt and freshly ground pepper, to taste
- 2 medium zucchini, sliced lengthwise
- 2 small Japanese eggplants, halved lengthwise
- 1 large yellow summer squash, quartered lengthwise
- 2 medium red bell peppers, halved lengthwise and seeded
- Parmesan shavings

COOK:

Stir together ¹/₄ cup (60 ml) soy sauce and ¹/₂ cup (120 ml) maple syrup in small saucepan for glaze. Bring to a simmer over medium-high heat and cook until slightly thickened, 3 to 4 minutes. Measure 4 tablespoons (60 ml) glaze into small bowl and set aside.

PREP:

Whisk ¹/₃ cup (80 ml) soy sauce and ¹/₃ cup (80 ml) maple syrup in 13" x 9" (32.5 x 22.5 cm) baking dish until combined; carefully place fillets, flesh side down, in single layer in marinade (do not coat salmon skin with marinade). Refrigerate while preparing grill.

GRILL:

Remove salmon from marinade and sprinkle flesh side liberally with pepper. Using long-handled tongs, dip a wad of paper towels in vegetable oil and wipe hot side of grill grate. Place fillets flesh side down on hot side of grill and cook until grill-marked, about 1 minute. Using tongs, flip fillets skin side down, still on hot side of grill; brush flesh with glaze and cook until salmon is opaque about halfway up thickness of fillets, 3 to 4 minutes. Using long-handled tongs, dip wad of paper towels in vegetable oil and wipe cooler side of grill grate. Brush flesh again with glaze, then turn fillets flesh side down onto cooler side of grill; cook until deeply browned, crust has formed, and center of thickest part of fillet is still translucent when cut into with paring knife, about 1¹/₂ minutes. Transfer fillets to platter, brush with reserved 4 tablespoons (60 ml) glaze, and serve with lemon wedges.

While salmon is grilling, combine the oil, garlic, and salt and pepper in a resealable plastic bag, and add zucchini, yellow squash, eggplants, and red bell peppers; toss to coat. Remove vegetables from bag. Lay vegetables on grill and brush with maple-soy glaze. Leave without moving for 5 to 6 minutes, or until good grill marks show. Turn vegetables and brush with glaze and cook 5 to 6 minutes, or until tender. Arrange on a serving platter and top with Parmesan shavings.

Grilled Salmon with Tarragon Reduction Glaze

SERVES 4

- ¼ cup (60 ml) Marsala
- ¾ cup (175 ml) sherry vinegar
- 2½ tablespoons (10 g) fresh French tarragon, diced finely
- 2 tablespoons (30 g) Dijon mustard
- ¼ cup (85 g) honey
- 1 tablespoon (14 g) butter, softened
- Salt and freshly ground pepper, to taste
- 4 salmon fillets (about 6 ounces [170 g] each)

PREHEAT:

Preheat grill to 400°F (200°C).

COOK:

In a small saucepan over high heat, reduce the Marsala and sherry vinegar to ½ cup (120 ml). Add the tarragon and reduce to ¼ cup (60 ml).

PREP:

Combine the Dijon mustard and honey in a small bowl. Add the tarragon reduction and blend well. As soon as the temperature of the mixture cools to 140°F (60°C), whisk in the butter. Add salt and pepper to taste. Let rest for 30 minutes.

GRILL:

Brush both sides of the salmon liberally with the glaze. Let stand for 15 minutes. Grill for 3 to 5 minutes on each side for a medium doneness. Baste liberally with the remaining glaze while cooking.

Salmon Marinated in Wine

SERVES 4

- 2 cups (475 ml) white wine
- 1 cup (235 ml) olive oil
- ⅓ cup (80 ml) lemon juice
- 1 large clove garlic, chopped finely
- 2 pounds (905 g) salmon
- Salt and pepper

PREHEAT:

Preheat grill to medium.

MARINATE:

Mix wine, olive oil, lemon juice, and garlic in a casserole dish and lay salmon skin side down for 30 minutes; let sit in refrigerator. Turn salmon over and do same for 30 minutes on opposite side.

GRILL:

Salt and pepper lightly, then place on grill skin side up for 2 minutes and flip over to seal in the juices. Continue to cook until fish is flaky, flipping if needed.

Simple Lemon-Butter Salmon

SERVES 4

- Freshly cut lemon slices
- 4 (8-ounce [225 g]) salmon steaks, skin removed
- Lemon juice from another lemon
- Freshly ground sea salt
- Freshly ground pepper
- Fresh large sprigs rosemary
- 2 pats butter per each salmon fillet

PREHEAT:

Preheat grill to medium.

PREP:

Tear off four large squares of aluminum foil, four times the size of each of the steaks. You will use these to bake the steaks on the grill. Line the aluminum foil squares with enough lemon slices to cover the bottoms of each of the steaks. Pour over each of the steaks some of the lemon juice, and then sprinkle with some of the freshly ground salt and pepper. Place a sprig of fresh rosemary over each of the steaks and then top each steak with two pats of butter. Bring the ends of the aluminum foil upward together and begin turning the fold over, inward toward you.

GRILL:

Once you have completely wrapped the foil closed, wrap the ends upward from the outside to the middle, and put the packet on the grill. Cooking time will vary between 15 and 25 minutes. Open carefully; escaping steam will be hot.

Teriyaki Salmon with Cabbage-Fennel Slaw

SERVES 6

- 6 salmon steaks
- I cup (235 ml) teriyaki sauce
- 1/2 cup (120 ml) water
- 1/2 cup (115 g) brown sugar
- 4 cloves garlic , crushed
- I medium head green cabbage
- I head fennel, bulb only
- 1/2 medium red onion
- 6 tablespoons (90 ml) cider vinegar
- 4 teaspoons (17 g) sugar
- 2 tablespoons (28 ml) extra-virgin olive oil
- 2 teaspoons (12 g) salt
- 2 teaspoons (4 g) ground black pepper
- Pinch red pepper flakes

PREHEAT:

Preheat grill to medium-high.

MARINATE:

Place salmon steaks in a large resealable plastic bag; combine teriyaki sauce, water, brown sugar, and garlic, and pour marinade over salmon. Seal bag tightly, and refrigerate for 1 hour.

PREP:

Meanwhile, remove core from cabbage. Cut cabbage into quarters, and slice into fine shreds; place cabbage into a large bowl. Remove core from fennel, and slice into fine shreds; add to cabbage. Remove ends and peel from onion, and cut into quarters. Slice into fine shreds and add to cabbage and fennel. Combine cider vinegar, sugar, olive oil, salt, pepper, and pepper flakes; pour over cabbage, and stir to coat. Leave at room temperature, stirring occasionally, while salmon marinates and cooks.

GRILL:

Grease a large sheet of foil, and place on grill. Remove salmon steaks from marinade, and place on grill. Cook for 5 to 7 minutes per side, depending upon thickness and desired doneness.

SERVE:

Place salad on a large serving platter, and place steaks around edge (slightly overlapping salad).

Glazed Salmon with Mango Salsa

SERVES 4

Mango Salsa:

- Whole lemon, well washed
- I large ripe mango, peeled, pitted, and cut into 1/2" (1.3 cm) chunks
- 1/2 cup (70 g) chopped seedless cucumber
- 3 tablespoons (30 g) finely minced sweet onion
- I tablespoon (4 g) chopped fresh mint leaves
- 4 blades fresh chives, chopped finely
- 1/8 teaspoon (0.8 g) salt

Glaze:

- 3 tablespoons (45 g) packed light brown sugar
- I tablespoon (20 g) honey
- 5 tablespoons (75 ml) olive oil
- 1/4 cup (60 g) Dijon mustard
- 2 tablespoons (28 ml) soy sauce

Salmon:

- 4 salmon fillets (about 6 ounces [170 g] each)
- Salt and freshly ground pepper

PREHEAT:

Preheat grill to medium.

TO PREPARE SALSA:

Grate 1/2 teaspoon (3 g) peel from lemon and squeeze 1 tablespoon (15 ml) juice; refrigerate remaining lemon for other uses. In medium bowl, toss lemon peel and juice with mango, cucumber, onion, mint, chives, and salt. Cover and refrigerate if not serving immediately.

TO PREPARE GLAZE:

In small saucepan, combine brown sugar, honey, and 2 tablespoons oil (28 ml). Cook over medium heat, stirring constantly, until sugar melts. Remove from heat and whisk in the mustard, soy sauce, and 2 tablespoons (28 ml) of the oil. Set aside until cool.

Use direct medium heat. Brush salmon with remaining oil; season with salt and pepper to taste. Place salmon between two cake-cooling racks or in a perforated grilling wok or grilling skillet; place on grate over heat. Brush salmon with glaze; turn and brush second side. Grill for 10 to 12 minutes, or until desired doneness, turning fish and brushing with glaze several times. Serve salmon topped with mango salsa.

To remove the sharpness from an onion, soak it in ice water for 10 minutes

Salmon or Trout Niçoise

SERVES 2

Dressing:

- 1 tablespoon (10 g) drained capers
- ½ cup (120 ml) extra-virgin olive oil
- 3 tablespoons (45 ml) red wine vinegar
- 1 teaspoon (5 g) Dijon mustard
- Small clove garlic, pressed
- Salt and pepper, to taste

Salad:

- 2 small beets
- 8 ounces (225 g) new red or fingerling potatoes
- 1 hard-boiled egg (optional)
- 4 ounces (115 g) fresh green beans, ends trimmed
- 3 cups (25 g) torn mixed salad greens
- 1 ripe, top-quality tomato, cored and seeded, cut into 8 wedges
- ¼ cup (45 g) roasted red bell pepper strips
- 1 (12-ounce [340 g]) portion boneless, skinless salmon or trout
- 1 teaspoon (5 ml) olive oil
- Salt and pepper
- 10–12 whole black olives, preferably oil-cured
- 4 anchovy fillets, optional

PREHEAT:

Preheat grill to medium.

PREP:

To prepare dressing, mash capers slightly with a fork, then transfer to small glass jar. Add remaining ingredients. Cover jar tightly and shake to blend. Set aside.

COOK:

Add beets to saucepan of boiling water and cook until tender, about 35 minutes. Meanwhile, boil or steam potatoes in another pan until tender; drain and set aside to cool, then cut into quarters. Hard-boil the egg; peel while still warm and set aside to cool. Steam, microwave, or boil the green beans just until tender-crisp; refresh under cold running water and drain well. When beets are tender, hold under cold running water and slip skin off (use a fork to hold a hot beet, or wear rubber gloves to protect your hands from the heat).

PREP:

Cut each beet into eight wedges; set aside to cool to room temperature. Divide greens between two individual serving plates. Arrange potatoes, green beans, beet pieces, tomato wedges, and roasted pepper strips attractively around the edges of the plates, keeping the center clear for the salmon (there should be lettuce in the center, but none of the other ingredients). Quarter the egg, then divide between the plates. Set plates aside.

GRILL:

Lightly oil salmon; season with salt and pepper to taste. Place on grate over heat, flesh side down, and cook for 5 minutes, turning once to create cross hatch grill marks. Turn fish over and cook on second side until flesh is just opaque, 5 to 10 minutes longer.

SERVE:

Divide salmon into two pieces, and place onto plates in the center so salmon is surrounded by vegetables. Divide olives evenly between the two plates; cross two anchovy strips over each piece of salmon. Serve prepared dressing on the side.

Grilled Salmon Burgers

SERVES 4

- 1 pound (455 g) boneless, skinless salmon fillets
- 2 teaspoons (6 g) minced shallots
- 1 teaspoon (1.3 g) minced fresh parsley
- 2 tablespoons (5 g) minced fresh basil
- Kosher salt and freshly ground pepper
- 2–3 tablespoons (28–45 ml) olive oil
- 2 cloves garlic, minced
- 3 whole tomatoes, peeled, seeded, and chopped

PREHEAT:

Preheat grill to medium.

PREP:

Place salmon in food processor and process with 1-second pulses until coarsely chopped. Transfer salmon to mixing bowl; add shallots, parsley, 1 tablespoon (2.5 g) of the basil, and salt and pepper to taste. Mix well. If mixture is too dry, add a little olive oil as needed. Divide mixture into four equal portions. Shape into patties, packing well; set aside.

COOK:

In small saucepan, heat 1 tablespoon (28 ml) oil over medium heat. When hot, add garlic and sauté for about a minute. Add tomatoes and remaining 1 tablespoon (2.5 g) basil. Stir to mix well and let simmer for 5 to 10 minutes. Set aside and keep warm.

GRILL:

Brush all sides of the burgers with oil and place them in hinged grilling basket. Place basket on grate over heat. Cook for 2 to 3 minutes per side, or until cooked through; drizzle a little more oil on the burgers as they cook, if you like. To serve, spoon some of the warmed tomato mixture onto each individual serving plate, and position a salmon burger alongside sauce.

Lime-Grilled Salmon

SERVES 4

- 4 boneless salmon fillet portions, skin on (5–6 ounces [140–170 g] each)
- 1/4 cup (60 ml) olive oil
- 1/4 cup (16 g) snipped fresh dill weed
- 2–3 limes, peeled and sliced very thinly
- 1 red bell pepper, cored, seeded, and cut into thin strips
- 1 yellow bell pepper, cored, seeded, and cut into thin strips

PREHEAT:

Preheat grill to medium.

PREP:

Rub each side of salmon fillets with olive oil; place on platter, skin side down. Cover each fillet with dill. Completely cover with lime slices and top with thin strips of red and yellow bell peppers.

GRILL:

Place salmon on grate over heat, skin side down; cover grill. Cook for about 15 minutes (without turning), or until fish flakes.

Lemon-Dill Poach Grill

SERVES 6

- 1½ pounds (680 g) salmon fillet
- ½ cup (115 g) mayonnaise
- ½ teaspoon (1.3 g) paprika
- 1 teaspoon (2 g) ground black pepper
- ¼ cup (60 ml) lemon juice
- 1 teaspoon (1 g) dried dill weed
- 3 tablespoons (18 g) chopped green onion
- Oil, for grilling
- 6 sprigs fresh parsley
- 6 sprigs fresh mint

PREHEAT:

Preheat grill to 375°F (190°C).

PREP:

Cut salmon into six equal portions. Combine remaining ingredients (except parsley and mint). Lay out two sheets of tin foil, each large enough to wrap three fillet pieces.

Place a dollop of sauce on each piece of foil and spread around center of foil with spoon.

Place three fillets on the foil, and pour equal measures of remaining sauce over fish. Securely wrap both pieces of foil, folding tops and edges for a tight seal.

GRILL:

Place foil packages on grill for 4 minutes. Turn and cook for an additional 4 minutes.

Carefully open foil packages and, using a spatula, transfer fish to oiled grill. Cook for 1 minute, turn, and cook for an additional minute. Transfer to plate or platter, and place an intertwined sprig of parsley and mint on each portion.

Grilled Tuna Teriyaki with Pepper and Fruit Kabobs

SERVES 4

- 1–1½ tuna loin cuts
- 1 large can pineapple chunks, or use fresh
- 12 small white mushrooms
- 12 baby bella mushrooms
- 3 tablespoons (45 ml) reduced-sodium soy sauce
- 3 tablespoons (45 ml) sherry, such as mellow Oloroso
- 1 tablespoon (6 g) minced fresh gingerroot
- 1½ teaspoons (4.5 g) dry mustard
- 2 cloves garlic, minced
- 1 tablespoon (15 g) brown sugar
- 2 tablespoons (28 ml) vegetable oil
- 1 large red bell pepper, cut into large pieces and seeded
- 1 large orange bell pepper, cut into large pieces and seeded

PREHEAT:

Preheat grill to medium.

MARINATE:

Make the marinade by combining the reserved pineapple juice, soy sauce, sherry, ginger, mustard, garlic, brown sugar, and oil. Mix well and pour over the tuna steaks. Cover and let marinate in the refrigerator for 1½ hours, turning once.

PREP:

Rinse tuna with cold water. Pat dry and set aside. Drain pineapple, reserving ¼ cup (60 ml) of the juice. Set aside the chunks. Wash and clean the mushroom caps and set aside.

ASSEMBLE:

Make the kabobs by using bamboo skewers, which have been soaked for 30 minutes. Alternate pineapple, red pepper, white mushroom, orange pepper, and mushrooms. Set aside.

GRILL:

Drain the tuna, reserving the marinade. Place tuna on a well-oiled grate, 4" to 5" (10 to 13 cm) from hot coals, and cook 4 to 5 minutes. Baste with the marinade and turn. Cook for an additional 4 to 5 minutes, or until tuna flakes, but take care not to overcook.

Baste the kabobs with some of the marinade and place on the grill. Cook 1 to 2 minutes on each side until lightly browned.

Sesame Encrusted Tuna Steaks

Sesame Encrusted Tuna Steaks with Grilled Asparagus

SERVES 2

- 2 tuna steaks, 1"–1½" (2.5–3.8 cm) thick
- Soy sauce
- 1 red bell pepper
- 1 bunch asparagus
- Sesame seeds
- Freshly ground black pepper
- 1 cup (225 g) mayonaise
- 1 teaspoon (5 ml) apple cider vinegar

PREHEAT:

Preheat grill to medium.

MARINATE:

Place tuna steaks in a bowl and cover them completely with soy sauce; allow 15 to 30 minutes marinade time.

GRILL:

Turn on the grill and while it is heating, grill the red pepper to blacken the skin. Remove the red pepper from grill, place it in a bowl, and cover bowl with plastic wrap, to loosen the skin. Place asparagus on grill, and cook it on medium-high until it is tender and slightly blackened.

Remove tuna steaks from soy sauce and cover top side only with sesame seeds. Using pepper mill, sprinkle with black pepper, about four turns per steak. Place steaks, sesame seed side down, on a medium-high flame on your grill and cook for 5 to 7 minutes on each side.

COOK:

Peel the red pepper, cut it up, and remove the seeds .Place it in a food processor to chop it almost to a liquid. Place mayonnaise, pepper, and apple cider vinegar in a saucepan and warm.

SERVE:

Serve tuna and asparagus with sauce poured over the asparagus.

Grilled Tuna with Orange-Basil Sauce

SERVES 2

- 2 tuna fillets, 1" (2.5 cm) thick (about 6 ounces [170 g] each)
- Juice from 1 orange
- Juice from 1 lemon
- ½ cup (120 ml) extra-virgin olive oil
- 6 heaping tablespoons (15 g) finely chopped fresh basil
- ¼ teaspoon (1.5 g) kosher salt, plus additional for seasoning
- ¼ teaspoon (0.5 g) freshly ground pepper, plus additional for seasoning

PREHEAT:

Preheat grill to medium.

MARINATE:

Place tuna fillets in resealable plastic bag. In mixing bowl, combine remaining ingredients and mix with a whisk. Pour mixture over tuna and marinate at room temperature for 30 minutes.

GRILL:

Shake marinade from fish, reserving marinade. Season fish with salt and pepper to taste. Place fish on grate over heat. Cook for 4 to 5 minutes per side, or until desired doneness (do not cook more than a total of 10 minutes per 1" [2.5 cm] of thickness). While fish is cooking, heat marinade to boiling on stovetop; cook until slightly reduced. Pour hot cooked marinade over fish to serve.

Thai-Grilled Hot Spot Rainbow Trout

SERVES 6

- I cup (230 g) plain yogurt
- 2¼ cup (24 g) finely chopped fresh gingerroot
- 4 teaspoons (9 g) ground turmeric
- 2 tablespoons (26 g) sugar
- 2 tablespoons (28 ml) rice vinegar
- I tablespoon (5 g) finely grated lime zest
- 2 teaspoons (12 g) fine sea salt
- 6 natural trout fillets, cut lengthwise into 4 strips
- 24 lettuce leaves, torn into small curly pieces
- I½ cups (248 g) cooked jasmine rice
- Lime-Ginger Dipping Sauce, as needed (right)
- Torn orange leaves for garnish

PREHEAT:

Preheat grill to medium.

MARINATE:

Mix yogurt and next 6 ingredients and set aside to marinate at room temperature. Toss trout strips to cover completely before putting on the grill.

GRILL:

Grill marinated trout strips, flesh side down, for 1 minute. Turn and grill just until firm (about 30 seconds).

SERVE:

Make six nests of four lettuce leaves each. Put equal amount of rice into each. Drizzle each with dipping sauce, add four grilled trout strips. Garnish with torn orange leaves. Serve remaining dipping sauce on the side.

Lime-Ginger Dipping Sauce:

- I½ cups (355 ml) Asian fish sauce
- I cup (200 g) sugar
- I cup (235 ml) ginger ale
- ¾ cup (175 ml) fresh lime juice
- ⅓ cup (32 g) chopped fresh gingerroot
- ⅓ cup (20 g) fresh cilantro leaves
- 4 cloves garlic
- about 6 Thai bird chiles

PREP:

Puree all ingredients.

Crab-Stuffed Rainbow Trout

SERVES 2

- 1 tablespoon (15 ml) olive oil, plus additional for rubbing fish
- 1 tablespoon (10 g) finely diced onion
- 1 tablespoon (8 g) finely diced celery
- 2 tablespoons (28 g) butter
- 1 cup (135 g) shredded crabmeat (about 5 ounces)
- 1/4 cup (30 g) Italian-seasoned bread crumbs
- 1/4 cup (25 g) crushed saltine crackers
- 1 tablespoon (15 ml) lemon juice
- 1/4 teaspoon (0.5 g) Old Bay Seasoning
- 1/4 teaspoon (0.5 g) freshly ground pepper, plus additional for seasoning trout
- 5–6 small wild rainbow trout, or 2 farm-raised rainbow trout (about 1 1/2 pounds [680 g])
- Kosher salt

PREHEAT:

Preheat grill to medium.

COOK:

In saucepan, heat oil over medium heat. Add onion and celery; sauté for about 2 minutes. Add butter, crabmeat, bread crumbs, cracker crumbs, lemon juice, Old Bay Seasoning, and 1/4 teaspoon pepper; mix gently but thoroughly. Spoon stuffing into the cavity of each fish. Rub both sides of each fish with additional olive oil and place in grilling basket. Sprinkle fish with salt and pepper to taste.

GRILL:

Place on grate over heat and cook for about 10 minutes, or until fish are golden and flake when tested with a fork; turn basket several times during cooking.

Coconut-Basted Fish

SERVES 4

- 4 boneless, skinless walleye or other mild fish fillets (4–6 ounces [115–170 g] each)
- 1/4 cup (60 ml) freshly squeezed lime juice (from about 1 lime)
- 1/4 cup (60 ml) Asian fish sauce (nuoc mam or nam pla)
- 1/2 cup (120 ml) thick unsweetened coconut milk
- 3 tablespoons (45 g) packed brown sugar
- 1 tablespoon (6 g) finely minced fresh gingerroot
- 1/4 cup (18 g) flaked unsweetened coconut, lightly toasted

PREHEAT:

Preheat grill to medium-high.

PREP:

Arrange fillets in glass baking dish. In measuring cup, combine lime juice and fish sauce; pour over fillets, turning to coat. Set aside to marinate at room temperature for 15 to 30 minutes. Combine coconut milk, brown sugar, and gingerroot in small bowl, stirring to blend; set aside.

GRILL:

Remove fish from marinade; pat dry. Place fish between two cake-cooling racks; secure edges. Place rack of fish on grate over heat. Cook for about 1 minute, then flip rack and brush fish with coconut-milk mixture. Cook for about 1 minute longer, then flip rack and brush second side of fish with coconut milk mixture. Continue cooking, flipping rack every 2 minutes and brushing fish with coconut milk mixture, until fish is cooked through and beginning to brown in spots; total cooking time will be about 10 minutes. Open rack carefully, loosening fish from top rack as you open. Loosen fish from bottom rack; transfer to serving plate. Sprinkle with toasted coconut.

Marinated Trout Rolls

SERVES 4

- 4 boneless, skinless lake trout fillets, $3/4"$ (1.9 cm) at the thickest point (5–6 ounces [140–170 g] each)
- $1\frac{1}{2}$ cups (90 g) tightly packed fresh parsley leaves
- 2 cloves garlic
- $1/2$ lemon
- 1 tablespoon (15 ml) olive oil
- 1 teaspoon (6 g) coarse salt
- $1/4$ teaspoon (1.3 g) cracked peppercorns
- 8 slices thick-cut bacon
- Mustard Cream Sauce (page 42) (optional)
- 8 wooden toothpicks

PREHEAT:

Preheat grill to medium.

PREP:

Rinse fillets and trim away any dark lateral line. Pat fillets dry with paper towels; place in glass baking dish big enough to hold fillets in a single layer. Combine parsley and garlic in food processor and process with on-and-off pulses until finely chopped. Trim and discard all rind, including the white inner rind, from the lemon. Cut lemon into chunks and remove seeds. Add lemon, oil, salt, and peppercorns to food processor and pulse a few times to chop lemon. Pour parsley mixture over fillets, turning fillets to coat evenly. Cover and refrigerate for about an hour. While the fillets marinate, soak the toothpicks in a bowl of cold water.

ASSEMBLE:

Roll each fillet into a spiral, starting with the tail end; dab the parsley mixture over the fish as you roll so there's a good amount inside each roll. As each roll is made, circle it with two slices of bacon, securing with toothpicks.

GRILL:

Place rolls on grate over heat and cook, turning every 4 or 5 minutes, until bacon is crisp and fish is cooked through; cooking time should be 20 to 25 minutes. (If the bacon is overcrisping before the fish is done, move the rolls off to the sides of the grill where it is cooler.) Test doneness with an instant-read thermometer; the center should be 140°F (60°C). If you don't have an instant-read thermometer, you can pierce a roll with a thin metal skewer. Leave it in place for 15 seconds, then remove it and touch the tip with your finger; if the fish is cooked, the skewer will be warm to the touch. Serve fish rolls with Mustard Cream Sauce or a lemon sauce.

Grilled Flounder on Tomato Sauce

SERVES 4

Sauce:

- 1 tablespoon (15 ml) olive oil
- 2 tablespoons (12 g) minced gingerroot
- 1 tablespoon (10 g) minced garlic
- 1 tablespoon (10 g) minced shallot
- 4 tomatoes, peeled, seeded, and diced
- Salt, to taste
- $1/4$ cup (60 ml) dry white wine
- 1 quart (940 ml) tomato sauce
- 1 cup (235 ml) water
- 4 fresh basil leaves
- 8 boneless, skinless flounder fillets (2–3 ounces [55–85 g] each)
- $1/2$ cup (50 g) chopped green onions (white and green parts)
- Freshly ground pepper

PREHEAT:

Preheat grill to medium-high.

COOK:

In saucepan, heat oil over medium-high heat. Add gingerroot, garlic, and shallot; sauté until soft, about 5 minutes. Add tomatoes and salt; cook for about 3 minutes, stirring occasionally. Add wine and cook for 3 to 5 minutes longer. Add tomato sauce, water, and basil; heat to a gentle boil. Reduce heat slightly and simmer for about 1 hour, stirring occasionally.

GRILL:

Place flounder fillets in grilling basket or between two cake-cooling racks. Place on grate over heat and cook for about 1 minute per side, or until the fish flakes.

SERVE:

Spoon some warm tomato sauce on each individual serving plate; top with two pieces of grilled flounder. Garnish with chopped green onions and pepper to taste.

Herb-Marinated Red Snapper

SERVES 4

- 1 cup (60 g) tightly packed fresh parsley leaves
- 2 fresh basil leaves
- 2 sprigs fresh thyme
- 2 sprigs fresh rosemary
- 2 tablespoons (6 g) dried oregano
- 1 tablespoon (18 g) kosher salt
- 1 teaspoon (2 g) freshly ground pepper
- 1/2 cup (120 ml) olive oil
- 4 boneless red snapper fillets, skin on (about 6 ounces [170 g] each)

PREHEAT:

Preheat grill to medium.

PREP:

Place parsley and basil in food processor. Strip thyme and rosemary leaves from the stems and add leaves to processor. Add oregano, salt, and pepper. Start processing and slowly drizzle in the olive oil from the top. Process until mixture is well blended. Place snapper in baking dish; cover with herb mixture. Cover dish and refrigerate for 3 hours.

When you're almost ready to cook, remove dish from refrigerator and let stand at room temperature.

GRILL:

Place snapper fillets in grilling basket or between two cake-cooling racks. Place on grate away from heat and cook for about 5 minutes. Turn fish, and cook for an additional 3 to 5 minutes, or until fish is just opaque.

Stir-Fried Marlin and Peppers

SERVES 4

- 2 tablespoons (28 ml) hot pepper oil or dark sesame oil
- 1 teaspoon (3 g) chopped garlic
- 1/2 teaspoon (3 g) salt
- 1/2 teaspoon (1.3 g) ground cumin
- 1/4 teaspoon (0.5 g) coarsely ground pepper
- 1 small orange, peeled, seeded, and sectioned
- 3/4–1 pound (340–455 g) marlin steaks, cut into 3/4" (1.9 cm) cubes
- 1 red or orange bell pepper, cored, seeded, and cut into 3/4" (1.9 cm) cubes
- 1 green or yellow bell pepper, cored, seeded, and cut into 3/4" (1.9 cm) cubes
- 1 small white onion, cut into 3/4" (1.9 cm) pieces
- 1 small zucchini, halved lengthwise and sliced 1/4" (.6 cm) thick
- 2 tablespoons (8 g) chopped fresh cilantro (optional)

PREHEAT:

Preheat grill to medium.

PREP:

In large nonreactive bowl, combine oil, garlic, salt, cumin, and pepper. Break or cut orange segments into bowl into 1/2" (1.3 cm) pieces, holding segments over bowl to allow juices to drip into oil mixture. Stir to blend. Add cubed marlin, bell peppers, onion, and zucchini; stir to coat. Set aside at room temperature to marinate for about 30 minutes, stirring occasionally.

GRILL:

Place perforated grilling wok on grate; heat for about a minute. Add marlin mixture. Cover grill and cook for about 15 minutes, stirring every few minutes with wooden spatula. Transfer mixture to serving bowl; sprinkle with cilantro.

Stir-Fried Marlin and Peppers

Corn-Roasted Whole Fish

SERVES 2 TO 3

- 2–3 ears fresh corn, unhusked
- $1/2$ cup (75 g) diced and seeded red bell pepper
- $1/2$ cup (80 g) diced onion
- I teaspoon (3 g) chopped garlic
- $1/2$ fresh hot pepper, seeded and minced
- I tablespoon (14 g) butter
- 1–2 teaspoons (5–10 ml) water
- 2 tablespoons (8 g) chopped fresh cilantro
- I whole, dressed walleye, trout, or other fish, boned but intact, skin on (scaled, $1^1/2$–2 pounds [680–905 g] dressed weight)
- Salt and black pepper
- 6–8 pieces heavy kitchen string (each about 12 inches [30 cm] long)

PREHEAT:

Preheat grill to high.

PREP:

Husk the corn, retaining husks; discard silk. Cut kernels from one ear corn; wrap and refrigerate remaining peeled ears for another use (or plan to cook to accompany fish meal). Place husks in sink of cold water to soak while you prepare stuffing. Add kitchen string to sink to soak also.

COOK:

For stuffing, sauté bell pepper, onion, garlic, and hot pepper in butter in small skillet over medium heat until just tender, about 5 minutes. Add corn kernels and 1 to 2 teaspoons (5 to 10 ml) of water; cook for 1 minute longer. Remove from heat. Stir in cilantro; set aside to cool.

ASSEMBLE:

Make a layer of corn husks on work surface by overlapping two husks as necessary to slightly exceed length of fish; lay a second row of husks next to the first, overlapping by 1" (2.5 cm) or so. Open up boned fish, cavity side up, over husks. Sprinkle flesh with salt and pepper to taste. Pack cooled corn stuffing into cavity. Fold fish over to enclose filling. Arrange more husks around fish to enclose it completely. Tie fish off firmly at 2" (5 cm) intervals with wet kitchen string. If necessary, tuck additional husks underneath string to cover any gaps.

GRILL:

Position filled water pan between coal banks or away from heated area of gas grill. Place wrapped fish on grate over water pan. Cover grill. Cook until fish reaches 140°F (60°C) in center, about 30 minutes (check temperature with instant-read thermometer pushed into center of stuffing). Remove from grill; let stand for 3 or 4 minutes before unwrapping and serving.

Ask the fish seller to bone or "butterfly" the fish. When boning a fish yourself, use a sharp fillet knife, slipping the tip of the knife between the ribs and flesh near the head of the fish. Continue working the knife between the ribs and flesh until you've cleaned away the ribs, staying as close to the bone as possible. Repeat on other side. Lift the ribcage up and cut along the bony ridge between the backbone and the dorsal fin to remove rib bones and backbone completely. Scrape the bonesto remove any flesh that remains and place the boneless flesh into the cavity of the fish before stuffing.

Grilled Fish and Vegetable Soup

SERVES 4

- 1 large ear fresh corn (or 2 small), unhusked
- 4 medium red-skinned potatoes, quartered
- 2 shallots, peeled but whole
- $^1/_4$ cup (60 ml) olive oil
- Salt and coarsely ground pepper
- 1 small red bell pepper
- 1 quart (940 ml) chicken broth
- 2 carrots, diced
- 1 rib celery, diced
- 8–10 ounces (225–280 g) boneless, skinless walleye, trout, salmon, char, or other fillet, $^1/_2"$–$^3/_4"$ [1.3–1.9 cm] thick)
- 2 tablespoons (8 g) chopped fresh cilantro or flat-leaf parsley

PREHEAT:

Preheat grill to medium-high.

PREP:

Soak unhusked corn in sinkful of water for 30 minutes. Combine potatoes and shallots in mixing bowl. Add about 2 tablespoons (28 ml) oil to bowl, tossing vegetables to coat. Sprinkle with a little salt and pepper; toss again.

GRILL:

When grill is ready, place drained corn and whole pepper on grate over hottest part of fire. Arrange potatoes and shallots around cooler parts of fire. Cover grill to begin cooking. Meanwhile, combine broth, carrots, and celery in saucepan; place on stove over medium heat. Keep an eye on the stock; it should simmer gently but not boil while the vegetables are on the grill.

After vegetables have been on grill for a few minutes, rearrange with tongs, turning corn and pepper but keeping them over hottest part of fire. Re-cover grill. Rearrange and turn vegetables every few minutes until potatoes are rich golden brown and shallots are soft, a total of about 20 minutes. Remove individual pieces of potatoes and shallots as each piece is just cooked through. When cool enough to handle, chop potatoes coarsely into $^3/_4$" (1.9 cm) chunks and add to simmering soup; slice shallots and chop to medium consistency, then add to soup.

When skin of pepper is completely black, remove from grill and set aside to cool for 5 to 10 minutes. Continue grilling the corn until tender, a total of 25 to 35 minutes; husk will be burned and blackened, but the corn inside will remain unburned (it should have a few brown spots on it). Peel blackened skin from pepper; cut open and remove seeds and stem. Dice pepper; add to soup.

When corn is done, remove from grill and set aside to cool slightly. Brush fillets with oil; sprinkle with salt and pepper to taste. Brush a little oil over grill grate also. Place fish on oiled grate; cover grill. Cook until fish is just cooked through, 5 to 10 minutes, depending on thickness; use spatula to gently turn fish once during cooking. When fish is just cooked through, transfer to plate.

COOK:

Peel burned husks from corn; the silk should strip away with the husks. Cut kernels from cob and add to simmering soup. Chop fish coarsely with spatula; add to soup.

Simmer soup for about 5 minutes, stirring gently several times. Stir in cilantro just before serving.

Whole Fish with Chinese Flavors

SERVES 4

- 1 whole, dressed 18"–20" (45–51 cm) lake trout, salmon, or similar fish (about 2 pounds [900 g] dressed weight)
- 3 tablespoons (45 ml) soy sauce
- 3 tablespoons (45 ml) hoisin sauce
- 2 tablespoons (28 ml) black bean sauce with garlic
- 1 tablespoon (15 ml) dark sesame oil
- 1 tablespoon (15 ml) dry sherry
- 1 teaspoon (2 g) finely minced fresh gingerroot

PREHEAT:

Preheat grill to medium. Place coals in a line up the center of the grill or along one side, so there is an area of the grill with no coals (for gas grill, leave one bank unlit).

PREP:

Rinse fish inside and out; pat dry. Make deep slashes through the skin on both sides, cutting parallel with the gill edge and spacing the slashes about 2" (5 cm) apart; you will have four or five slashes per side. Tear off a piece of heavy-duty foil that is 4 inches (10 cm) longer than the fish. Fold foil in half lengthwise; turn up edges slightly, forming a shallow rim. Place foil on a baking sheet, and place the fish on the foil. In small bowl, mix together remaining ingredients. Pour one-quarter of the mixture over one side of the fish and rub it into the slits with your fingers. Turn fish over and pour a similar amount over the second side, rubbing it into the slits. Cover and refrigerate for 15 minutes to as long as 2 hours; reserve remaining soy sauce mixture.

GRILL:

Carefully lift the foil-cradled fish onto the grate over heat. Pour half of the remaining soy sauce mixture over the fish. Cover grill and cook for 15 minutes. Pour remaining soy sauce mixture over the fish; re-cover grill and cook for 10 minutes longer. Now, carefully pull the foil-cradled fish to the side of the grill so the back part of the fish is still partially over the heat; the belly side should not be over the hot area. Re-cover grill and cook until the fish is just cooked through, 10 to 15 minutes longer.

Mustard-Tarragon Fish

SERVES 4

- 4 salmon or other fillet portions, skin on (5–6 ounces [140–170 g] each)
- 1/4 cup (60 g) Dijon mustard
- 2 tablespoons (28 ml) olive oil
- 2 tablespoons (8 g) finely chopped fresh tarragon (do not substitute dried)
- 1 teaspoon (2 g) coarsely ground pepper

PREHEAT:

Preheat grill to high.

PREP:

Rinse fillets; pat dry with paper towels. Arrange in single layer in glass baking dish, skin side down. In small bowl, combine remaining ingredients. Divide mustard mixture evenly among fish portions, spreading over flesh to cover completely. Cover dish and refrigerate for 1 hour. Remove dish from refrigerator 15 minutes before cooking.

GRILL:

Place fish, skin side down, on grate away from heat. Cover grill; cook until thickest portion of fish is barely opaque, 12 to 18 minutes. Remove from grill; let stand for 3 or 4 minutes before serving.

Fish-Stuffed Pepper Cups

SERVES 4

- 2 tablespoons (20 g) drained capers
- ¹/₂ cup (115 g) mayonnaise
- 2 teaspoons (2.6 g) snipped fresh dill weed
- 2 teaspoons (10 g) Dijon mustard
- ¹/₂ teaspoon (3 g) salt
- 1 pound (455 g) boneless, skinless fish fillets, at least ¹/₂" (1.3 cm) thick
- 2 bell peppers (for an attractive presentation, use 2 different colors)
- 1 teaspoon (5 ml) olive oil
- 2 tablespoons (14 g) bread crumbs
- 2 teaspoons (10 g) butter, melted

PREHEAT:

Preheat grill to medium-high.

PREP:

Add capers to medium bowl and mash slightly with a fork. Add mayonnaise, dill, mustard, and salt; stir to mix well. Cut fish into ¹/₂" (1.3 cm) cubes and add to mayonnaise mixture. Stir gently to blend; set aside. Carefully cut stems from peppers, removing as little of the pepper flesh as possible. Cut peppers into halves. Remove and discard seeds and membranes, again removing as little of the pepper flesh as possible.

GRILL:

Place peppers, cut side up, on grate directly over heat. Brush insides of peppers with oil. Grill for about 5 minutes, or until pepper skins have colored in spots and peppers are somewhat soft. Transfer peppers to plate. Divide fish mixture evenly between the peppers. In small bowl, toss together bread crumbs and butter, then sprinkle mixture evenly over fish. Place peppers on grate away from heat. Cover grill and cook for 25 minutes; the crumb mixture should be golden and the fish cooked through.

Grilled Striper with Crusty Topping

SERVES 2

- 1 (12-ounce [340-g]) portion striped bass fillet, skin on about 1" (2.5 cm) thick
- 2 tablespoons (28 ml) dry vermouth
- 4¹/₂ teaspoons (22.5 g) Dijon mustard
- 1 small shallot, minced
- 3 tablespoons (21 g) Italian-seasoned bread crumbs
- 2 tablespoons (20 g) crumbled feta cheese

PREHEAT:

Preheat grill to medium-high.

PREP:

Rinse fish; pat dry and place in glass baking dish. In small jar, combine vermouth, mustard, and shallot; cover tightly and shake to blend. Pour vermouth mixture over fish. Set aside to marinate at room temperature for about 30 minutes, or refrigerate for up to 1 hour. Meanwhile, combine bread crumbs and feta in small bowl. Crumble together with a fork to break up the feta into small pieces, then rub with your fingers until the mixture is the consistency of coarse sand. Set aside.

GRILL:

Place fish, skin side up, on grate over heat. Cook for about 4 minutes. Turn fish skin side down. Spoon bread crumb mixture over fish flesh, patting into place. Cover grill and cook until fish is just opaque; total cooking time should be 10 to 13 minutes. Let fish stand for 5 minutes before serving.

Cedar Planked Fish

SERVES 4 TO 6

- 2 pounds (900 g) salmon, char, halibut or trout fillets, skin on or skinless
- 2 teaspoons (10 ml) canola oil, if using skinless fillets
- All-Purpose Seasoning (page 55), or other, to taste
- I red cedar plank, about ¹/₂″ (1.3 cm) thick and large enough to hold fish in single layer

PREHEAT:

Preheat grill to high.

PREP:

Soak plank for 8 hours, or overnight, in bucket of plain water (weight with brick to keep plank submerged). Drain plank and pat dry. If using skinless fish, rub one side with oil; place on plank, oiled side down. If using unskinned fish, place on plank, skin side down. Sprinkle fish generously with seasoning.

GRILL:

Place plank on grate over heat. Cover grill and cook until fish is just opaque, 15 to 25 minutes, depending on thickness of fish (the plank may catch on fire around the edges near the end, and this is okay; if fire becomes too strong, spray plank with water bottle).

SERVE:

Serve on plank, or transfer fish to serving dish if you prefer. When you transfer fish from plank, work spatula between fish skin and flesh so skin remains on plank. Discard plank after use.

Variations

ONION PLANKED FISH

Use skinless fish fillets; omit oil. Place a layer of chopped green onions or sliced globe onions on soaked plank before adding fish. Place fish atop onions; season as directed. Sprinkle additional onions on top of fish; cook as directed.

GINGER PLANKED FISH

Omit seasoning blend. Chop together a 1" (2.5 cm) chunk of peeled fresh gingerroot and several strips of orange zest. Combine chopped mixture in small bowl with 1 teaspoon (5 ml) dry sherry, 1 teaspoon (5 ml) soy sauce, and ¹/₂ teaspoon (2.5 ml) dark sesame oil. Place fish on soaked plank as directed. Brush with ginger mixture; cook as directed.

CITRUS PLANKED FISH

Use skinless fish fillets; omit oil and seasoning blend. Place a layer of orange and lemon slices on soaked plank before adding fish. In small bowl, combine 2 tablespoons (28 ml) thawed orange juice concentrate and ¹/₂ teaspoon each olive oil (2.5 ml), Dijon mustard (2.5 g), dried oregano (0.5 g), and salt (3 g); mix well and brush over fish. Top fish with a few additional orange and lemon slices, arranging attractively. Cook as directed.

GARLIC-CAJUN PLANKED FISH

Omit seasoning blend. In small bowl, combine 2 tablespoons (8 g) chopped fresh parsley, 1 tablespoon (11 g) chopped garlic, and 1¹/₂ teaspoons (7 ml) olive oil. Place fish on soaked plank as directed. Sprinkle fish generously with any Cajun-style seasoning blend; spread garlic mixture evenly over fish. Cook as directed.

MAPLE-GLAZED PLANKED FISH

Omit seasoning blend. Slice 2 green onions thinly; set aside. In small saucepan, combine ¹/₄ cup (60 ml) pure maple syrup and 1 tablespoon each of butter (14 g), lemon or lime juice (15 ml), and soy sauce (15 ml). Add 2 teaspoons (4 g) minced fresh gingerroot, 1 teaspoon (3 g) minced garlic, and ¹/₄ teaspoon (0.3 g) hot red pepper flakes. Heat to boiling over medium-high heat; reduce heat slightly and cook until reduced by half, stirring occasionally. Place fish on soaked plank as directed. Brush generously with maple mixture; sprinkle with green onoins Cook as directed.

To keep the fish from falling apart: Sandwich fish between two cake-cooling racks; place wired-together racks over coals and cook for about 4 minutes on each side. Or, run thin skewers lengthwise through fish strips before placing on oiled grate; remove skewers before serving.

Fish Tacos

SERVES 4

- $^1/_2$ cup (120 ml) dry white wine
- 2 tablespoons (28 ml) freshly squeezed lime juice
- 2 tablespoons (28 ml) canola or olive oil
- I tablespoon (4 g) chopped fresh cilantro
- $^1/_8$ teaspoon (.3 g) ground cumin
- 2 cloves garlic, minced
- 1–1$^1/_4$ pounds (455–560 g) boneless, skinless marlin, mahi mahi, halibut, or other firm fish, about I" (2.5 cm) thick
- I$^1/_2$ cups (105 g) finely shredded cabbage, preferably a mix of red and green
- 2 teaspoons (10 ml) cider or wine vinegar
- I teaspoon (6 g) salt
- $^1/_4$ cup (60 g) mayonnaise
- 3 tablespoons (45 g) tomato-based salsa
- 4 (10" [25 cm]) flour tortillas, warmed in oven or microwave just before serving

PREHEAT:

Preheat grill to medium.

PREP:

In glass dish, combine wine, lime juice, oil, cilantro, cumin, and garlic; beat with fork until well blended. Cut fish with the grain into strips that are 3" to 4" (7.5 to 10 cm) long and roughly $^1/_2$" (1.3 cm) wide. Add fish strips to wine mixture, turning gently to coat. Cover dish and refrigerate for 1 to 2 hours (but no longer or the fish will become mushy).

Meanwhile, combine cabbage, vinegar, and salt in nonreactive mixing bowl, tossing to mix well. Let stand at room temperature for about 30 minutes. Drain, rinse briefly, and drain again. In same bowl, stir together mayonnaise and salsa. Add well-drained cabbage; stir well. Cover and refrigerate until serving time.

GRILL:

Drain fish strips, discarding marinade. Place on grate over heat (see page 182 for some alternatives that help the fish hold together during grilling). Cook for 7 to 8 minutes total, turning carefully so each side is exposed to heat; fish should be just opaque in center. To serve, place fish strips in warmed flour tortilla, top with cabbage mixture, and roll up like a burrito.

Grilled Marinated Fish Fillets

SERVES 3 PER POUND

- Boneless salmon fillets, skin on or skinless, plus marinade, of choice (each marinade recipe below works for I pound [455 g] fish fillets)

Parsley-Ginger Marinade:

- 2 tablespoons (8 g) minced fresh parsley
- 2 tablespoons (28 ml) olive oil
- 2 tablespoons (28 ml) lemon juice
- I teaspoon (2 g) minced fresh gingerroot
- I teaspoon (3 g) minced shallot

Sweet Lemon-Dill Marinade:

- $^1/_4$ cup (60 ml) freshly squeezed lemon juice
- 2 tablespoons (30 g) packed light brown sugar
- $^1/_2$ teaspoon (0.7 g) snipped fresh dill weed
- $^1/_4$ teaspoon (1.5 g) kosher salt
- $^1/_8$ teaspoon (0.3 g) pepper

Vermouth-Maple Marinade:

- I cup (235 ml) sweet (red) vermouth, boiled until reduced to $^1/_3$ cup (80 ml)
- 2 tablespoons (28 ml) real maple syrup
- 2 teaspoons (10 ml) soy sauce
- I teaspoon (3 g) dry mustard
- $^1/_4$ teaspoon (0.5 g) ground ginger
- A few grindings of pepper

PREHEAT:

Preheat grill to medium-high.

PREP:

In small bowl, whisk together marinade ingredients, stirring until any sugar or salt dissolves. Place fish in shallow nonreactive dish. Pour marinade over fish, turning to coat. Cover and let stand for 10 to 45 minutes (don't overmarinate fish, especially if the fillets are thin; acids in the marinade will begin to "cook" the fish after too long).

GRILL:

If you like, place trout fillets in lightly oiled hinged grilling basket, or between two cake-cooling racks; this is particularly helpful if cooking skinless or thin fillets (if you're not using a basket or racks, lightly oil grate). Place on grate over heat and cook until fish is just opaque .

Cajun Shrimp

SERVES 6

- 1½ pounds (680 g) peeled and deveined large raw shrimp, tail on
- ¼ cup (60 ml) olive oil

Cajun Spice Blend:

- 1 teaspoon (3 g) onion powder
- 1 teaspoon (3 g) garlic powder
- 1 teaspoon (2.5 g) paprika
- 1 teaspoon (1.8 g) ground dried oregano
- ½ teaspoon (3 g) kosher salt
- ½ teaspoon (0.9 g) cayenne pepper

PREHEAT:

Preheat grill to medium.

PREP:

In large bowl, combine shrimp and oil, tossing to coat well. In resealable plastic bag or another large bowl, mix together all spice-blend ingredients. Add shrimp, tossing to coat shrimp evenly with spices. Thread shrimp on skewers.

GRILL:

Place skewers on grate over heat. Cook until shrimp are pink and opaque, about 3 minutes per side, turning once.

Quick Shrimp

SERVES 4

- 1 chipotle chile in adobo sauce
- 3 cloves garlic
- 1 tablespoon (13 g) sugar
- Pinch salt
- 1 cup (235 ml) pineapple juice
- 2 limes
- About 24 medium-size shrimp

PREHEAT:

Preheat grill to medium.

PREP:

Chop chipotle and garlic and then combine in a medium bowl with the sugar, salt, pineapple juice, and the juice from both limes

Place shrimp in a resealable plastic bag and then pour marinade into bag. Coat all shimp and refrigerate for 30 minutes.

GRILL:

Heat grill to 400°F (200°C). Thread the shrimp onto skewers. Oil the grates and place the shrimp on the grill. Turn after 2 minutes and remove from heat when pink.

Cedar Planked Shrimp

SERVES 4

- 4 tablespoons (55 g) garlic butter
- 2 lemons
- 2 tablespoons (28 ml) citrus-flavored olive oil
- 16 (medium-size) cooked shrimp, tail on
- 1 cedar plank
- 4 long bamboo skewers

PREHEAT:

Preheat grill to medium.

PREP:

Soak the cedar plank and the bamboo skewers in a container of cold, salted water

for at least 1 hour. Melt the garlic butter in a small pan and keep warm.

Slice 1 lemon into quarters. Cut the other into ⅛" (.3 cm) slices. Light your grill and set it to high heat.

Take the cedar plank out of the water, drain it, and coat the top with the olive oil. Place it on the grill over direct high heat until it begins to steam.

ASSEMBLE:

Take the skewers out of the water and thread four of the shrimp onto each one. Place one lemon quarter on the end of each skewer.

Lay the lemon slices on the hot plank and coat each skewer with melted garlic butter.

Place each skewer of shrimp and lemon on the bed of lemon slices on the plank.

GRILL:

Close the lid and let them steam in the cedar and lemon smoke. Baste often with remaining garlic butter and cook 12 to 15 minutes.

Basil Shrimp with Pineapple

SERVES 2 TO 3

Marinade:

- ¼ cup (60 ml) freshly squeezed lemon juice
- ¼ cup (60 ml) olive oil
- 1 tablespoon (15 ml) pineapple juice
- 1 tablespoon (6 g) finely grated fresh lemon zest
- 2 tablespoons (8 g) chopped fresh parsley, or 1 tablespoon (0.4 g) dried
- 1 tablespoon (2.5 g) chopped fresh basil
- 1 teaspoon (6 g) kosher salt
- ¼ teaspoon (0.6 g) paprika
- ⅛ teaspoon (0.2 g) hot red pepper flakes
- 1 clove garlic, minced

Shrimp with Pineapple:

- 12 ounces (340 g) peeled and deveined large raw shrimp
- 1 (20-ounce [560 g]) can pineapple chunks, drained, or 1 cup (155 g) cut-up fresh pineapple

PREHEAT:

Preheat grill to medium.

PREP:

In mixing bowl, whisk together marinade ingredients. Place shrimp in shallow dish and add marinade, stirring to coat. Cover and refrigerate for 1 hour. If using bamboo skewers, soak in water while shrimp marinates.

ASSEMBLE:

Alternate shrimp and pineapple on skewers.

GRILL:

Place skewers on grate over heat. Cook until shrimp are pink and opaque, about 3 minutes per side, turning once.

Cedar Planked Shrimp

Tropical Shrimp and Sausage Kabobs

Tropical Shrimp and Sausage Kabobs

SERVES 4

- 2 Italian or other sausages (about 6 ounces [170 g] each), skin-on; venison works fine
- 8 ounces (225 g) fresh pineapple chunks (approximately $1/2$" x 1" x 1" (1.3 x 2.5 x 2.5 cm)
- $3/4$ pound (340 g) peeled and deveined raw shrimp
- $1/4$ cup (60 ml) gold rum
- 2 tablespoons (28 ml) orange juice
- 1 tablespoon (15 ml) canola oil
- 1 teaspoon (2 g) minced fresh gingerroot
- 1 teaspoon (3 g) minced garlic
- $1/4$ teaspoon (0.3 g) hot red pepper flakes
- $1/4$ teaspoon (0.3 g) dried marjoram
- $1/4$ teaspoon (1.5 g) salt
- Metal skewers or $1/4$ (4-ounce [115 g]) package sugarcane swizzle sticks

PREHEAT:

Preheat grill to medium.

PREP:

Cut sausages into $3/4$" (1.9 cm) rounds, discarding ends.

ASSEMBLE:

Thread pineapple chunks, shrimp, and sausage slices (thread sausage through the cut ends, not through the skin) alternately onto skewers or sugarcane swizzle sticks, presoaked for 30 minutes, placing in 9" x 13" (22.5 x 32.5 cm) baking dish as you make each one. Combine remaining ingredients in small glass jar; cover tightly and shake to emulsify. Pour rum mixture over assembled kabobs, turning carefully to coat. Cover and refrigerate for 1 hour, turning kabobs occasionally.

GRILL:

Place kabobs on grate over heat. Cover grill and cook until sausages and shrimp are just cooked through, about 10 minutes, turning every few minutes.

Grilled Shrimp with Garlic–White Wine Sauce

SERVES 6

- ¼ cup (40 g) chopped onion
- 6 cloves garlic, minced
- ¼ cup (60 ml) olive oil
- ⅓ cup (80 ml) dry white wine
- 2 tablespoons (28 g) unsalted butter
- 2 tablespoons (28 ml) lemon juice
- 2 tablespoons (6 g) snipped fresh chives
- 1 tablespoon (15 ml) Worcestershire sauce
- 2 pounds (905 g) peeled and deveined jumbo raw shrimp, tail on
- 1 teaspoon (1.8 g) cayenne pepper
- Salt and freshly ground black pepper
- 1 tablespoon (4 g) minced fresh flat-leaf parsley
- skewers

PREHEAT:

Preheat grill to medium.

PREP:

If using bamboo skewers, soak in cold water for 30 minutes while you prepare sauce. In nonreactive bowl, combine shrimp, remaining tablespoons (28 ml) oil, cayenne pepper, and salt and black pepper to taste; toss to coat shrimp thoroughly. Thread shrimp on skewers. In skillet, sauté onion and garlic in 2 tablespoons (28 ml) of the oil over medium-high heat until just soft. Add wine, butter, lemon juice, chives, and Worcestershire sauce. Simmer for about 3 minutes. Strain sauce; set aside and keep warm.

GRILL:

Place skewers on grate over heat. Cook until shrimp are pink and opaque, 3 to 4 minutes per side, turning once. To serve, spoon some of the warm sauce onto each individual serving plate and place four or five shrimp on top of the sauce. Sprinkle with parsley.

Summer Paella

SERVES 6

- ½ cup (120 ml) lemon juice
- 1 cup (235 ml) chicken broth
- ¼ teaspoon (0.2 g) saffron
- ½ teaspoon (3 g) salt
- ½ teaspoon (0.5 g) pepper
- 2 tablespoons (28 g) butter
- 1 clove garlic, minced
- 2 boneless chicken breasts
- 2 sun-dried tomato sausages
- 3 cups (495 g) cooked rice
- 1 cup (130 g) frozen peas
- 20 shrimp, peeled and cleaned
- ½ cup (120 ml) tomato sauce

PREP:

In a foil roasting pan, combine lemon juice, chicken broth, saffron, salt, pepper, butter, and garlic. Boil for 5 minutes and set aside.

Chop up chicken and sausages, and brush with ¼ cup (60 ml) of the boiled mixture. Grill for 7 to 10 minutes.

Add chicken and sausage to roasting pan along with rice, peas, shrimp, and tomato sauce. Toss ingredients together, then seal with aluminum foil and continue grilling for 10 minutes.

Citrus-Maple Bacon-Wrapped Scallop Skewers

SERVES 4

- ³/₄ cup (175 ml) real maple syrup
- ¹/₄ cup (60 ml) fresh orange juice
- 2 tablespoons (28 g) butter, melted
- ¹/₄ teaspoon (1.5 g) salt
- 16 large scallops, cleaned and muscles removed if necessary
- 8 slices bacon, cut in half

PREHEAT:

Preheat grill to medium-high.

PREP:

Mix together ¹/₂ cup (120 ml) maple syrup, orange juice, butter, and salt in large mixing bowl until well combined. Add scallops and toss to coat. Refrigerate for 30 minutes. Spread remaining ¹/₄ cup (60 ml) maple syrup over bacon to coat on both sides. Wrap ¹/₂ piece of bacon around each scallop, then thread onto lightly oiled skewers.

GRILL:

Place scallops onto oiled grill grates over medium-high heat and cook about 2 to 4 minutes per side or until scallops are opaque and slightly browned.

Grilled Scallops with Lime and Garlic Butter

SERVES 6

- 1–1¹/₂ pounds (455–680 g) large scallops
- 3 limes
- Kosher salt
- Freshly ground black pepper
- 2 egg yolks
- 2 cloves garlic, finely grated
- 8 tablespoons (112 g [1 stick]) salted butter
- Bamboo skewers, soaked in water for 30 minutes to prevent them from burning

PREHEAT:

Preheat grill to medium-high.

PREP:

Clean the scallops by running under water and remove the tough muscle. Rinse and dry. Place the cleaned scallops along with the zest and juice of 1 lime in a resealable plastic bag or other nonreactive container. Season well with salt and pepper. Whisk the egg yolks and the zest and juice of the second lime until pale and smooth. Gently sauté the grated garlic in the butter; be careful not to burn the garlic! (That will make it bitter.) Gradually whisk the butter and garlic into the egg yolk mixture until thick and smooth. Season to taste. It will thicken as it cools. Whisk again just before serving. Thread scallops onto skewers, and pat the assembled skewers dry with paper towels before grilling.

GRILL:

Grill over medium direct heat, turning two or three times, until just opaque throughout and lightly browned, taking care not to overcook. Cut the third lime into wedges and serve with the scallops and garlic and butter mixture.

Grilled Scallops with Grilled Zucchini and Eggplant

SERVES 6

- I medium zucchini
- I medium eggplant
- Olive oil
- Kosher salt and pepper, to taste
- Fresh basil, coarsely chopped
- 12 medium or 6 large sea scallops
- 6 romaine lettuce leaves
- 24 tomato slices
- 18 thin slices of lemon cucumber
- 6 tablespoons (90 g) Grilled Red Bell Pepper Mayonnaise (page 68)

PREP:

Cut off the ends of the zucchini and eggplant. Cut into slices long enough for two slices per plate. Pour some olive oil into a nonreactive pan. Season with salt and pepper. Sprinkle with basil. Place the slices of the zucchini and eggplant in the oil. Turn over and sprinkle with more basil. Place the washed scallops in the olive oil. Let the scallops and vegetables marinate for about 30 minutes.

GRILL:

Heat a grill to about 400°F (200°C). Lay the vegetables and the scallops on a vegetable grilling pan. Grill until the vegetables are golden brown, about 4 minutes per side. Grill the scallops until they are golden brown. Remove from grill.

SERVE:

Place the romaine leaf on a plate. Place four slices of tomato on the lettuce. Sprinkle with salt and pepper. Sprinkle with chopped basil. Lay three slices of cucumber on the salad.

Arrange the vegetables on the platter surrounding the scallops. Place 1 tablespoon (15 g) of Grilled Red Bell Pepper Mayonnaise in the center of the scallops.

Wasabi Oysters with Sweet Fennel

SERVES 4

- 8 tablespoons (112 g [1 stick]) unsalted butter, softened
- 1 tablespoon (10 g) wasabi paste
- 2 cloves garlic, chopped
- Black pepper, to taste
- 8 oysters (opened and the muscle loosened; placed on the half shell)
- 1 bunch fennel, sliced thickly lengthwise
- 1 cup (235 ml) sake
- ¼ cup (60 g) brown sugar
- 1 tablespoon (15 ml) soy sauce
- Fresh herbs, cherry tomatoes, sesame seeds, and sliced green onions, for garnish
- Rock salt

PREHEAT:

Preheat grill to high.

PREP:

Mix softened butter with wasabi paste, 1 chopped clove of garlic, and black pepper to taste. Put dollops of this on each of the eight prepared oysters and then let sit in the refrigerator while preparing fennel. Mix sake, brown sugar, soy sauce, the remaining garlic, and some pepper in a small bowl. Pour over sliced fennel.

GRILL:

Have grill on medium heat and place the fennel on the grill first for a few minutes or so until it has some nice grill marks. Then turn and brush with the marinade.

Place the prepared oysters on the half shell on the grill. Let cook until the oysters look done and the butter has melted. Take off grill and place on platter lined with rock salt. Garnish, with fresh herbs and cherry tomatoes. Take fennel off grill and place on a platter, sprinkle with sesame seeds and sliced green onions.

Traditional Southern Oyster Roast

VARIABLE SERVINGS

- 12–24 live oysters per person
- Accompaniments: Hot sauce or seafood sauce, crackers
- Tow sacks

PREHEAT:

Preheat grill to high.

PREP:

Soak the tow sacks in saltwater for 15 minutes. Scrub oysters with a stiff wire brush and then pile them onto the grate over the heat. Cover immediately with soaked tow sacks.

GRILL:

Cook until oysters show a hint of opening, using long-handled tongs to turn them once. Do not overcook to the point that the juice contained inside the shell evaporates. As soon as they are ready, remove from heat and eat at once. Serve with hot sauce and crackers.

Seafood Stir-Fry

SERVES 4 TO 6

- 6 large onions
- I green bell pepper, seeded
- I red bell pepper, seeded
- I yellow bell pepper, seeded
- I tablespoon (14 g) butter
- ¼ cup (30 g) chopped celery
- 2 cloves garlic, crushed
- ½ cup (120 ml) white wine
- 2 tablespoons (12 g) dehydrated chicken stock
- I cup precooked tiger shrimp
- I cup precooked frozen scallops
- ¼ cup (35 g) pine nuts
- I teaspoon (I g) dried dill leaves
- Fresh lemon juice
- Ground pepper, to taste
- I cup cherry tomatoes

PREHEAT:

Preheat grill to medium.

PREP:

Cut the onions into rings and cube the three peppers. Toss into a grilling pan greased with nonstick cooking spray. Add the butter, celery, garlic, white wine, and dehydrated chicken stock. Stir.

COOK:

Turn down the heat to medium-low. Simmer until onions are softened and the liquid has reduced to one-third. Add the shrimp, scallops, and pine nuts. Stir. Cook for approximately 3 minutes, stirring often.

GRILL:

Turn off the grill burner and add in the dill, lemon, and pepper. Stir.

Add in the cherry tomatoes and combine before serving on a bed of rice.

CHAPTER NINE
SANDWICHES AND PIZZA

Black Bean and Roasted Corn Pizza, page 221

THE TERM "FAST FOOD" HAS COME IN FOR A GREAT DEAL OF

criticism over the past several decades, but quickly prepared food doesn't have to be tasteless or boring. The sandwich is the world's "fastest" food offering, but sandwiches can be marvelous in their taste and texture. Pizza can be ready, whether you make it at home or buy it ready-made, in 20 minutes or less, and pizza has become one of the most tasty and anticipated dishes on the modern menu. A pizza can come in any size and be served as an appetizer, a main course, or even a dessert. Fast and fantastic, sandwiches and pizza are also great items for grilling.

Sandwiches: Meals on the Go

The ubiquitous sandwich has become one of the world's favorite meals, partly because of our increasingly busy, on-the-go lifestyles and partly because of the incredible variety of sandwiches that have been invented or adopted from other cultures to satisfy our love for this fast food. Today's sandwiches range from cheese between a couple of slices of bread to hamburgers, clubs, panini, pitas, tacos, and wraps. They can be plain and simple fare or as exotic a dish as one can imagine.

Grilled sandwiches are one of the most popular sandwich categories. From the grilled cheese of our childhood, we have progressed to grilling sandwiches made with ciabatta bread, multigrain breads, pita bread, French baguettes, and more. We stuff these sandwiches with spicy beef and black bean pesto or we go back to cheese with a grilled Italian version featuring mozzarella, tomatoes, and basil oil.

If you love the seashore, you'll love a picnic on the beach with Grilled Summer Sandwiches. If you like to live dangerously, you might go for Chicken Soprano Panini (page 199), named after the infamous TV mobster. And if you want a taste of the Caribbean to get into the mood while planning a tropical trip, how about a Jerked Chicken Breast Sandwich with Grilled Plantain, Sliced Mango, and Coconut-Cilantro Spread (page 202)? No matter how you slice them, grilled sandwiches are very much on the menu of any great outdoor chef.

Grilled Vegetable Panini with Herbed Feta Spread

SERVES 4

- 1 Italian eggplant, sliced into $1/2$" (1.3 cm) -thick slices horizontally
- 1 small zucchini, sliced into $1/2$" (1.3 cm) -thick slices horizontally
- 1 red onion, sliced into $1/2$" (1.3 cm) -thick slices
- 2 portobello mushroom caps, stems trimmed
- $1/2$ cup (120 ml) olive oil, plus extra for brushing
- Salt
- Coarsely ground black pepper
- 8 slices crusty ciabatta or other sandwich bread
- $1/3$ cup (100 g) Herbed Feta Spread (page 78)
- 4 pieces red leaf lettuce
- 1 red bell pepper, roasted, seeded, and sliced

PREHEAT:

Preheat grill to medium-high.

PREP:

Brush eggplant, zucchini, onion slices, and portobello mushrooms evenly with olive oil, then season with salt and pepper.

GRILL:

Place on hot grill and cook until browned and tender, about 4 minutes per side for eggplant and zucchini, 6 minutes per side for the onion, and 8 minutes per side for the mushrooms. Remove from grill or pan and let cool. Peel the purple skin off the eggplant slices. Cut the onion rings in half and slice the mushroom into thin slices.

SERVE:

Lay out bread, and then spread bottom with Herbed Feta Spread, and layer with eggplant, lettuce, zucchini, onion, mushroom, and red pepper. Spread second bread slice with feta spread and place on top of sandwich, feta side down. Brush both sides of sandwich evenly and generously with olive oil and grill with the lid down approximately 3 to 5 minutes per side with aluminum foil wrapped brick pressed on top.

Grilled Summer Sandwiches

SERVES 4

- 4 chicken breasts
- Seasoning salt
- $1/4$ cup (60 g) chicken and rib barbecue sauce
- 8 slices Calabrese loaf
- Olive oil
- $1/2$ cup (60 g) sliced zucchini
- 8 slices Havarti cheese

PREHEAT:

Preheat grill to medium.

GRILL:

Place the chicken breasts on the grill over medium heat. Cook on each side for 8 minutes, sprinkling with seasoning salt and coating with barbecue sauce. When cooked, place on the side of the grill.

Coat each loaf slice with olive oil and brown on the grill (oiled side down). Grill zucchini at the same time.

SERVE:

Place one slice of Havarti cheese on each browned slice of loaf, then add one chicken breast to four of the slices. Top with zucchini and place remaining slices of bread on top of each sandwich.

Close grill and allow sandwiches to heat for 2 to 3 minutes, watching closely. When cheese has melted, remove from heat.

Slice sandwiches into halves. Serve with Garlic-Herb Mayonnaise, (page 73).

Grilled Tuna Panini with Wasabi-Ginger Mayonnaise

SERVES 4

- 1/4 cup (60 ml) extra-virgin olive oil
- 1 teaspoon (2 g) coarsely ground black pepper
- 1/2 teaspoon (3 g) kosher salt
- 1/2 teaspoon (0.6 g) ground dried lemongrass (optional)
- 4 (1/4-pound [115 g]) tuna steaks
- 1/4 cup (60 g) mayonnaise
- 1 tablespoon (10 g) wasabi paste
- 1 teaspoon (2.7 g) freshly grated gingerroot
- 1/2 teaspoon (2.5 ml) lemon juice
- Softened butter, for spreading on English muffins
- 4 English muffins
- 4 leaves Bibb lettuce
- 1 English cucumber, sliced thin

PREHEAT:

Preheat grill to high.

PREP:

Combine olive oil, pepper, salt, and lemongrass in a small mixing bowl. Brush each side of the tuna steaks with the olive oil mixture. Place mayonnaise, wasabi paste, ginger, and lemon juice in a second mixing bowl; stir to combine; and refrigerate for at least 30 minutes.

GRILL:

Place on hot grill and cook until browned but still pink in the middle, about 5 minutes per side.

SERVE:

Butter both sides of English muffins and grill until toasted on both sides, about 5 minutes. Lay out bottom of English muffin and layer with lettuce, cucumber, wasabi mayonnaise, and tuna steak. Add additional mayonnaise and top of muffin.

Paris Texas Panini

SERVES 4

- 1 (6-ounce [170 g]) can green enchilada sauce
- 1 teaspoon (5 ml) hot sauce
- 1 teaspoon (2.5 g) ground cumin
- 1/4 teaspoon (0.3 g) dried oregano
- 1 teaspoon (2 g) coarsely ground black pepper
- 3 tablespoons (30 g) chopped fresh garlic
- 3 (6-ounce [170 g]) boneless, skinless chicken breasts
- 4 poblano peppers
- 1 large white onion, sliced thinly
- Olive oil
- 1 French baguette
- 6 ounces (170 g) Monchego cheese, sliced
- 8 ounces (225 g) Monterey Jack cheese, sliced

PREHEAT:

Preheat grill to high.

MARINATE:

Combine enchilada sauce, hot sauce, cumin, oregano, pepper, and garlic in a large bowl, and stir. Add chicken and toss to coat. Refrigerate for at least 30 minutes.

GRILL:

Rub poblano peppers and onions with olive oil and place on hot grill. Grill onions for about 4 minutes on each side, until browned. Remove and set aside. Grill peppers, charring all sides, until skin is black and blistered, about 15 minutes. Transfer to a paper bag and seal, then let rest for about 5 minutes. Remove peppers from bag and peel away charred skin. Remove stem, seeds, and membranes, then set aside.

Remove chicken from refrigerator and grill for about 7 minutes on each side, until cooked through and browned (the internal temperature should reach 165°F [74°C]). Remove from grill and set aside.

SERVE:

Cut baguette vertically in four equal pieces, then slice open horizontally, but not all the way through. Fold bread open and with inside facing up, press down to flatten. On bottom half of bread, layer Monchego and Monterey Jack cheese. Close bread inside out. Spread butter on top half and grill until browned and cheese is melted through, about 5 minutes. Slice chicken in thin strips with the grain. Remove sandwiches from grill. Open up and layer with poblano peppers, onion, and chicken. Close sandwich and slice in half.

Grilled Salmon and Pepper-Smoked Bacon Club

SERVES 6

- 6 (4-ounce [115 g]) fillets fresh salmon
- Olive oil
- Salt
- Coarsely ground black pepper
- 6 French baguette rolls
- ⅓ cup (75 g) Lemon-Dill Mayonnaise (below)
- 6 leaves red leaf lettuce
- 2 large tomatoes, sliced thinly
- 12 slices smoked bacon, cooked

PREHEAT:

Preheat grill to medium-high.

PREP:

Trim salmon fillets of any fatty pieces. Rub with olive oil and season with salt and pepper.

GRILL:

Grill salmon skin side down until pink and meat begins to flake, about 6 minutes per side. Remove from grill and set aside.

SERVE:

Slice baguette roll open lengthwise, taking care not to slice all the way through. Spread mayonnaise on bread and layer with 1 lettuce leaf, tomato, salmon, and two slices of bacon.

Lemon-Dill Mayonnaise

- ½ cup (115 g) mayonnaise
- 1 teaspoon (5 ml) fresh lemon juice
- 2 teaspoons (2.6 g) chopped fresh dill weed
- Salt
- Coarsely ground black pepper

PREP:

Combine all ingredients and refrigerate until use.

Chicken Soprano Panini

SERVES 4

- 4 (8-ounce [225 g]) boneless, skinless chicken breasts
- ¼ cup (60 g) olive oil, plus more for brushing
- 1 tablespoon (6 g) coarse ground black pepper
- 2 tablespoons (20 ml) chopped fresh garlic
- 2 medium red peppers
- 4 ciabatta rolls
- ¼ cup (60 g) Roasted Garlic Aioli (page 72)
- 8 ounces (225 g) sharp provolone cheese, sliced thinly
- 12 leaves fresh basil
- 8 ounces (225 g) sliced pepperoni
- 8 ounces (225 g) mozzarella cheese, sliced thin

PREHEAT:

Preheat grill to medium.

PREP:

Combine chicken breasts with ¼ cup (60 ml) of olive oil, pepper, and garlic. On a platter, brush each red pepper generously with olive oil. Place mayonnaise, wasabi paste, ginger, and lemon juice in a second mixing bowl; stir to combine; and refrigerate for at least 30 minutes.

GRILL:

Place chicken and red peppers on grill. Grill chicken for 7 minutes on each side, until browned and cooked through (the internal temperature should reach 165°F [74°C]). Transfer chicken to a cutting board and let cool. When cool enough to handle, cut into thin strips and set aside. Grill red peppers, charring the skin black all over, about 20 minutes total. Transfer to a paper bag and seal, then let rest for about 5 minutes. Remove peppers from bag and peel away charred skin, leaving bright red flesh. Remove stem, seeds, and membranes, then cut into thick strips and set aside.

SERVE:

Brush inside of each roll with olive oil, place on grill oiled side down, and toast until golden brown. Transfer to plate. Lay out bottom half of roll, toasted side up, and spread with Garlic Aioli. Top with provolone, basil, pepperoni, chicken, red pepper, mozzarella, and finally top of roll, toasted side down. Wrap sandwich in aluminum foil. Reduce heat on grill to low. Place sandwich on grill and cook for 7 minutes, turning once, until cheese is melted. Remove from foil and slice in half.

Asian Pork Tenderloin Wraps

SERVES 8

Marinade:

- ¹/₂ cup (120 ml) soy sauce
- ¹/₄ cup (60 ml) orange juice
- 3 tablespoons (60 g) honey
- ¹/₄ cup (60 g) packed brown sugar
- 2 tablespoons (28 ml) Scotch whiskey
- 3 tablespoons (45 ml) hoisin sauce
- I tablespoon (8 g) grated fresh gingerroot
- I teaspoon (3 g) Chinese five-spice powder
- I teaspoon (6 g) salt
- I tablespoon (6 g) coarsely ground black pepper
- 2 tablespoons (28 ml) toasted sesame oil
- 2 tablespoons (28 ml) vegetable oil

Pork Wraps:

- 2 pork tenderloins (about 2¹/₂ pounds [1.1 kg])
- 2 cups (40 g) shredded Bibb lettuce
- I cup (120 g) shredded carrots
- 4 scallions, sliced thinly on the diagonal
- ¹/₃ cup (20 g) fresh cilantro leaves
- ¹/₂ cup (75 g) chopped dry roasted peanuts
- ¹/₃ cup (80 ml) Asian Lime Vinaigrette (right)
- 8 red pepper or rice paper wraps

PREHEAT:

Preheat grill to medium-high.

MARINATE:

Place the first ten ingredients in a mixing bowl and whisk to combine. While whisking, gradually add sesame and olive oils in a thin, steady stream. Add pork tenderloin, toss to coat, then cover and refrigerate for at least 1 hour.

GRILL:

Remove pork from refrigerator and let come to room temperature. Place on grill and sear all around, about 4 minutes on each side, then reduce heat to medium-low and cook until internal temperature reaches 125°F (52°C), turning periodically to cook evenly. Remove from heat and let rest 10 minutes, then slice pork thinly.

SERVE:

Lay out wrap on a clean, dry, and flat work surface. If using rice paper, dampen with a cloth until tender and pliable, then lay out flat. Layer wrap with lettuce, carrots, scallions, pork, cilantro leaves, and peanuts, then drizzle with Asian Lime Vinaigrette. Roll wrap one-quarter turn, then fold in sides and continue to roll up. Slice in half on the diagonal and serve. Extra vinaigrette can be served on the side.

Asian Lime Vinaigrette

YIELD: 2 CUPS (475 ML)

- I clove garlic, minced finely
- I fresh red chile pepper, stem end removed, seeded and minced
- ¹/₄ cup (50 g) sugar
- ¹/₄ cup (60 ml) lime juice, including pulp
- 5 tablespoons (75 ml) Thai fish sauce
- ¹/₂ cup (120 ml) water
- I cup (235 ml) olive oil
- ¹/₄ cup (15 g) chopped fresh cilantro

PREP:

Combine garlic, chile pepper, and sugar in a small bowl, then use a fork to mash together and form a paste. Add lime juice and pulp, fish sauce, and water, then stir to dissolve the sugar. Strain the sauce, then whisk with olive oil to thicken, and add cilantro. Cover and refrigerate until ready to use. The dressing can be covered and refrigerated for up to 1 week.

Border Turkey Wrap

SERVES 6

- 2 ears fresh corn, husked
- 2 tablespoons (28 g) butter
- 2 tablespoons (20 g) chopped fresh garlic
- Salt
- Black pepper
- 1 teaspoon (1.3 g) chopped fresh flat-leaf parsley
- 1 teaspoon (1.3 g) chopped fresh cilantro
- 2 tablespoons (19 g) chopped red pepper
- 2 tablespoons (20 g) chopped red onion
- 1 tablespoon (15 ml) red wine vinegar
- Juice from 1 lime
- 6 tomato wraps
- 4 ounces (115 g) Pepper Jack cheese, sliced thinly
- 4 ounces (115 g) Muenster cheese, sliced thinly
- 6 leaves red leaf lettuce
- 1 avocado, sliced thinly
- Chipotle Spread (right)
- 1 pound (455 g) smoked deli turkey breast, sliced thinly

PREHEAT:

Preheat grill to high.

PREP:

Place corn on piece of heavy-duty aluminum foil and top with butter pieces, garlic, salt, and pepper. Wrap tightly.

GRILL:

Grill corn for 20 minutes, turning occasionally. Remove, unwrap, and let cool.

SERVE:

When cool enough to handle, cut kernels from cob into a mixing bowl and remove any silk. Combine with parsley, cilantro, red pepper, red onion, vinegar, and lime juice, then refrigerate for at least 30 minutes. Lay out wrap on flat, clean, and dry work surface, then layer with cheeses, lettuce, corn relish, and avocado; drizzle with Chipotle Spread; and top with turkey.

Chipotle Spread

YIELD 1/2 CUP (100 G)

- 1 tablespoon (15 g) cream cheese, softened
- 2 tablespoons (30 g) mayonnaise
- 2 tablespoons (30 g) sour cream
- 1 teaspoon (5 ml) red wine vinegar
- 1 chipotle pepper in adobo sauce, seeded and chopped finely

PREP:

Combine all ingredients in a small mixing bowl, then cover and refrigerate for at least 30 minutes.

Jerked Chicken Breast Sandwich with Grilled Plantain, Sliced Mango, and Coconut Cilantro Spread

SERVES 4

- 4 (4-ounce [115 g]) boneless, skinless chicken breasts
- 3 tablespoons (45 ml) olive oil, plus more for brushing
- 1/4 cup (20 g) Jamaican jerk seasoning
- I tablespoon (20 g) honey
- 2 ripe plantains
- 8 slices large peasant bread
- 1/3 cup (80 ml) Coconut-Cilantro Spread (below)
- I mango, peeled, pitted, and sliced thinly

PREHEAT:

Preheat grill to high, then reduce heat to medium-high.

PREP:

Place chicken in a bowl and add olive oil, jerk seasoning, and honey. Marinate for at least 1 hour. Peel plantains and slice into 1/4" (0.6 cm) -thick slices on the diagonal. Brush slices with olive oil and set aside.

GRILL:

Grill chicken until cooked through, about 7 minutes per side. Remove and let cool for about 5 minutes. Slice thinly, cutting with the grain of the meat. Grill plantain slices until golden and tender, about 3 minutes per side.

SERVE:

Lay out bread slices and spread evenly with Coconut-Cilantro Spread, then layer chicken, plantains, and mango. Add second slice of bread and slice in half.

Coconut-Cilantro Spread

YIELD: 1/2 CUP (120 ML)

- 1/4 cup (60 ml) Thai coconut sauce
- 1/4 cup (15 g) fresh cilantro leaves, chopped coarsely
- 2 tablespoons (28 ml) lime juice

PREP:

Combine all ingredients in a small mixing bowl, then cover and refrigerate for at least 30 minutes.

Monterey Chicken Club

SERVES 4

- 1/2 cup (120 ml) orange juice
- 1/2 cup (120 ml) ginger ale or 7-Up
- I teaspoon (2 g) black pepper
- I tablespoon (1.7 g) chopped fresh rosemary
- I tablespoon (4 g) chopped fresh flat-leaf parsley
- I tablespoon (15 ml) Worcestershire sauce
- 1/4 cup (60 ml) extra-virgin olive oil
- 3 (6-ounce [170 g]) boneless, skinless chicken breasts
- Butter for bread, softened
- 12 slices whole wheat bread, or other favorite bread
- 1/4 cup (60 g) Tarragon Mayonnaise (page 75)
- 6 leaves green lettuce, torn
- 6 slices smoked bacon, cooked
- 6 ounces (170 g) Monterey Jack cheese, sliced
- 2 vine-ripened tomatoes, sliced thinly

PREHEAT:

Preheat grill to high.

MARINATE:

Combine orange juice, ginger ale, pepper, rosemary, parsley, and Worcestershire sauce in a mixing bowl, then whisk in olive oil in a steady stream to emulsify. Add chicken and refrigerate for at least 1 hour and up to 2 days.

GRILL:

Grill chicken until browned and cooked through, about 7 minutes per side. Transfer to cutting board and let cool. When cool enough to handle, slice into thin strips, cutting with the grain.

SERVE:

Preheat oven broiler or toaster. Butter one side of eight bread slices, then place butter side up on sheetpan and toast until browned, about 2 minutes. Remove and let cool. Repeat with remaining bread, but toast both sides. Working on a clean, dry, and flat surface, lay out four slices of single-side-toasted bread, toasted side down. Coat each evenly with Tarragon Mayonnaise, then layer with lettuce, bacon, cheese, double-toasted bread, mayonnaise, lettuce, tomato, chicken, and cheese. Spread Tarragon Mayonnaise on untoasted side of remaining slice of bread, then place on top of sandwiches, toasted side up. Place four long toothpicks in the center of each quarter of the sandwiches.

Grilled Spring Vegetable Wrap

SERVES 8

- 1 zucchini, sliced thinly lengthwise
- 1 summer squash, sliced thinly lengthwise
- 2 large carrots, peeled and sliced thickly diagonally
- ¼ cup (60 ml) extra-virgin olive oil
- Kosher salt
- Coarsely ground black pepper
- 2 avocados, peeled and sliced thinly
- Juice of 1 lemon
- 8 whole wheat or other flavor wraps
- 1 (12-ounce [340 g]) container hummus
- 8 leaves green or red leaf lettuce
- 1 English cucumber, sliced thinly diagonally
- 1 head radicchio, sliced in half and then into thinly strips (optional)
- 4 ounces (115 g) alfalfa sprouts
- 8 ounces (225 g) bottled ranch dressing

PREHEAT:

Preheat grill to medium-high.

PREP:

Toss zucchini, summer squash, and carrot slices with olive oil on a large platter. Sprinkle with salt and pepper.

GRILL:

Grill the vegetables until browned and tender, about 3 minutes per side, and a few minutes longer for the carrots. Remove from grill and let cool.

SERVE:

Sprinkle avocado slices with lemon juice, salt, and pepper, then set aside. Lay out wrap on a flat, clean, and dry surface. Spread hummus in an even layer on the wrap, leaving a 1" (2.5 cm) border dry around the edges. Layer with lettuce, grilled vegetables, cucumber, avocado, radicchio, and alfalfa sprouts. Top with 2 tablespoons (28 ml) ranch dressing. Fold the left and right sides in and over the other fold, then roll the wrap.

Barbecue Chicken and Gouda on Ciabatta

SERVES 6

- 1½ cups (375 g) barbecue sauce
- 1 tablespoon (15 ml) liquid smoke
- 1 tablespoon (15 ml) Worcestershire sauce
- 1 tablespoon (20 g) honey
- 1 tablespoon (10 ml) minced fresh garlic
- 1 tablespoon (6 g) coarsely ground black pepper, plus more for sprinkling
- 6 (8-ounce [225 g]) boneless, skinless chicken breasts
- 1 large red onion, sliced thinly
- Olive oil, for brushing
- 6 ciabatta rolls, sliced open horizontally
- ½ cup (25 g) loosely packed cilantro leaves
- 6 ounces (170 g) smoked Gouda or mozzarella cheese, sliced thinly

PREHEAT:

Preheat grill to high.

MARINATE:

Combine barbecue sauce, liquid smoke, Worcestershire sauce, honey, garlic, and pepper in a large bowl. Set aside half of the sauce mixture. Add chicken to original bowl of sauce mixture, toss to coat, then cover and marinate for at least 30 minutes.

GRILL:

Grill chicken on high heat until tender and cooked through, about 7 minutes per side. Remove from grill and set aside. Thinly coat the onion slices with olive oil and sprinkle with black pepper. Grill until tender, about 4 minutes on each side. Remove from heat and let cool. Once chicken is cool enough to handle, pull strips of chicken apart or slice thinly and toss in ¼ cup (65 g) of reserved barbecue sauce.

SERVE:

Lay out bottom of roll, coat with a thin layer of barbecue sauce, and top with cilantro leaves, red onions, chicken, and cheese. Brush inside of top half of roll with remaining barbecue sauce and top sandwich.

> **Typically, chicken is grilled** on high heat until cooked through, about seven minutes per side. However, the cooking time will vary according to the thickness of the chicken and the temperature of the grill. If in doubt, the internal temperature of the cooked chicken should reach 165°F (74°C).

Antipasta-Stuffed Focaccia Party Sandwich

SERVES 6 TO 8

- I medium red bell pepper
- I medium yellow bell pepper
- I medium orange bell pepper
- Olive oil, for brushing
- 1½ teaspoons (7.5 g) Dijon mustard
- I tablespoon (15 ml) balsamic vinegar
- I tablespoon (4 g) chopped fresh parsley
- I tablespoon (7 g) finely minced sun-dried tomato
- I teaspoon (3 g) finely minced fresh garlic
- ½ cup (120 ml) extra-virgin olive oil
- I teaspoon (6 g) kosher salt
- Coarsely ground black pepper
- I (9" [23 cm]) round loaf focaccia
- ⅓ cup (85 g) prepared black olive paste
- 4 ounces (115 g) goat cheese, crumbled
- ½ medium red onion, sliced thinly (optional)
- 6 ounces (170 g) marinated artichoke hearts
- 8 ounces (225 g) fresh buffalo mozzarella cheese, sliced thinly
- 6 ounces (170 g) prosciutto, sliced thinly
- 6 ounces (170 g) peppered salami, sliced thinly
- 4 ounces (115 g) pepperoni, sliced thinly
- ½ cup (20 g) loosely packed fresh basil leaves
- 2 tablespoons (6 g) chopped fresh chives

PREHEAT:

Preheat grill to high.

GRILL:

Brush peppers with olive oil, then place on hot grill and cook until charred, turning frequently so all sides cook evenly, 8 to 10 minutes. Remove from heat and place in a brown paper bag. Seal bag by rolling top and set aside for 5 to 10 minutes.

PREP:

Remove peppers from bag and use fingers to rub charred skin away from flesh. Remove seeds and stems, then slice peppers into 1" (2.5 cm) strips and set aside. Combine mustard, balsamic vinegar, parsley, sun-dried tomato, and garlic in the bowl of a food processor fitted with the blade attachment and pulse until pureed. With the processor running slowly, add the olive oil in a steady stream to emulsify. Transfer to bowl, season with salt and pepper, cover, and refrigerate.

SERVE:

Slice focaccia in half horizontally. Remove top and set aside. Drizzle bottom of focaccia with one-third of the vinaigrette, then layer with an even coat of olive paste followed by roasted peppers, goat cheese, red onion, and artichoke hearts. Arrange the mozzarella cheese over the artichoke hearts and layer with prosciutto, salami, and pepperoni. Drizzle with one-third of the vinaigrette and top with basil and chives. Drizzle inside of top half of focaccia with remaining vinaigrette. Place on sandwich, vinaigrette side down. Wrap sandwich in parchment paper and refrigerate for at least 1 hour before serving. If making sandwich in advance, reserve vinaigrette for dipping or drizzle the insides of the top and bottom of the focaccia just before serving.

Folded Greek Pita with Traditional Tzatziki Sauce

SERVES 6

- 2 Japanese eggplants, peeled and sliced $1/2''$ (1.3 cm) thick
- Olive oil, for grilling
- Freshly ground black pepper
- 6 large pita breads
- $1/2$ cup (30 g) loosely packed Italian flat-leaf parsley
- 1 pound (455 g) shaved roasted leg of lamb or deli roast beef, sliced thinly
- 8 ounces (225 g) feta cheese, crumbled
- 2 small vine-ripened tomatoes, sliced thinly
- 1 cup (235 g) Tzatziki Sauce (right)

PREHEAT:

Preheat grill to high.

PREP:

Rub eggplant slices with olive oil and sprinkle with pepper.

GRILL:

Grill eggplant until golden, about 4 minutes per side. Remove from heat and set aside to cool.

SERVE:

Place eggplant slices on one half of pita bread. Top with parsley, shaved lamb or roast beef, feta cheese, and tomatoes. Drizzle with Tzatziki Sauce and fold pita over.

Tzatziki Sauce

YIELD: 1 CUP (235 G)

- $1/2$ cup (70 g) peeled, seeded, and finely chopped cucumber
- $1/2$ cup (115 g) plain yogurt
- 1 teaspoon (5 ml) olive oil
- 1 teaspoon (5 ml) lemon juice
- $1/4$ teaspoon (1.5 g) kosher salt
- $1/2$ teaspoon (0.7 g) chopped fresh oregano
- 1 teaspoon (3 g) minced fresh garlic
- 1 teaspoon (1.3 g) minced fresh dill weed (optional)

PREP:

Combine all ingredients in a bowl, cover, and refrigerate for at least 1 hour.

Pizza: The Universal Dish

Pizza has become a universal food and the toppings and crusts of our pizzas seem to be reinvented every day. The early residents of Naples who first created this marvelous dish would be astounded—and perhaps appalled—by the variety of pizzas today. The most common picture of pizza preparation that would come to most minds would be this pie cooking inside a brick oven, but pizza is another of the many popular foods that can be grilled to flavorful perfection.

You can make your own pizza dough or buy ready-made dough or premade crusts from almost any supermarket and some bakeries. The type of flour in the dough determines whether your pizza crust is thick or thin, tender or chewy, so choose your ingredients carefully. Toppings, as we said, range, literally, all over the map from a traditional buffalo mozzarella cheese to ... well ... to almost any meat, poultry, fish, vegetable, or fruit. Here's a recipe for basic pizza dough in case you just can't wait to get to your market.

BASIC PIZZA DOUGH

- Start with $1^1/2$ cups (355 ml) warm water
- 1 (.25-ounce [7 g]) package active dry yeast
- 1 teaspoon (4 g) sugar
- $3^1/2$ cups (440 g) all-purpose flour
- $1/2$ cup (60 g) semolina flour or finely-ground yellow cornmeal
- $1/3$ cup (80 ml) olive oil
- 1 teaspoon (6 g) salt

PREP:

1. Combine $1^1/2$ cups (355 ml) of warm water, 1 (.25–ounce [7 g]) package of active dry yeast, and 1 teaspoon (4 g) sugar in a large mixing bowl. Stir to dissolve the yeast, and set aside until foamy on top (about 5 minutes).

2. Add 1 1/2 cups (190 g) of all-purpose flour, 1/2 cup (60 g) of semolina flour or fine-ground yellow cornmeal, 1/3 cup (80 ml) of olive oil, and 1 teaspoon (6 g) of salt. Mix by hand using a wooden spoon until smooth.

3. Work another 2 cups (250 g) of flour into the dough, 1/4 cup (30 g) at a time, until all the 3 1/2 cups (440 g) of flour are incorporated but the dough is still slightly sticky.

4. Turn the dough out onto a lightly floured work surface and knead for 3 to 5 minutes, until smooth but still tacky.

5. Coat a large mixing bowl with oil, place the dough in the bowl, and turn the dough around to coat all sides with the oil.

6. Cover the bowl with plastic wrap or a clean kitchen towel and place it in a warm, draft-free area for 1 to 1 1/2 hours, until the dough is double in size.

7. Punch down the dough and divide it into two equal portions. Roll each portion into a ball and store in airtight bags in the refrigerator or use it for a great grilled pizza.

You can freeze pizza dough in plastic wrap or a freezer bag for up to 4 months. Thaw it in your refrigerator or at room temperature for several hours until it doubles in size; punch it down and use it in some of the super recipes in this chapter.

Some of the recipes in this chapter also call for Sweet Pizza Dough. Whether used as a crust for a dessert pizza or as a twist for a savory pie, this dough will boost any flavor.

SWEET PIZZA DOUGH

YIELD: 1–16" (41 CM) PIZZA

- 1 cup (235 ml) warm water (about 110°F to 115°F [43°C to 46°C])
- 1 (1/4-ounce [7 g]) package active dry yeast
- 1 tablespoon (20 g) honey
- 1/4 cup (60 g) sugar
- 3 cups (330 g) all-purpose flour
- 1/2 cup (38 g) semolina flour
- 1/2 teaspoon (3 g) salt
- 1/4 cup (60 ml) canola oil

PREP:

1. Combine the water, yeast, sugar, and honey in small bowl and stir to combine and dissolve yeast. Set aside until a foamy top forms, about 5 minutes.

2. Combine the 2 1/2 cups (275 g) flour, semolina, and salt in a large mixing bowl, then make a well in the center.

3. Pour the yeast mixture into the well, then use a wooden spoon to stir the flour vigorously into the well, starting in the center and gradually working out to the sides of the bowl, until the flour is incorporated and the dough begins to hold together.

4. Turn the dough out onto a lightly floured work surface. Knead dough, gradually working in remaining 1/2 cup (55 g) of flour until the dough is no longer sticky, about 5 minutes.

5. Continue kneading until the dough is smooth elastic, and shiny about 10 minutes. Coat a large mixing bowl with oil, place the dough into the bowl, and turn to coat all sides. Cover with plastic wrap or clean kitchen towel and place in a warm, draft-free area to double in size, about 1 1/2 hours. Punch down the dough.

If not using immediately, cover and refrigerate up to 36 hours. If using immediately, turn dough out and prepare according to the recipe. If refrigerating before use, remove from refrigerator and bring to room temperature before continuing with recipe. The dough can be kept refrigerated for about 2 days, although you may have to punch it down once or twice during that time. To freeze, place the dough in airtight bags for up to 3 months.

Add a baking stone to the grill as you heat it to turn your grill into a pizza oven. Or cook pizza on a ceramic pizza plate, preheated on the grill for a crisp crust and evenly cooked pizza. Sprinkle the cooking surface with cornmeal.

Some recipes call for grilling of toppings like chicken strips; red, green, and yellow peppers; sausage; or asparagus spears. If you have a single-burner gas grill, you may have to finish your pizza in a conventional oven, but if you have a gas grill that offers both hot and cool zones, you can cook the pizza on your grill from start to finish. Just preheat your grill to high, oil your dough well to eliminate sticking to the grates, and flip the pizza oil side down onto the grate. Reduce your heat, close the lid, and grill the pizza crust for about 3 minutes; then open the grill, oil the pizza top, and flip it over, with a spatula or tongs, to cook the other side. Immediately add your toppings and move the pizza to the cool zone of your grill to finish baking. You can also close the lid of the grill and turn the heat to low or off to finish the pizza.

Meatball and Tomato Stew Grilled Pizza

SERVES 4

Sauce:

- I (28 ounce [784 g]) can diced tomatoes
- I (28 ounce [784 g]) can tomato sauce
- ¹/₂ cup (20 g) packed coarsely-chopped fresh basil leaves
- I (6-ounce [170 g]) can baby bella mushrooms, chopped, stems reserved
- 6 cloves garlic, sliced thinly
- I (6-ounce [170 g]) can small ripe olives, chopped
- 3 tablespoons (45 ml) red wine vinegar
- ¹/₄ teaspoon (1.5 g) kosher salt
- ¹/₂ teaspoon (1 g) coarsely ground black pepper
- ¹/₄ teaspoon (0.3 g) crushed red pepper flakes

Meatballs:

- 2 tablespoons (28 ml) olive oil
- ¹/₃ cup (55 g) finely chopped red onion
- I tablespoon (10 g) chopped garlic
- Reserved stems from baby bella mushrooms from sauce, chopped finely
- I pound (455 g) ground sirloin
- ¹/₂ pound (225 g) ground sweet Italian sausage, removed from casing
- 2 large eggs
- I tablespoon (4 g) chopped fresh Italian flat-leaf parsley
- 3 tablespoons (15 g) freshly grated Parmesan cheese
- ¹/₄ cup (30 g) seasoned bread crumbs
- ¹/₈ teaspoon (0.3 g) ground nutmeg
- ¹/₂ teaspoon (0.5 g) dried oregano
- ¹/₂ teaspoon (3 g) kosher salt
- ¹/₄ teaspoon (0.5 g) coarsely ground black pepper
- 2 tablespoons (28 ml) vegetable oil, for frying

Pizza:

- I tablespoon (9 g) coarse cornmeal
- Basic Pizza Dough (page 206)
- ¹/₃ cup (85 g) ricotta cheese
- I egg
- 2 tablespoons (5 g) chopped fresh basil
- ¹/₄ teaspoon (3 g) kosher salt
- ¹/₄ teaspoon (0.5 g) coarsely ground black pepper
- 2 tablespoons (13 g) grated Parmesan cheese
- ¹/₄ cup (25 g) shredded Asiago cheese
- 2 cups (230 g) shredded mozzarella cheese

Sauce and Meatballs:

PREHEAT:

Preheat grill to madium.

PREP:

Heat the olive oil in a large skillet over medium-high heat. Add the onion, garlic, and mushroom stems, and sauté until tender, about 5 minutes. Remove and let cool. place the sirloin, sausage, eggs, parsley, Parmesan cheese, bread crumbs, nutmeg, oregano, salt, pepper, and cooled mushroom mixture in a large mixing bowl. Use your hands to combine all the ingredients thoroughly, then form into 2" (5 cm) round balls and set aside.

COOK:

Combine all ingredients for the sauce in a large stockpot and bring to a boil. Reduce heat and simmer for 1 hour. Heat the vegetable oil in a large skillet over medium heat, then sauté first batch of meatballs, turning to cook on all sides. Once browned on all sides, transfer meatballs directly to pot of sauce; do not drain or let cool. Repeat to cook remaining meatballs, adding vegetable oil as needed. Mix meatballs to cover with sauce and cook for 45 minutes to 1 hour.

Pizza:

Preheat oven to 450°F (230°C) with pizza stone (if using). Dust peel or pan with cornmeal. Stretch the dough into a large disk and place on pizza pan or peel. Combine the ricotta, egg, basil, salt, and pepper in a small mixing bowl and stir to incorporate egg thoroughly. Top dough with 1 cup (250 g) tomato sauce in an even layer, then sprinkle with Parmesan, Asiago, and mozzarella cheeses. Remove meatballs from sauce and slice. Add sliced meatballs to pizza, then top randomly with spoonfuls of ricotta cheese mixture. Transfer to stone or oven and bake until golden and cheese is bubbling, about 15 minutes. Remove from oven and let rest for 5 minutes.

Wood-Grilled Chicken Pizza with Radicchio and Feta

SERVES 4

- 2 (8-ounce [225 g]) boneless, skinless chicken breasts
- Asian ginger hibachi grilling sauce
- 2 tablespoons (28 g) butter
- 2 tablespoons (28 ml) olive oil
- 1 medium red onion, sliced
- 4 ounces (115 g) shiitake mushrooms, sliced thinly
- 3 cloves roasted garlic
- Basic Pizza Dough (page 206)
- 1 tablespoon (9 g) coarse cornmeal
- 1 cup (260 g) Basil Pesto (page 58)
- 4 ounces (115 g) shredded Asiago cheese
- 6 ounces (170 g) shredded mozzarella cheese
- 1 cup (40 g) shredded radicchio
- 8 leaves fresh basil, torn

To roast garlic heads, drizzle with olive oil, season with salt and pepper, and place with cuts ends up in a dish to roast in oven for 35 to 40 minutes. Remove roasted cloves by pinching skin of each clove.

PREHEAT:

Preheat grill to high. Preheat oven to 450°F (230°C) with pizza stone (if using).

MARINATE:

Toss chicken breast with grilling sauce in a mixing bowl. Cover and refrigerate for at least 30 minutes.

COOK:

Melt the butter with the olive oil over high heat in a large skillet, then sauté the onion for 3 minutes. Add the mushrooms and roasted garlic, and continue to sauté until the mushrooms and onion are tender, 3 minutes more. Transfer to bowl and set aside.

GRILL:

Stretch dough to a large rectangular shape. Oil and grill one side at a time until golden and crisp, about 3 minutes per side. Dust pan or peel with cornmeal. Transfer grilled dough to a pizza stone or pan. Grill chicken until cooked through, about 7 minutes on each side. Remove and let cool. When cool enough to handle, slice into thin strips.

SERVE:

Top grilled dough with Basil Pesto followed by Asiago and mozzarella cheeses, mushroom mixture, and sliced chicken. Bake on stone or pan until cheese is melted and bubbling, about 10 minutes. Remove and top with radicchio and basil.

Caramelized Leek and Golden Potato Grilled Pizza

SERVES 4

- Basic Pizza Dough (page 206)
- 2 tablespoons (28 ml) olive oil, plus extra for brushing dough
- 3 tablespoons (42 g) butter
- 4 leeks, cleaned, white parts sliced thinly
- 1/4 cup (50 g) sugar
- 1/4 cup (60 ml) heavy cream
- Salt
- Black pepper
- 3 tablespoons (15 g) grated Parmesan cheese
- 8 ounces (225 g) shredded Gruyère cheese
- 2 pounds (905 g) Yukon Gold potatoes, sliced thinly
- 1/4 cup (25 g) sliced scallions, green and white parts

PREHEAT:

Preheat grill to high. Preheat oven to 450°F (230°C) with pizza stone (if using).

PREP:

Stretch dough into a large rectangle.

GRILL:

Oil and grill one side at a time until golden and crisp, about 3 minutes per side. Transfer to a pizza pan or peel.

COOK:

Heat olive oil and butter in a large skillet over medium-high heat, then add leeks and sauté on high for 3 minutes, until just tender. Reduce heat to medium, add sugar, stir to combine, and cook, stirring occasionally, for about 10 minutes, to caramelize leeks. Don't let leeks burn or get crisp. Once browned, add heavy cream and reduce to a thick consistency, about 2 minutes. Season with salt and pepper. Remove from heat and set aside.

SERVE:

Sprinkle grilled dough with an even layer of Parmesan, followed by Gruyère; then top with an even layer of potatoes, followed by leeks. Transfer to oven and bake until golden and bubbling, about 15 minutes. Remove, sprinkle with scallions, and let rest for 5 minutes.

Roasted Wild Mushroom Pizza with Pancetta and Feta

SERVES 6

- 12 ounces (340 g) assorted wild mushrooms, such as shiitake, oyster, and baby bella
- 3 tablespoons (30 g) chopped fresh garlic
- 1 teaspoon (2 g) coarsely ground black pepper
- ½ teaspoon (3 g) kosher salt
- 3 tablespoons (45 ml) olive oil, plus extra for grilling dough
- 2 tablespoons (28 g) butter
- 4 ounces (115 g) pancetta, chopped
- Basic Pizza Dough (page 206)
- ½ cup (50 g) grated Romano cheese
- 8 ounces (225 g) shredded mozzarella cheese
- ¼ cup (40 g) crumbled feta cheese

PREHEAT:

Preheat grill to high. Preheat oven to 350°F (180°C) with pizza stone (if using).

COOK:

Remove the stems and slice mushrooms thin, then transfer to a roasting pan and toss with garlic, black pepper, salt, and olive oil. Dot the mushrooms with butter and roast, stirring occasionally, until tender and browned, about 30 minutes. Remove from oven and let cool. Pan-fry the pancetta in a small skillet over medium-high heat until browned, about 7 minutes. Transfer to bowl and let cool.

GRILL:

Stretch dough into thin disk. Oil and grill one side of dough until browned and crisp, about 4 minutes. Turn dough over, reduce grill heat to low.

SERVE:

Top pizza with even layers of Romano, mozzarella, and mushroom mixture. Sprinkle with pancetta and feta cheese. Close grill lid and cook until cheeses are melted. Remove from grill and let rest for 5 minutes.

BBQ Chicken Pizza with Smoked Gouda and Grilled Pineapple

SERVES: 6

- 2 (8-ounce [225 g]) boneless, skinless chicken breasts
- 1 cup (250 g) favorite barbecue sauce
- 1 teaspoon (2 g) coarsely ground black pepper
- Basic Pizza Dough (page 206)
- Olive oil, for brushing dough
- 1 tablespoon (9 g) coarse cornmeal
- 1 golden pineapple, peeled and cut into ½" (1.3 cm) -thick slices
- 2 tablespoons (28 ml) vegetable oil
- 4 ounces (115 g) shredded mozzarella cheese
- 6 ounces (170 g) shredded smoked Gouda cheese
- 4 ounces (115 g) Canadian bacon, chopped
- ¼ cup (15 g) loosely packed cilantro leaves

PREHEAT:

Preheat grill to high. Preheat oven to 450°F (230°C) with pizza stone (if using).

MARINATE:

Toss the chicken breast with ½ cup (125 g) of the barbecue sauce and the black pepper in a large mixing bowl. Cover and refrigerate for at least 30 minutes. Stretch dough to a 16" (40 cm) round.

GRILL:

Oil and grill one side at a time until golden and crisp, about 2 minutes per side. Dust peel or pan with cornmeal. Transfer to pizza pan or peel. Coat pineapple slices with vegetable oil, place on hot grill, and cook until browned on each side, about 5 minutes per side. Transfer to dish and let cool. When cool enough to handle, remove and discard core section of each slice and chop into large chunks. Grill chicken until cooked through, about 7 minutes per side. Transfer to plate and let cool. When cool enough to handle, cut or shred into strips.

SERVE:

Top grilled dough with mozzarella cheese and half of Gouda. Add chopped pineapple, chicken, and Canadian bacon, then sprinkle with remaining Gouda. Transfer to pizza stone and cook until cheese is bubbling, about 5 minutes. Remove from oven and let rest for 5 minutes, then top with cilantro.

Cheesiest Cheesy and Herb Pizza

SERVES 4

- 1 tablespoon (9 g) coarse cornmeal
- Basic Pizza Dough (page 206)
- Olive oil, for brushing
- ¼ cup (25 g) grated Pecorino Romano cheese
- 6 ounces (170 g) shredded mozzarella cheese
- ½ cup (30 g) chopped mixed fresh herbs (such as rosemary, flat-leaf parsley, chives, and basil)
- 4 ounces (115 g) shredded Asiago cheese
- 4 ounces (115 g) shredded creamy Havarti cheese
- ½ cup (75 g) crumbled feta cheese

PREHEAT:

Preheat grill to high. Preheat oven to 450°F (230°C) with pizza stone (if using).

PREP:

Dust peel or pan with cornmeal. Stretch or roll dough into a large rectangular shape. Toss together mozzarella, fresh herbs, and Asiago cheese in a small mixing bowl.

GRILL:

Oil and grill dough one side at a time until golden and crisp, about 3 minutes per side. Transfer dough to a pizza pan or peel.

SERVE:

Brush grilled dough with olive oil, then sprinkle evenly with Pecorino cheese. Spread mixture evenly over the top of Pecorino, then top with Havarti and sprinkle with feta. Transfer to pizza stone or bottom rack of oven and bake until cheese is bubbling and golden. Remove and let rest 5 minutes.

Tenderloin and Portobello Mushroom Pizza with Roasted Garlic

SERVES 4

- 1 tablespoon (9 g) coarse cornmeal
- 1 tablespoon plus 1 teaspoon (8 g total) coarsely ground black pepper
- 2 tablespoons (3.4 g) chopped fresh rosemary
- 8 ounces (225 g) portobello mushroom caps, stems and gills removed
- 1 medium red onion, sliced thinly
- 2 tablespoons (28 ml) olive oil
- 8 ounces (225 g) beef tenderloin
- ¼ cup (60 ml) Worcestershire sauce
- 1 teaspoon (5 ml) truffle oil (optional)
- 2 tablespoons (28 g) butter
- ½ cup (120 ml) Madeira wine
- Basic Pizza Dough (page 206)
- 1 bulb roasted garlic
- 2 tablespoons (13 g) grated Romano cheese
- 4 ounces (115 g) Muenster cheese, sliced thinly
- 3 green onions, sliced thinly lengthwise

PREHEAT:

Preheat grill to high. Preheat oven to 450°F (230°C) with pizza stone (if using).

PREP:

Dust peel or pan with cornmeal. Rub beef tenderloin with 1 tablespoon (6 g) coarsely ground black pepper and 1 tablespoon (1.7 g) rosemary. Toss portobello mushrooms and onion with olive oil and remaining black pepper in a mixing bowl.

COOK:

Coat a roasting pan with nonstick vegetable spray, then place portobello mushrooms and red onion slices in pan. Set the tenderloin on top of the mushroom mixture and drizzle tenderloin with Worcestershire sauce. Drizzle mushroom mixture with truffle oil and dot with butter. Place pan on middle rack of oven. Cook until internal temperature of the tenderloin reaches 130°F (54°C) and the mushrooms and onions are tender, about 45 minutes; stir mushrooms and onions occasionally. Remove from oven and let tenderloin rest for at least 10 minutes. Transfer tenderloin to cutting board and slice thinly. Transfer mushrooms and onions to a bowl. Add Madeira wine to roasting pan, return to oven and deglaze, scraping pan periodically; reduce by half. Remove and set aside.

GRILL:

Heat grill to high. Stretch dough to a thin, rough disk and oil one side. Place on grill oiled side down, then oil remaining side and close grill. Cook until browned on both sides. Remove grilled dough and place on pizza peel. Rub generously and evenly with roasted garlic.

SERVE:

Sprinkle with Romano cheese, Muenster cheese, mushroom mixture, and tenderloin. Sprinkle with scallions and remaining rosemary, and drizzle with Madeira wine sauce. Place in oven and cook for 30 minutes, or until bubbling and cheese is melted. Remove and let rest for 5 minutes.

Garlic-Grilled Chicken and Pepperoni Pizza with Smoked Gouda

SERVES 6

- 3 (6-ounce [170 g]) boneless, skinless chicken breasts, trimmed and cut in half
- 3 tablespoons (30 g) chopped fresh garlic
- 3 tablespoons (45 ml) olive oil, plus extra for grilling dough
- 2 teaspoons (4 g) coarsely ground black pepper
- Basic Pizza Dough (page 206)
- 1 tablespoon (9 g) coarse cornmeal
- 2 tablespoons (13 g) grated Romano cheese
- 6 ounces (170 g) shredded white Cheddar cheese
- 3 ounces (85 g) sliced pepperoni
- 2 ounces (55 g) baby spinach leaves
- 6 ounces (170 g) shredded smoked Gouda cheese

PREHEAT:

Preheat grill to high. Preheat oven to 450°F (230°C) with pizza stone (if using).

PREP:

Toss chicken with garlic, olive oil, and black pepper in a mixing bowl. Cover and refrigerate for at least 30 minutes.

GRILL:

Stretch dough into a thin, rough circle. Oil and grill one side at a time until golden and crisp, about 3 minutes per side. Dust peel or pan with cornmeal. Place on peel and then transfer to pizza stone or pan. Grill chicken for 7 minutes on each side, until browned and tender. Remove from grill and let cool. When cool enough to handle, slice into thin strips.

SERVE:

Top grilled dough with even layers of Romano, Cheddar, pepperoni, spinach, and Gouda. Add shredded chicken, then place on middle rack of oven and bake until cheese is melted and starting to brown, about 15 minutes. Remove and let rest for 5 minutes.

Grilled Asparagus and Cheese Pizza with White Truffle Oil

SERVES 6

- ¹/₂ pound (225 g) thick asparagus spears
- Extra-virgin olive oil
- Coarsely ground black pepper
- Basic Pizza Dough (page 206)
- 2 tablespoons (13 g) freshly grated Romano cheese
- 8 ounces (225 g) shredded mozzarella cheese
- 3 ounces (85 g) crumbled goat cheese
- I teaspoon (1.3 g) chopped fresh tarragon
- I teaspoon (1.3 g) chopped fresh Italian flat-leaf parsley
- White truffle oil
- I ounce (28 g) shaved fresh Parmigiano-Reggiano cheese

PREHEAT:

Preheat grill to high. Preheat oven to 450°F (230°C) with pizza stone (if using).

PREP:

Holding each asparagus spear in both hands, snap the spear in half; the spear should break at the natural place where the tough end meets the tender top. Rinse spears and pat dry. Place snapped spears on cutting board and line up tops, then trim all spears to the same length. Place spears on a platter, drizzle with olive oil, and sprinkle generously with black pepper.

GRILL:

Grill spears until tender, turning periodically, about 10 minutes. Remove and let cool. When cool enough to handle, slice in half lengthwise and set aside. Stretch dough to a thin rectangle. Oil and grill one side at a time until golden and crisp, about 3 minutes per side.

SERVE:

Transfer to pizza stone or baking sheet. Top grilled dough with Romano, mozzarella, and sliced asparagus spears. Top with goat cheese and sprinkle with tarragon and parsley. Place on middle rack of hot oven and bake until cheese is melted and starting to brown, about 15 minutes. Remove and let rest for 5 minutes. Drizzle with truffle oil, sprinkle with shaved fresh Parmigiano-Reggiano.

Individual Grilled Greek-Style Pizza

SERVES 6

- 1 pound (455 g) beef flank steak or skirt steak
- Coarsely ground black pepper
- 1 pint (300 g) grape tomatoes
- 1 cup (100 g) kalamata olives, pitted and chopped
- 1 tablespoon (3 g) dried oregano
- 4 tablespoons (60 ml) olive oil, plus extra for grilling dough
- 1 eggplant, peeled and sliced in 1/2" (0.3 cm) -thick slices
- Basic Pizza Dough (page 206)
- Cilantro-Mint Pesto (right)
- 8 ounces (225 g) shredded mozzarella cheese
- 8 ounces (225 g) feta cheese, cut into chunks or crumbled
- 1 tablespoon (4 g) chopped fresh cilantro

PREHEAT:

Preheat grill to high. Preheat oven to 375°F (190°C) with pizza stone (if using).

PREP:

Place beef on a plate, coat aggressively and evenly with coarsely ground black pepper, then set aside. Toss tomatoes, olives, oregano, and 2 tablespoons (28 ml) olive oil in medium mixing bowl. Place tomatoes and olives on a baking sheet in a single, even layer, then roast for about 15 minutes, or until tomatoes begin to blister and pop. Place eggplant slices on a plate and coat evenly with remaining olive oil.

GRILL:

Grill for about 5 minutes per side, or until browned and tender. Remove from grill and let cool. When cool enough to handle, cut into cubes and set aside. Clean grill grates after cooking eggplant. Stretch or roll the dough into a thin rectangle. Brush one side of dough evenly with olive oil, and then grill for 3 minutes. While grilling, oil other side. Flip dough over and reduce heat to low. Top grilled dough with even coating of Cilantro-Mint Pesto, then sprinkle on mozzarella cheese, tomatoes, and olives, followed by sliced beef, feta cheese, and chopped cilantro. Close grill and let cook until cheese is melted. If the bottom of the dough starts to get overbrowned, turn off heat and leave lid closed until cheese is melted. Remove pizza and let rest for 5 minutes.

Cilantro-Mint Pesto

YIELD: 1 CUP (260 G)

- 1 cup (60 g) chopped fresh cilantro
- 1/4 cup (15 g) chopped fresh mint
- 3 cloves fresh garlic, peeled
- 2 tablespoons (28 ml) freshly squeezed lemon juice
- Pinch of salt
- 1/4 teaspoon (0.5 g) coarsely ground black pepper
- 1 cup (235 ml) extra-virgin olive oil
- 1 tablespoon (15 g) plain yogurt
- 1/4 cup (25 g) grated Parmesan cheese
- 2 tablespoons (13 g) grated Asiago cheese

PREP:

In the bowl of a food processor fitted with the blade attachment, combine the cilantro, mint, garlic, lemon juice, salt, and black pepper. Pulse to chop the ingredients. With the processor running, add the olive oil in a steady stream. Blend until achieving a thick puree. Scrape from processor into a small mixing bowl. Add the yogurt, Parmesan, and Asiago cheese, and mix to combine. Set aside until needed. Can be covered tightly and refrigerated for up to 1 week.

SERVE:

Top grilled dough with equal amounts of mozzarella and fontina cheese, then add sliced ham and eggs. Dust peel or pan with cornmeal. Place on pizza stone or pan and cook until cheese is melted and starting to brown around the edges, about 10 minutes. Remove from oven and sprinkle with fresh chives and hollandaise sauce (or serve hollandaise on the side).

Western Omelet Grilled Pizza

SERVES 6

- 1 tablespoon (9 g) coarse cornmeal
- Basic Pizza Dough (page 206)
- Olive oil, for brushing dough
- 6 slices bacon
- ¼ pound (115 g) ground breakfast sausage
- 1 small red bell pepper, diced
- 1 small green bell pepper, diced
- 1 small yellow onion, diced
- 2 tablespoons (20 g) chopped garlic
- 3 green onions, chopped
- 4 Roma tomatoes, seeded and sliced thinly
- 5 eggs
- 2 tablespoons (28 ml) heavy cream
- Salt
- Freshly ground black pepper
- 4 ounces (115 g) shredded Monterey Jack cheese
- 6 ounces (170 g) shredded white Cheddar cheese (preferably Vermont sharp)
- ¼ cup (15 g) cilantro leaves, torn

PREHEAT:

Preheat grill to high.

GRILL:

Dust peel or pan with cornmeal. Stretch dough to thin 16" (40 cm) rectangle. Oil and grill one side at a time until golden and crisp, about 3 minutes per side. Remove and transfer to pizza peel.

COOK:

Fry bacon over medium-high heat in a large skillet until browned and crisp, about 6 minutes. Transfer to paper towel and let cool, reserving cooking fat. When cool enough to handle, crumble bacon into small pieces and set aside. Fry sausage in same skillet until browned, about 6 minutes, then transfer to plate. Clean skillet of drippings. Add two tablespoons (28 ml) bacon fat back to skillet,

Brunch Pizza with Scrambled Eggs and Tasso Ham

SERVES 4

- Basic Pizza Dough (page 206)
- Olive oil, for brushing dough
- 4 eggs
- 2 tablespoons (28 ml) heavy cream
- Salt
- Black pepper
- 2 tablespoons (28 g) butter
- 6 ounces (170 g) shredded mozzarella cheese
- 6 ounces (170 g) shredded fontina cheese
- 6 ounces (170 g) tasso ham or Canadian-style bacon, sliced
- 1 tablespoon (9 g) coarse cornmeal
- 2 tablespoons (6 g) chopped fresh chives
- Hollandaise sauce (optional)

PREHEAT:

Preheat grill to high.

GRILL:

Divide dough into four individual balls, then stretch each to about an 8" (20 cm) thin circle. Brush all circles with olive oil and grill, oil side down, until golden brown, about 4 minutes on each side. Remove from grill and set aside.

PREP:

Whip the eggs with the heavy cream in a mixing bowl, then season with salt and pepper. Melt the butter in a skillet over medium heat, add eggs, and scramble until just beginning to brown, about 4 minutes. (Take care not to overcook the eggs, as they will continue to cook on the pizza.)

adjust to medium-high heat, and sauté red and green peppers with onion until just tender, about 3 minutes. Add garlic, scallions, and tomatoes, and sauté 3 minutes more, then transfer to plate to cool. Whip the eggs with the heavy cream in a mixing bowl, then season with salt and pepper. Add 3 additional tablespoons (45 ml) bacon fat to skillet, add eggs, and scramble until tender. Remove and set aside.

SERVE:

Top grilled dough with Monterey Jack cheese and 4 ounces (115 g) Cheddar cheese, then add pepper-onion mixture, crumbled bacon, sausage, eggs, and remaining Cheddar cheese evenly over top. Grill on pizza stone or pan until golden and bubbling, about 7 minutes. Remove, sprinkle with cilantro, and let rest for 5 minutes.

Pizza with Rosemary Shrimp and Spicy Golden Potatoes

SERVES 6

Shrimp:

- I pound (455 g) peeled and deveined large shrimp
- 2 tablespoons (28 ml) olive oil
- 2 tablespoons (28 ml) cider vinegar
- ¼ cup (85 g) honey
- 2 teaspoons (I.4 g) fresh chopped rosemary
- ½ teaspoon (I g) coarse ground black pepper

For the Roasted Potatoes:

- I pound (455 g [about 3]) Yukon Gold potatoes, washed and cut into I" (2.5 cm) cubes
- 2 tablespoons (28 ml) olive oil
- 2 tablespoons (10 g) freshly grated Parmesan cheese
- 2 tablespoons (20 g) fresh chopped garlic
- ½ teaspoon (3 g) kosher salt
- ½ teaspoon (I g) coarsely ground black pepper
- ¼ teaspoon (0.5 g) cayenne pepper

Pizza:

- Basic Pizza Dough (page 206)
- Olive oil, for brushing dough
- I tablespoon (9 g) coarse cornmeal
- 2 tablespoons (28 ml) olive oil
- ½ cup (125 g) Basic Tomato Sauce (page 34)
- I cup (110 g) shredded fontina cheese
- ¾ cup (90 g) shredded provolone cheese
- 2 scallions, sliced into thin strips

PREHEAT:

Preheat grill to high. Preheat oven to 375°F (190°C).

MARINATE:

Combine shrimp with 2 tablespoons (28 ml) olive oil, vinegar, honey, rosemary, and black pepper in a mixing bowl. Cover and refrigerate for at least 1 hour or overnight.

PREP:

In a large cast-iron or other ovenproof skillet, mix potatoes with 2 tablespoons (28 ml) olive oil, Parmesan, garlic, salt, black pepper, and cayenne pepper.

BAKE:

Place in oven and bake for about 45 minutes, scraping and stirring every 15 minutes, until golden and tender.

GRILL:

Stretch dough to a thin round. Oil and grill one side at a time until golden and crisp, about 3 minutes per side. Dust peel or pan with cornmeal. Transfer dough to pizza stone or pan and set aside. In a large skillet over medium-high heat, add 2 tablespoons (28 ml) olive oil, then sauté shrimp until pink and tender. Remove from heat and set aside, reserving pan drippings.

SERVE:

Top grilled dough with tomato sauce, fontina, provolone, sautéed shrimp, and scallions. Bake on middle rack of oven until cheese is melted and begins to brown, about 15 minutes. Remove and let rest for 5 minutes, then drizzle with reserved pan drippings.

German Sausage and Sauerkraut Pizza

SERVES 6

- 2 tablespoons (30 g) German-style mustard
- ¼ cup (60 g) Russian dressing
- I tablespoon (15 ml) olive oil, plus extra for brushing
- Basic Pizza Dough (page 206)
- I tablespoon (9 g) coarse cornmeal
- 8 ounces (225 g) shredded mozzarella cheese
- I pound (455 g) bratwurst, grilled and sliced thinly
- I medium white onion, sliced thinly
- ½ cup (115 g) sauerkraut
- 4 ounces (115 g) shredded Gruyère cheese

PREHEAT:

Preheat grill to high. Preheat oven to 450°F (230°C) with pizza stone (if using).

PREP:

Combine mustard, Russian dressing, and olive oil in a small mixing bowl and set aside. Divide dough in half, return one half to refrigerator for another use, and stretch dough to a thin round.

GRILL:

Oil and grill one side at a time until golden and crisp, about 3 minutes per side.

BAKE:

Dust peel or pan with cornmeal. Remove dough from grill and transfer to pizza peel. Top dough with even layer of the mustard mixture, then add mozzarella, sausage, onion, and sauerkraut, and top with Gruyère. Place on pizza stone in oven and bake until golden and bubbling, about 15 minutes. Remove and let rest for 5 minutes.

Hummus and Grilled Eggplant Pizza with Feta and Oven-Dried Tomatoes

SERVES 6

- I tablespoon (9 g) coarse cornmeal
- I large eggplant, sliced lengthwise into ½" (1.3 cm) -thick slices
- 2 tablespoons (28 ml) olive oil, plus extra for brushing dough
- Basic Pizza Dough (page 206)
- 6 ounces (170 g) hummus
- 2 tablespoons (6 g) chopped fresh chives
- 6 ounces (170 g) creamy Havarti cheese, sliced thinly
- Oven-dried tomatoes
- 4 ounces (115 g) feta cheese, cut into chunks

PREHEAT:

Preheat grill to high. Preheat oven to 350°F (180°C).

GRILL:

Dust peel or pan with cornmeal. Coat the sliced eggplant with 2 tablespoons (28 ml) olive oil, then place on hot grill and cook until browned on both sides, about 5 minutes per side. Remove from grill and let cool. When cool enough to handle, remove skin from sides and cut into large chunks, then set aside. Stretch pizza dough to a 16" (40 cm) round. Oil and grill one side at a time until golden and crisp, about 3 minutes per side.

ASSEMBLE:

Remove dough from grill and transfer to pizza peel. Combine hummus with 1 tablespoon (3 g) chives in a small bowl, then spread hummus evenly over grilled dough. Top with Havarti cheese, eggplant, and oven-dried tomatoes, then sprinkle evenly with feta cheese.

BAKE:

Transfer to pizza stone and bake until bubbling, about 7 minutes. Remove from oven, sprinkle with remaining chives, and let rest for 5 minutes.

Fontina and Gruyère Pizza Shell with Skirt Steak Salad

SERVES 6

Rub:

- **3 cloves fresh garlic**
- **1½ teaspoons (9 g) kosher salt**
- **1½ teaspoons (3.8 g) paprika**
- **1½ teaspoons (3.8 g) ground cumin**
- **1½ teaspoons (3 g) ground coriander**
- **1 teaspoon (2 g) coarsely ground black pepper**
- **1 tablespoon (15 g) Dijon mustard**
- **2 tablespoons (28 ml) canola oil**
- **2 dashes hot sauce**

Steak:

- **1¼ pound (560 g) skirt steak**
- **Olive oil, for rubbing steak and grill grates**

Salad:

- **4 ounces (115 g) mixed salad greens**
- **2 ounces (55 g) baby spinach**
- **3 tablespoons (9 g) chopped, fresh chives**
- **¼ cup (10 g) loosely packed fresh basil leaves, coarsely chopped or torn**

- **¼ cup (15 g) loosely packed fresh Italian flat-leaf parsley, coarsely chopped or torn**
- **⅓ cup (80 ml) balsamic vinaigrette dressing**
- **Basic Pizza Dough (page 206)**
- **8 ounces (225 g) shredded fontina cheese**
- **6 ounces (170 g) shredded Gruyère cheese**
- **¼ cup (25 g) shaved Parmigiano-Reggiano cheese**

PREHEAT:

Preheat grill to high, then reduce to medium.

COOK:

In a small bowl, mash garlic and salt to form a paste. Combine paprika, cumin, coriander, and black pepper in small skillet and toast over medium heat, stirring constantly until aromatic, about 3 minutes. Transfer to medium mixing bowl and add garlic paste, Dijon mustard, oil, and hot sauce. Stir to combine. Rub mixture over skirt steak, working it into the meat, then cover with plastic wrap and refrigerate for at least 6 hours or overnight. Bring steak to room temperature.

GRILL:

Soak mesquite wood chips in water, fully submerged, for at least 30 minutes. If using a charcoal grill, prepare and light coals. Sprinkle moist wood chips over charcoal. Place moist wood chips into a firebox and place to one side of grill. Once wood chips are smoking, lightly oil the grill grates and grill steak, turning only once, until medium-rare, about 7 minutes on each side. Meanwhile, toss mixed greens and spinach with fresh herbs and vinaigrette. Stretch dough out to a rough circle and oil one side. Remove steak from grill and set aside to rest for about 5 minutes. Clean grill grates, then place dough on hot grill, oiled side down. Oil remaining side, then close grill and cook until golden and crisp, about 3 minutes. Reduce heat to low, flip over dough, and top with cheeses. Grill until cheeses are melted. Cut steak diagonally against the grain into ¼" (.6 cm) -thick slices. Place greens atop grilled cheese pizza and top with skirt steak.

Pizza Montreal

SERVES 4

- I tablespoon (9 g) coarse cornmeal
- Basic Pizza Dough (page 206)
- Oil, for brushing
- I cup (235 ml) Béchamel Sauce (right)
- 8 ounces (225 g) white Cheddar cheese
- 4 ounces (115 g) baby spinach
- 8 slices bacon, cooked and chopped
- I small red onion, chopped
- 3 ounces (85 g) Monterey Jack cheese
- 8 ounces (225 g) smoked salmon
- 2 tablespoons (6 g) fresh chopped chives

PREHEAT:

Preheat grill to high. Preheat oven to 450°F (230°C) with pizza stone (if using).

GRILL:

Dust peel or pan with cornmeal. Stretch dough to a thin 16" (40 cm) round. Oil and grill on both sides until golden, about 3 minutes per side.

ASSEMBLE:

Transfer to pizza pan or peel, top with Béchamel Sauce, Cheddar cheese, spinach, bacon, onion, and Monterey Jack cheese, then finish with salmon.

BAKE:

Bake until golden and bubbling, about 10 minutes. Remove, sprinkle with chives, and let rest 5 minutes.

Béchamel Sauce

YIELD: 3 CUPS (710 ML)

- I cup (235 ml) whole milk
- 3 tablespoons (42 g) unsalted butter
- 3 tablespoons (24 g) flour
- I cup (235 ml) dry white wine
- I tablespoon (15 g) Dijon mustard
- $\frac{1}{4}$ teaspoon (0.6 g) ground nutmeg
- Salt
- White pepper

PREP:

In a medium saucepan, scald the milk over medium heat, stirring occasionally, until bubbles form around the sides, then turn off the heat. Melt the butter in a medium skillet over medium-high heat. Add flour and whisk thoroughly to combine. Cook until just turning tan in color, about 3 minutes, stirring constantly. Once roux has reached a light tan color, reduce heat to low, add the white wine, and stir vigorously to incorporate without lumps. Once sauce is thick and wine is incorporated, gradually add scalded milk $\frac{1}{3}$ cup (80 ml) at a time, stirring vigorously and continuously between additions to prevent lumps. Add Dijon mustard and nutmeg, and season with salt and pepper. The sauce is done when it coats the back of a wooden spoon. If it appears too thick, add more milk.

Black Bean and Roasted Corn Pizza with Seared Mexican Shrimp and Monchego Cheese

SERVES 6

- 1 tablespoon (9 g) coarse cornmeal
- 3 ears fresh corn, husked
- 4 tablespoons (55 g) butter
- 2 tablespoons (20 g) chopped fresh garlic
- Salt
- Black pepper
- 1 pound (455 g) large shrimp, peeled and deveined
- 1 tablespoon (7.5 g) ancho chile powder
- 1 teaspoon (3 g) garlic powder
- 1 teaspoon (2.5 g) ground cumin
- 1 teaspoon (2 g) ground coriander
- 2 teaspoons (10 ml) hot sauce
- $\frac{1}{2}$ teaspoon (1 g) black pepper
- 3 tablespoons (45 ml) olive oil
- 1 (10-ounce [284 g]) can black beans, drained
- 1 small red pepper, diced
- $\frac{1}{2}$ teaspoon (0.9 g) cayenne pepper
- $\frac{1}{2}$ teaspoon (1.5 g) onion powder
- 1 teaspoon (2.6 g) chile powder
- Basic Pizza Dough (page 206)
- 4 ounces (115 g) shredded Monterey Jack cheese
- 6 ounces (170 g) shredded Monchego cheese
- $\frac{1}{4}$ cup (15 g) fresh cilantro, chopped coarsely

PREHEAT:

Preheat grill to high. Preheat oven to 450°F (230°C) with pizza stone (if using).

PREP:

Dust peel or pan with cornmeal. Tear off three sheets of aluminum foil large enough to wrap the ears of corn completely. Place one ear of corn on each piece of foil, top with equal amounts butter and garlic, and season generously with salt and pepper. Wrap foil by bringing front and back together and rolling down toward the ear; keep a loose fit (like a tent) at the top, then fold in the sides tightly.

GRILL:

Place corn on grill, reduce heat to medium, close lid, and grill corn for about 15 to 20 minutes, turning every 5 minutes. Remove from grill, open foil packets, and set aside to cool.

COOK:

Toss the shrimp with ancho chile powder, garlic powder, cumin, coriander, hot sauce, and $\frac{1}{2}$ teaspoon (1 g) black pepper in a mixing bowl, coating evenly. Heat 2 tablespoons (28 ml) olive oil in large skillet over medium-high heat. Sauté shrimp in skillet until just pink, but still tender, about 6 minutes; do not overcook. Transfer to bowl and set aside. Place corn ear on cutting board and cut away the kernels. Repeat with remaining two ears, then place corn kernels in a mixing bowl. Add black beans, red pepper, remaining olive oil, cayenne pepper, onion powder, and chile powder to corn kernels, toss to combine, and set aside.

ASSEMBLE:

Stretch the dough to a 16" (40 cm) round. Place dough on peel, then top with even layers of shredded Monterey Jack and Monchego cheeses, followed by black bean mixture and seared shrimp.

BAKE:

Transfer to pizza stone or pan and bake until golden and cheese is bubbling, about 7 minutes. Remove from oven, top with cilantro, and let rest for 5 minutes.

Chicken Caesar Salad Pizza

SERVES 6

- Basic Pizza Dough (page 206)
- Olive oil, for brushing dough
- ¹/₂ cup (130 g) Basil Pesto (page 58)
- ¹/₄ cup (25 g) grated Parmesan cheese
- 8 ounces (225 g) shredded mozzarella cheese
- 1 (8-ounce [225 g]) boneless, skinless chicken breast, cooked and shredded
- 1 small head romaine lettuce, chopped
- 1 cup (40 g) Garlic Croutons (below)
- 6 slices good-quality, thickly-cut bacon, cooked and crumbled
- ¹/₃ cup (80 ml) Caesar Dressing (right)

PREHEAT:

Preheat grill to high. Preheat oven to 450°F (230°C) with pizza stone (if using).

GRILL:

Stretch dough to a thin round. Oil and grill one side at a time until golden and crisp, about 3 minutes per side.

BAKE:

Transfer to a pizza stone or pan. Top with Basil Pesto, Parmesan, and mozzarella cheese. Place in oven or on stone and bake until cheese is melted and begins to brown, about 15 minutes. Remove and let rest for 5 minutes.

SERVE:

Meanwhile, combine chicken, romaine lettuce, croutons, and bacon in large mixing bowl, then toss with Caesar Dressing. Top pizza with salad.

Garlic Croutons

- 1 day-old loaf French bread, cut into 1" (2.5 cm) cubes
- 2 tablespoons (20 g) fresh chopped garlic
- 1 tablespoon (2.5 g) Italian seasoning
- ¹/₂ teaspoon (3 g) kosher salt
- ¹/₄ teaspoon (0.5 g) coarse ground black pepper
- 3 tablespoons (42 g) butter, melted

PREHEAT:

Preheat oven to 350°F (180°C). Place bread, garlic, Italian seasoning, salt, and black pepper in a mixing bowl, then toss to combine. Drizzle with butter and toss vigorously to coat evenly. Transfer to a baking sheet and place on middle rack of oven. Bake until browned and crisp, about 45 minutes; stir and rotate pan every 15 minutes. Remove and let cool. Use immediately or place in an air tight container and store for up to 2 weeks.

Chicken Caesar Salad Pizza

Caesar Dressing

YIELD: 2 CUPS (475 G)

- 1 tablespoon (15 g) mayonnaise
- 1 teaspoon (5 g) Dijon mustard
- 2 cloves fresh garlic, chopped finely
- 1 teaspoon (6 g) kosher salt
- 4 anchovy fillets (optional)
- 1 teaspoon (1.7 g) lemon zest
- ¹/₄ cup (60 ml) freshly squeezed lemon juice (about 1 large lemon)
- ¹/₄ teaspoon (0.5 g) coarsely ground black pepper
- ³/₄ cup (175 ml) mild olive oil
- ¹/₄ cup (25 g) freshly grated Parmigiano-Reggiano cheese

PREP:

Combine mayonnaise, mustard, garlic, salt, anchovies, lemon zest, lemon juice, and black pepper in the bowl of a food processor fitted with the blade attachment. Pulse until well combined, then, with motor running, add olive oil in a steady stream, blending to emulsify. Remove and stir in Parmigiano-Reggiano cheese. Cover and refrigerate until ready to use.

Ancho-Seared Shrimp and Spicy Caesar Pizza

SERVES 6

- 1 pound (455 g) large shrimp, peeled and deveined
- 1 tablespoon (7.5 g) dried ancho chile powder
- ¹/₂ teaspoon (1 g) coarsely ground black pepper
- 3 tablespoons (45 ml) canola oil
- Basic Pizza Dough (page 206)
- Olive oil, for brushing dough
- 1 tablespoon (9 g) coarse cornmeal
- 8 ounces (225 g) shredded mozzarella cheese
- ¹/₄ cup (25 g) shredded Asiago cheese
- 6 ounces (170 g) shaved Parmigiano-Reggiano cheese

- ½ cup (120 g) Caesar Dressing (page 222)
- 2 chipotle peppers in adobo sauce, chopped
- 1 head romaine lettuce, chopped
- 2 ounces (55 g) fresh arugula leaves, torn
- ¼ cup (15 g) fresh cilantro leaves, coarsely chopped

PREHEAT:

Preheat grill to high. Preheat oven to 450°F (230°C) with pizza stone (if using).

MARINATE:

Combine shrimp with ancho chile powder, pepper, and 2 tablespoons (28 ml) canola oil in mixing bowl; toss to combine; then cover and refrigerate for at least 30 minutes or overnight.

GRILL:

Stretch dough to a thin round. Oil and grill one side at a time until golden and crisp, about 3 minutes per side. Dust peel with cornmeal. Transfer grilled dough to pizza stone or pan. Top with mozzarella, Asiago cheese, and half of Parmigiano-Reggiano cheese.

BAKE:

Place on middle rack of oven and bake until cheese is melted and begins to brown, about 15 minutes. Remove and let rest.

COOK:

Heat remaining canola oil over medium-high heat in medium-size skillet, then add shrimp and sear on each side until pink. Remove from heat and let cool.

SERVE:

In a small mixing bowl, combine Caesar Dressing with chipotle peppers, then cover and refrigerate. In a large mixing bowl, combine romaine lettuce, arugula, and cilantro, then toss with Caesar Dressing. Add shrimp and combine. Top pizza with shrimp salad.

Ancho-Seared Shrimp and Spicy Ceasar Pizza

Grilled Vegetable Salad Pizza with Parmesan Balsamic Vinaigrette

SERVES 4

- 1 zucchini, sliced lengthwise into ½" (1.3 cm) -thick slices
- 1 yellow squash, lengthwise sliced into ½" (1.3 cm) -thick slices
- 1 eggplant, sliced lengthwise into ½" (1.3 cm) -thick slices
- 1 red onion, sliced in half and then in thick slices
- 2 large carrots, peeled and sliced lengthwise into thick slices
- Olive oil, for drizzling over vegetables and brushing dough
- 2 portobello mushrooms, stems removed
- Basic Pizza Dough (page 206)
- 4 ounces (115 g) Parmesan cheese
- 8 ounces (225 g) shredded mozzarella cheese or Monterey Jack cheese
- 6 ounces (170 g) mixed greens (such as mesclun mix)
- 6 ounces (170 g) crumbled feta cheese
- ½ cup (120 ml) Parmesan Balsamic Vinaigrette (page 224)

PREHEAT:

Preheat grill to high.

PREP:

Place zucchini, yellow squash, eggplant, onion, and carrots in a large mixing bowl. Drizzle with olive oil. Repeat with whole mushroom caps.

GRILL:

Grill vegetables on hot grill until tender and browned, about 4 minutes each side; 6 minutes per side for the mushrooms. Remove vegetables from grill and set aside to cool. Meanwhile, stretch the dough into a rough thin rectangular shape measuring about 18" x 12" (45 x 30 cm). Place on a large sheet pan and oil one side. Let rest while grill reheats. Once all vegetables are cool enough to handle, chop into cubes and set aside. Place dough oiled side down on hot grill and let cook for about 3 minutes, until dough begins to rise and is crisp on the cooking side. Oil the uncooked side and flip the dough over. Reduce grill heat to low. Sprinkle dough evenly with Parmesan and mozzarella. Grill until cheese is melted. Remove from heat and set aside.

SERVE:

To prepare salad, combine chopped grilled vegetables, salad greens, and feta cheese in large mixing bowl, then toss with balsamic dressing. Place salad on top of grilled pizza, and then cut into individual portions. When eating, fold dough over in half like a sandwich to prevent contents from sliding out.

Asian Salad Grilled Pizza

SERVES 4

- Basic Pizza Dough (page 206)
- Olive oil, for brushing dough
- 8 ounces (225 g) shredded white sharp Cheddar cheese
- 4 ounces (115 g) shredded Asiago cheese
- 6 ounces (170 g) mixed salad greens
- 6 ounces (170 g) snow peas, sliced into thin strips
- 1 red bell pepper, sliced into thin strips
- 1 yellow bell pepper, sliced into thin strips
- 2 large carrots, shredded
- 1 cup (70 g) shredded Chinese cabbage
- 1/3 cup (80 ml) Sesame-Ginger Dressing (page 49)
- Vegetable oil for frying
- 6 ounces (170 g) square wonton wrappers

PREHEAT:

Preheat grill to high.

PREP:

Combine salad greens, snow peas, red and yellow peppers, carrots, and cabbage in large mixing bowl, then toss to combine. Drizzle with dressing and toss to coat just before ready to serve. Heat about 2" (5 cm) vegetable oil in a large saucepan to 375°F (190°C). Cut each wonton square into four wedges.

COOK:

Fry wontons in hot oil until crisp and browned. Remove and let drain.

GRILL:

Stretch dough out into a thin rectangle. Rub one side of dough with olive oil and place oiled side down on hot grill, then oil remaining side. Cook on medium-high heat, until golden, about 3 minutes. Turn dough and top with cheeses, reduce heat to low, cover, and continue to grill until cheese is melted. Remove and let rest for 5 minutes.

SERVE:

Toss wontons with salad, then place salad on top of cheese pizza.

Parmesan Balsamic Vinaigrette

YIELD: 1 CUP (235 ML)

- 2 cloves garlic, minced
- 1/2 teaspoon (3 g) salt
- 2 tablespoons (28 ml) balsamic vinegar
- 1 teaspoon (5 ml) fresh lemon juice
- 3 tablespoons (7.5 g) minced fresh basil
- 1/4 cup (25 g) finely grated Parmesan cheese
- 1/4 teaspoon (0.5 g) coarsely ground black pepper
- 1/2 cup (120 ml) extra-virgin olive oil

PREP:

Mash the garlic and salt together in a small bowl to form a paste. Using a whisk, combine the garlic paste with the balsamic vinegar, lemon juice, basil, Parmesan, and black pepper. Add oil in a steady stream while whisking to emulsify.

Asian Salad Grilled Pizza

Pizza Margherita

SERVES 4

Pizza Crust:

- ¾ cup (175 ml) warm water (110°F [43°C])
- 1¼ teaspoons (3.5 g) active dry yeast (about half of a ¼-ounce [7 g] package)
- A good pinch of sugar
- 2 cups (250 g) unbleached all-purpose flour, plus additional for working dough
- ¾ teaspoon (4.5 g) salt
- 1 tablespoon (15 ml) olive oil

Topping:

- 2 garden-fresh medium tomatoes
- 8 ounces (225 g) fresh, water-packed mozzarella balls, or shredded regular mozzarella cheese
- 2 tablespoons (28 ml) extra-virgin olive oil
- 1–2 cloves garlic, minced
- ¼ cup (25 g) grated Romano or Parmesan cheese
- 8 fresh basil leaves, torn

PREHEAT:

Preheat grill to medium-high.

TO MAKE THE CRUST:

In measuring cup, combine water, yeast, and sugar; let stand until mixture appears creamy on surface and begins to form a few small bubbles, about 5 minutes. (If the mixture doesn't begin to look creamy and bubbly, discard and start over with new yeast.) Combine flour and salt in food processor fitted with metal blade; pulse a few times to mix. With machine running, add creamy yeast mixture through feed tube. Process until mixture is smooth and well-mixed, then add olive oil and pulse a few times. Scrape the dough, which will be somewhat sticky, out onto work surface that has been generously dusted with flour. Knead a few times to incorporate any loose bits of flour that were not incorporated in the food processor, then divide into two equal portions. Shape each into a smooth ball; dust with flour. Cover with clean dish towel; let rise for 45 minutes to 1 hour.

PREP:

Peel and core tomatoes; slice thinly and set on a layer of paper towels to drain. If using fresh mozzarella balls, slice about ¼" (.6 cm) thick and set aside.

After rising, place balls of dough on floured work surface and shape each into a 9" (22.5 cm) round, pressing with your fingertips and palms; work from the center to the outside edge as you shape the dough. Transfer to floured baking sheet. Let rounds stand while you heat grill.

GRILL:

Place pizza rounds on grate away from heat. Grill until undersides are nicely browned and beginning to firm up. Turn with large spatula and cook until second side is browned. Transfer rounds to baking sheet. Brush tops with olive oil; scatter garlic over the top. Arrange drained tomato slices on crusts; top with mozzarella cheese, dividing evenly. Sprinkle with Romano cheese. Return pizzas to grate away from heat. Cover grill and cook until cheese melts and dough is cooked through, about 5 minutes. Scatter basil leaves over pizza before cutting.

To save time, you may use a loaf of frozen bread dough, thawed, instead of the homemade dough above; cut in half and shape into two smaller rounds, each about 8" (20 cm).

CHAPTER TEN
VEGETABLES

Simple Vegetable Grill, page 242

TO MANY PEOPLE, "GRILLING" INVOLVES THE COOKING OF

meat or poultry on a "barbecue." These people might widen their perspective once introduced to dishes like Parmesan Tomatoes (page 228) or Silver and Gold Corn with Blue Cheese Butter (page 232). Vegetarian cooking is not only "in" in the twenty-first century, it is also a fun and delicious way to sneak veggies into the diets of carnivorous friends and family.

Vegetables from all over the world are available in most local supermarkets, but the most flavorful and least expensive are usually locally grown. Grilling "in season" is not only an economical way to go, but it's a lot of fun when dinner parties have a corn-on-the-cob harvest festival theme or a first-of-the-season menu of stuffed peppers. Root vegetables can be grilled at any time: how about Grilled Sweet Potatoes (page 234)?

Cut vegetables into large slices to place on the grates. For example, instead of cutting rounds of zucchini, cut lengthwise into slices. Skewer smaller pieces of vegetables or place them in wire baskets for grilling so they won't end up as fuel instead of food. Marinate vegetables or coat them lightly with olive oil, using plastic bags to hold vegetables and marinade neatly and coat evenly. Some vegetables, like artichokes, should be boiled before grilling, but most veggies can be just grilled over medium direct heat. Grilling times will vary from 6 to 8 minutes for asparagus to about 30 minutes for corn in husks and up to 1 hour for garlic. Follow the recipe for appropriate times but make some allowances for the fact that each grill will cook differently and each chef has his or her own criteria for perfection.

Portobello Mushroom Burgers with Basil Aioli

SERVES 2

- 2 large portobello mushroom caps (4–5 ounces [115–140 g] each)

Marinade:

- $1/4$ cup (60 ml) balsamic vinegar
- 3 tablespoons (45 ml) olive oil
- 1 teaspoon (0.7 g) dried basil
- 1 teaspoon (1 g) dried oregano
- $1/2$ teaspoon (0.5 g) dried thyme
- $1/4$ teaspoon (1.5 g) kosher salt
- $1/4$ teaspoon (0.5 g) freshly ground pepper
- 1 clove garlic, finely minced

Basil Aioli:

- $1/2$ cup (115 g) good-quality mayonnaise
- 1 small clove garlic, minced finely
- 10–12 large fresh basil leaves, slivered thinly
- $1^1/2$ teaspoons (7.5 ml) freshly squeezed lemon juice
- $1/4$ teaspoon (1.5 g) kosher salt
- $1/4$ teaspoon (0.5 g) freshly ground pepper
- 2 slices cheese (1 ounce [28 g] each) (optional)
- 2 hamburger rolls, split
- Lettuce and sliced tomatoes, for serving

PREHEAT:

Preheat grill to medium.

MARINATE:

Cut stems off mushrooms and discard; clean caps with damp paper towels. Place smooth side up in shallow nonreactive dish. In small bowl, whisk together marinade ingredients. Pour over mushrooms and marinate at room temperature for 15 to 20 minutes.

PREP:

Combine all aioli ingredients in another small bowl; whisk to blend and set aside.

GRILL:

Place mushrooms on grate over heat and cook for 5 to 10 minutes or until tender, turning at least once. Top with cheese during the last 2 minutes of grilling, if desired.

SERVE:

Spread the insides of split hamburger rolls with a tablespoon (15 g) of Basil Aioli; top with grilled portobello, lettuce, and tomatoes. Refrigerate remaining aioli for other uses.

Grilled portobello mushrooms make a tossed salad special. Prepare a few extra mushrooms while you're making this dish, and refrigerate until needed.

Parmesan Tomatoes

SERVES 4

- 4 large tomatoes
- 2 tablespoons (28 ml) olive oil
- 1 clove garlic, minced
- 2 tablespoons (5 g) chopped fresh basil
- Kosher salt and freshly ground pepper
- $1/2$ cup (50 g) grated Parmesan cheese

PREHEAT:

Preheat grill to medium.

PREP:

Cut off and discard tops and cores from tomatoes. Brush cut sides of tomatoes with olive oil and sprinkle evenly with garlic, basil, and salt and pepper to taste.

GRILL:

Place on grate over heat. Cover and cook until almost tender, 5 to 10 minutes. Sprinkle each tomato with Parmesan cheese and cook a few minutes longer, until cheese melts and tomatoes are tender.

Grilled Artichokes

SERVES 2

- 1 (16-ounce [455 g]) can artichoke hearts, drained
- 1 tablespoon (15 ml) olive oil
- $1/4$ teaspoon (1.5 g) kosher salt
- $1/4$ teaspoon (0.5 g) freshly ground black pepper

PREHEAT:

Preheat grill to medium.

PREP:

Place artichoke hearts in bowl and toss with oil, salt, and pepper. Place artichoke hearts on grate over heat; cook until heated through and nicely browned, 10 to 15 minutes.

Portobellos au Gratin

SERVES 6

- ¹/₃ cup (75 g) unsalted butter
- 2 cloves garlic, minced
- 6 large portobello mushroom caps
- ¹/₂ cup (50 g) grated Parmesan cheese
- ¹/₄ cup (30 g) grated mozzarella
- 3 tablespoons (10 g) snipped fresh chives

PREHEAT:

Preheat grill to high.

COOK:

In small saucepan, melt butter over medium-low heat. Add garlic; cook for about 2 minutes, stirring occasionally (don't let the garlic brown).

GRILL:

Brush tops of mushroom caps with melted garlic butter and place, top side down, on grate over heat. Cook for about 2 minutes. Brush undersides with melted garlic butter, then turn top side up. Cook for about 2 minutes longer. Carefully sprinkle Parmesan and mozzarella cheeses over caps; sprinkle with chives. Cook until cheese melts.

Grilled Asparagus

SERVES 4

- 1 pound (455 g) fresh asparagus spears
- 1¹/₂ teaspoons (7.5 ml) olive or vegetable oil
- Kosher salt and freshly ground pepper
- 2 tablespoons (13 g) grated Parmesan or Romano cheese

PREHEAT:

Preheat grill to medium-high.

PREP:

Snap off and discard tough ends from asparagus. Place asparagus in perforated grilling wok; set wok on piece of waxed paper or a baking sheet. Drizzle oil over asparagus, tossing to coat; sprinkle with salt and pepper to taste.

GRILL:

Place wok on grate over heat. Cook until asparagus is tender-crisp, 5 to 7 minutes, turning frequently with wooden spatula or spoon. Sprinkle with Parmesan cheese and toss to distribute cheese.

Grilled Asparagus

Artichokes with Lemon Butter and Summer Savory

SERVES 4 (SIDE-DISH SERVINGS)

- 2 medium artichokes
- 1 tablespoon (15 ml) olive oil
- 2 tablespoons (28 g) unsalted butter
- 1 teaspoon (1.3 g) minced fresh summer savory
- Pinch salt
- 1 tablespoon (15 ml) freshly squeezed lemon juice
- 8 slices Italian-style country bread

PREHEAT:

Preheat grill to medium-high.

PREP:

Snap off the small, tough outer leaves at the base of the artichokes. Trim off about ¼" (6 mm) of the sharp points from the midrange leaves and from the top. Trim about ½" (1.3 cm) from the base of the stem.

COOK:

Put a steamer rack in a large saucepan that has a tight-fitting lid and place the artichokes on the rack, leaves pointing down. Add several inches of water to the saucepan and cover tightly. Place the saucepan on the stovetop and bring the water to a boil, reduce the heat to medium, and steam for about 25 minutes, until the bottoms of the artichokes are tender but not soft. Remove the artichokes from the saucepan to a cutting board. Let the artichokes cool for several minutes. Cut each artichoke in half lengthwise with a sharp knife. Spoon out and discard the choke (the fuzzy fibers), leaving the leaves attached to the bottom.

GRILL:

Rub the cut sides of the artichokes with the olive oil and place cut side down on the grill. Grill for 1 to 2 minutes on each side, to heat through and create grill marks.

Meanwhile, melt the butter in a small pan on the stovetop and add the savory and salt. Remove the pan from the heat and stir in the lemon juice.

SERVE:

Arrange the artichokes on a serving platter or individual appetizer plates. Drizzle with the butter mixture and set aside for a few minutes so some of the butter will soak in. Serve with bread.

Grill-Roasted Cauliflower

SERVES 4 TO 6

- ¾ cup (180 ml) chicken broth
- 1 tablespoon (14 g) butter
- 1 tablespoon (10 g) chopped garlic
- ½ teaspoon (1.5 g) dry mustard
- ¼ teaspoon (0.3 g) hot red pepper flakes, or to taste
- 1 head cauliflower

PREHEAT:

Preheat grill to medium-high.

COOK:

In small skillet, combine broth, butter, garlic, mustard powder, and pepper flakes; stir to blend. Heat to boiling over high heat; cook until reduced to ¼ cup (60 ml), 5 to 10 minutes.

PREP:

Meanwhile, remove any leaves from cauliflower. Cut core from underside of cauliflower head, taking care not to cut so deeply that head falls apart. Place on shiny side of 18" x 18" (45 x 45 cm) piece of heavy-duty foil; cup foil around base of cauliflower.

GRILL:

When broth mixture has reduced, pour evenly over cauliflower. Seal packet. Place on grate away from heat. Cover and cook until just tender when pressed with gloved fingers, 25 to 40 minutes (rotate packet once or twice during cooking, but do not turn over).

Baby Bok Choy with Lemon-Miso Sauce

SERVES 6 (SIDE-DISH SERVINGS)

- ¼ cup (60 ml) freshly squeezed lemon juice
- 2 tablespoons (35 g) white miso
- 2 cloves garlic, minced
- 6 tablespoons (90 ml) water
- 1 tablespoon (8 g) cornstarch
- 1 pound (455 g) baby bok choy
- 2 tablespoons (28 ml) toasted sesame oil

PREHEAT:

Preheat grill to medium-high.

COOK:

In a small saucepan, whisk together the lemon juice, miso, garlic, and ¼ cup (60 ml) water. Place on the stovetop over low heat and cook until steaming. Place 2 tablespoons (28 ml) water in a small jar with a tight-fitting lid and add the cornstarch. Cover tightly and shake to dissolve. Whisk the cornstarch mixture into the saucepan and cook over medium-low heat until thickened, about 1 minute. (Do not overcook or it will get gummy.) Remove the saucepan from the heat and set aside in a warm spot.

PREP:

Rinse the bok choy and shake to remove some of the water. Cut any larger heads in half lengthwise. Place the bok choy in a plastic bag and drizzle with the sesame oil. Twist the bag to seal, allowing some air to remain in the bag. Toss gently to coat the bok choy evenly.

GRILL:

Place the bok choy on the grill and grill for 3 to 5 minutes, turning frequently, until the leaves are limp and slightly charred. Remove the bok choy from the grill and place on a serving platter. Drizzle with the sauce.

Silver and Gold Corn with Blue Cheese Butter

SERVES 4

- 4 ears fresh silver and gold corn, husked
- ¼ cup (55 g) Blue Cheese Butter (page 75), divided into 4 portions

PREHEAT:

Preheat grill to high.

GRILL:

Place disposable pan on grate over heat. Add enough water to fill pan to about ⅛" (.3 cm). Heat until water begins to bubble from the bottom of the pan. Add corn and let simmer for about 10 minutes, turning corn occasionally.

After cooking for about 10 minutes, remove corn from pan and place directly on grate over heat (remove and discard the pan of water for more room). Cook corn on grate for about 5 minutes, turning several times; some of the kernels should turn nicely brown. Remove with long-handled tongs. Serve with a slice of Blue Cheese Butter on top.

Roasted Corn and Peppers with Black Beans

SERVES 4 TO 6

- 2 ears fresh corn, unhusked
- 1 red bell pepper
- 1 jalapeño pepper
- 2 tablespoons (28 ml) freshly squeezed lime juice
- 1 tablespoon (4 g) chopped fresh cilantro
- ¼ teaspoon (1.5 g) salt
- A pinch of ground cumin (optional)
- 1 (15-ounce [420 g]) can black beans, drained and rinsed briefly

PREHEAT:

Preheat grill to high.

PREP:

Soak corn for at least 30 minutes in cold water.

GRILL:

Place soaked corn, bell pepper, and jalapeño pepper on grate over heat. Cover and cook until pepper skins are completely blackened and corn husks are blackened, turning vegetables frequently; jalapeño will be done after about 10 minutes, while the bell pepper and corn will take 20 to 30 minutes. Remove peppers as they are done and transfer to paper bag for 5 to 10 minutes, then peel off skin.

SERVE:

Cut off stem ends of peppers. Chop jalapeño finely (for a milder dish, scrape away and discard seeds before chopping). Add chopped jalapeño to mixing bowl with lime juice, cilantro, salt, and cumin; mix well. Add drained beans. Remove and discard seeds from bell pepper. Dice pepper and add to bowl with beans. Peel blackened husks from corn. Cut corn from cobs, adding to bowl with beans. Stir well. Taste for seasoning and add more salt if desired.

White Corn with Chile Butter

SERVES 6 (SIDE-DISH SERVINGS)

- 6 ears white corn, unhusked
- 2 tablespoons (28 g) butter
- 1/2 teaspoon (1.5 g) crushed garlic
- 1/4 teaspoon (0.7 g) chile powder
- Pinch salt

PREHEAT:

Preheat grill to high.

PREP:

Place the corn in a plastic bag and fill the bag with water to soak the husks for about 15 minutes. Place the butter in a small dish and melt in the microwave oven. Add the garlic, chile powder, and salt and heat for several seconds. Set aside.

GRILL:

Remove the corn from the bag of water and place the corn on the grill. Turn every few minutes to evenly blacken all sides of the husks. Grill for 18 to 22 minutes. (The kernels will steam in the husks.) Remove the corn from the grill. Allow the corn to cool for a few minutes, then peel off the husks and remove the silk. Place the corn on a serving platter. Brush with the chile butter.

Parmesan Zucchini Spears

SERVES 3 TO 4

- 1½ pounds (680 g) medium zucchini or yellow summer squash
- 2 tablespoons (28 ml) Italian-style vinaigrette dressing
- Kosher salt and freshly ground pepper
- 3 tablespoons (15 g) grated Parmesan cheese

PREHEAT:

Preheat grill to medium-high.

PREP:

Trim ends of zucchini, then cut zucchini lengthwise into four spears each (six spears if zucchini are large). Place in baking dish. Drizzle with dressing, turning to coat; use pastry brush if necessary to coat all surfaces. Sprinkle with salt and pepper to taste.

GRILL:

Place zucchini directly on grate over heat, skin side down to start. Cook until tender-crisp, about 10 minutes, turning zucchini to expose each side to heat. Sprinkle each spear with a little Parmesan cheese. Cook for 2 to 3 minutes longer (covered if possible), or until zucchini is tender and cheese has melted somewhat to form a crust.

Grilled Sweet Potatoes

SERVES 6 (SIDE-DISH SERVINGS)

- 4 medium red-skinned sweet potatoes
- 2 tablespoons (28 ml) olive oil
- ½ teaspoon (1.5 g) granulated garlic
- ¼ cup (60 g) low-fat sour cream
- ¼ teaspoon (0.6 g) paprika

PREHEAT:

Preheat grill to medium-high.

PREP:

Scrub the sweet potatoes but do not peel them. Slice the potatoes crosswise into ½" (1.3 cm) rounds. Place the potatoes in a plastic bag and drizzle with the olive oil, then sprinkle with the garlic. Twist the bag to seal, allowing some air to remain in the bag. Toss gently to coat the sweet potatoes evenly.

GRILL:

Remove the potatoes from the bag and place on the grill. Grill for 10 to 12 minutes, turning frequently, until fork-tender and showing grill marks. Remove the potatoes from the grill and arrange on a large, warm platter. Spoon a small amount of sour cream on top of each sweet potato round. Sprinkle with the paprika.

The Best Grilled Peppers

SERVES 6

- 2 medium red or yellow bell peppers, nice and firm
- 3 tablespoons (45 ml) virgin olive oil
- 1 tablespoon (15 ml) walnut oil
- Salt and pepper, to taste
- 12 cooked asparagus spears, if desired

PREHEAT:

Preheat grill to medium-high.

PREP:

Wash red peppers.

GRILL:

Grill peppers evenly on both sides. Remove from grill and wrap in a clean dish towel. Wait 20 minutes for peppers to cool before removing skins.

SERVE:

Remove the seeds and cut out the yellowish veins. Cut peppers into strips.

Add olive and walnut oils, salt and pepper to taste, and mix. Serve warm or refrigerate for up to 2 days. If desired, these may be served wrapped around cooked asparagus spears.

Easy Vegetable Kabobs

SERVES 6

- 12 button mushrooms, washed, stems trimmed
- 12 large cherry tomatoes
- 3 medium red onions, peeled and quartered
- 3 small zucchini, cut into 1" (2.5 cm) chunks
- 1 yellow bell pepper, cored and cut into 12 chunks
- ¾ cup (175 ml) Italian-style vinaigrette dressing

PREHEAT:

Preheat grill to high.

PREP:

If using bamboo skewers, soak them in water for 30 minutes prior to starting. Thread all vegetables alternately on the skewers.

MARINATE:

Place filled skewers in shallow baking dish. Pour dressing over skewers and turn to coat evenly. Marinate at room temperature for 20 to 25 minutes, turning occasionally.

GRILL:

Place skewers on grate over heat. Cook until vegetables are tender-crisp, about 8 minutes, turning once.

Veggie Packets

SERVES 4

- 1 pound (455 g) small zucchini, halved lengthwise and sliced ½" (1.3 cm) thick
- 8 ounces (225 g) small-diameter asparagus, cut into 1" (2.5 cm) lengths
- 2 red onions, peeled and cut into eighths
- 1 pound (455 g) eggplant, quartered and cut into 1" (2.5 cm) pieces
- 2 tablespoons (28 ml) extra-virgin olive oil
- Kosher salt and freshly ground pepper, to taste

PREHEAT:

Preheat grill to high.

PREP:

In mixing bowl, combine all ingredients; stir gently to mix. Tear off four pieces of heavy-duty foil, each about 18" (45 cm) square (or use a double layer of regular-weight foil). Place one-quarter of the vegetable mixture on each piece of foil, shiny side up, and seal packets.

GRILL:

Place packets on grate over heat and cook for about 15 minutes, or until you hear a sizzling sound inside, turning packets once or twice. Transfer the packets to each person, open carefully, and enjoy. If you are using 12" (30 cm) -wide foil, tear off eight square pieces. Place one-quarter of the vegetable mixture on four pieces of foil, shiny side up. Cover each with remaining pieces of foil and roll-fold the edges on all sides.

Grilled Vidalia Onions

SERVES 4

- 2 Vidalia onions
- Olive oil
- Herbs of your choice (rosemary, garlic powder, or thyme)

PREHEAT:

Preheat grill to medium-high.

PREP:

Peel and cut onions in half. Put on nonstick aluminum foil. Drizzle with olive oil and sprinkle with spices.

GRILL:

Place onions (still on the foil) on the grill and cook for 10 minutes. Remove onions from the foil and then place onions directly on the grill for another 5 minutes to finish cooking.

Grilled Zucchini

SERVES 4 (SIDE-DISH SERVINGS)

- 6 small zucchini
- 1½ tablespoons (21 ml) olive oil
- 1 teaspoon (3 g) crushed garlic
- 1 tablespoon (15 ml) balsamic vinegar
- ⅛ teaspoon (0.8 g) salt
- Several grindings black pepper, to taste

PREHEAT:

Preheat grill to medium.

PREP:

Remove and discard the stem ends of the zucchini and cut lengthwise into ¼" (6 mm) slices. Place the zucchini in a plastic bag and drizzle with the olive oil and garlic. Twist the bag to seal, allowing some of the air to remain in the bag. Toss gently to coat the zucchini evenly. Remove from bag when ready to grill.

GRILL:

Place the zucchini on the grill and grill for about 10 minutes until tender-crisp, turning two to three times. Remove the zucchini from the grill to a serving platter. Drizzle with the balsamic vinegar and sprinkle with the salt and black pepper.

Russet Potato Wedges

SERVES 6 (SIDE-DISH SERVINGS)

- 4 medium russet potatoes
- 2 tablespoons (28 ml) olive oil
- $^1/_2$ teaspoon (1.3 g) paprika
- $^1/_4$ teaspoon (1.5 g) salt

PREHEAT:

Preheat grill to medium-high.

PREP:

Scrub the potatoes but do not peel. Cut the potatoes lengthwise into wedges and place in a plastic bag. Drizzle with the olive oil and sprinkle with the paprika and salt. Twist the bag to seal, allowing some of the air to remain in the bag. Toss gently to coat the potatoes evenly. Remove from bag when ready to grill.

GRILL:

Place the potatoes on the grill and cook for about 15 minutes, turning frequently. (The potatoes should be fork-tender but not falling apart.)

Peas in a Packet

SERVES:4

- 1 (10-ounce [280 g]) package frozen green peas
- 1 (3-ounce [85 g]) can mushrooms, drained
- 3 tablespoons (30 g) finely diced onion
- 3 tablespoons (27 g) finely diced ham
- 1 teaspoon (1.3 g) chopped fresh parsley
- 2 tablespoons (28 ml) olive oil
- $^1/_2$ teaspoon (0.5 g) pepper
- $^1/_4$ teaspoon (1.5 g) salt

PREHEAT:

Preheat grill to medium.

PREP:

Place block of frozen peas on large piece of heavy-duty foil, shiny side up. Top with mushrooms, onion, ham, and parsley. Drizzle with oil. Season with pepper and salt (adjust if ham is salty) and seal packet.

GRILL:

Place packet on grate over heat and cook for 15 to 20 minutes, turning packet occasionally.

Grilled Red Potatoes

SERVES 6 (SIDE-DISH SERVINGS)

- **6 red potatoes**
- **2 tablespoons (28 ml) olive oil**
- **¹/₂ teaspoon (1.5 g) crushed garlic**
- **¹/₈ teaspoon (0.8 g) salt**

PREHEAT:

Preheat grill to medium-high.

PREP:

Scrub the potatoes but do not peel them.

COOK:

Place the potatoes in the microwave oven and cook on high for 4 minutes, until slightly soft. Let the potatoes cool for a few minutes, then cut in half. Place the potatoes in a plastic bag and drizzle with the olive oil and garlic, then sprinkle with the salt. Twist the bag to seal, allowing some of the air to remain in the bag. Toss gently to coat the potatoes evenly.

GRILL:

Remove the potatoes from the bag, place on the grill, and grill for 5 minutes. Turn the potatoes and continue to grill for 5 more minutes. Turn the potatoes again and grill for about 5 additional minutes on each side, until the potatoes are fork-tender and lightly browned.

Corn Roas

SERVES 4

- 4 fresh corn ears, unhusked
- Butter, salt, and pepper, for serving

PREHEAT:

Preheat grill to medium-high.

PREP:

Place corn in a bucket or sink full of water; place weights such as plates, clean bricks, or whatever you can find on the corn to keep it submerged. Soak for at least 30 minutes or as long as 2 hours.

GRILL:

Place drained corn on grate over heat. Cook until husks char and begin to blacken and corn is tender, 20 to 30 minutes, turning corn frequently for even cooking. To check doneness, peel back a bit of husk from one ear and check kernels. They should be tender, and a few kernels should be browned.

SERVE:

Hold an ear with oven mitts and peel away the burned husks (and silk). For standard serving, snap off the bunch of peeled-back husks and place the corn on a platter. For a more casual backyard affair, hand the ear of corn, with the peeled-back husks at the bottom, to a diner; the peeled-back husks can be used like a handle to hold the corn. A container of melted butter offers an easy way for diners to dip their corn, but this is practical only for a large crowd).

Potato Packets

SERVES 4

- 2 tablespoons (28 ml) olive oil
- 4 medium baking potatoes
- ¹/₂ cup (80 g) finely diced onion
- ¹/₂–1 teaspoon (3–6 g) seasoned salt
- 1 teaspoon (2 g) freshly ground black pepper
- Several dashes of hot red pepper flakes

PREHEAT:

Preheat grill to medium.

PREP:

Tear off four large pieces of foil; brush the shiny side of each with a little oil. Scrub potatoes well and slice thinly. Divide potato slices evenly among prepared foil squares. Sprinkle each batch with oil, onion, seasoned salt, black pepper, and red pepper flakes, and seal packet.

GRILL:

Place packet on grate over heat and cook for 25 to 30 minutes, or until potatoes are tender, turning packets occasionally.

Salted Grilled Potatoes

SERVES 4

- 4 large baking potatoes
- 1 tablespoon (15 ml) olive oil, plus more as needed
- Kosher salt
- Accompaniments: Butter, sour cream, bacon bits, chopped chives

PREHEAT:

Preheat grill to high.

PREP:

Wash and dry potatoes, then pierce all over with a fork. Place a small amount of oil in the palm of your hand and coat potatoes, one at a time. Sprinkle each oiled potato with a generous amount of salt. Wrap each potato individually in heavy-duty foil (or a doubled layer of regular foil); use enough foil to wrap potato completely, sealing ends to trap steam.

GRILL:

Place wrapped potatoes on grate away from heat and cook for 30 to 60 minutes, depending upon the intensity of the heat and the size of the potato. To test for doneness, insert a sharp knife into the center; potato is done when knife pierces easily. When done, unwrap potatoes, cut them open on the top, and fill with accompaniments of your choice.

Simple Vegetable Grill

SERVES 4

- 1 medium yellow summer squash
- 1 medium zucchini
- 1 medium eggplant
- 1 red bell pepper
- 2–3 tablespoons (28–45 ml) olive oil
- 1 teaspoon (6 g) kosher salt
- 1/2 teaspoon (0.5 g) freshly ground pepper

PREHEAT:

Preheat grill to medium-high.

PREP:

Slice squashes and eggplant as you like; vegetables can be cut into larger chunks or slices if you are placing them directly onto grill grate. Place vegetables in a bowl; drizzle with oil and sprinkle with salt and pepper, stirring to coat.

GRILL:

Place in grill wok, on skewers, on grill screen, or directly on grate. Cook for 10 to 15 minutes, or until vegetables are tender and slightly charred; turn skewers or stir vegetables in wok several times.

Simple Vegetable Grill

Grilled Onions with Red Wine Vinaigrette

SERVES 4 (SIDE-DISH SERVINGS)

- **4 small yellow onions**
- **I tablespoon (15 ml) olive oil**
- **2 tablespoons (28 ml) extra-virgin olive oil**
- **I tablespoon (15 ml) red wine vinegar**
- **I tablespoon (15 ml) freshly squeezed lemon juice**
- **$\frac{1}{2}$ teaspoon (1.5 g) crushed garlic**
- **Pinch cayenne**
- **I small loaf country bread, sliced**

PREHEAT:

Preheat grill to medium-high.

PREP:

Trim off and discard the ends of the onions and peel them. Cut the onions in half across the middle. Rub equal amounts of the 1 tablespoon (15 ml) olive oil over the cut sides. Whisk together the extra-virgin olive oil, red wine vinegar, lemon juice, garlic, and cayenne in a small bowl.

GRILL:

Place the onions, cut side down, directly on the grill. Cover the grill and grill for about 45 minutes, turning every 10 to 12 minutes. (The onions are done when they are soft and slightly charred.)

SERVE:

Place the onions on a serving platter and drizzle with the olive oil mixture. Serve with passed bread.

Grilled Zucchini and Red Onions

SERVES 4

- 1 teaspoon (2.5 g) ground cumin
- ¹/₂ teaspoon (0.9 g) ground oregano
- ¹/₂ teaspoon (3 g) salt
- 2 medium zucchini, scrubbed and cut into ¹/₄" (.6 cm) rounds
- 2 medium red onions, peeled and quartered
- ¹/₄ cup (60 ml) olive oil
- About 8 wooden skewers, soaked in water for 30 minutes before grilling

PREHEAT:

Preheat grill to medium-high.

PREP:

Combine the cumin, oregano, and salt in a small bowl. Skewer the zucchini rounds and onion quarters loosely, without crowding them together. Brush the kebabs with half of the oil. Sprinkle evenly with the cumin mixture, reserving a little. Set aside on a baking sheet to marinate for 15 minutes at room temperature.

GRILL:

Grill skewers on an oiled rack for about 10 minutes total, turning often, until vegetables are tender and lightly charred.

SERVE:

Transfer to a platter to cool slightly. Unskewer vegetables into a large serving bowl. Drizzle with remaining olive oil and season with remaining cumin mixture to taste. Toss to combine and serve warm or at room temperature.

CHAPTER ELEVEN

SALADS

Spinach Salad with Spiced Walnuts & Fire-Roasted Red Bell Pepper, page 252

TODAY'S GRILLS AND OUTDOOR CHEFS CAN TURN OUT ANY

variation of any component of any meal, and salads are no exception. Grilled Spinach Salad with Spiced Walnuts and Fire-Roasted Red Bell Pepper (page 252)? Nothing to it on a modern grill. Tomato Salad with Fresh Mozzarella Cheese (page 252)? A cinch on a grill. Corn, Black Bean, and Avocado Salad (page 254)? The options are unlimited. The salads in this chapter will make memorable starters or hearty main courses.

We may not grill entire salads, but we grill enough of the salad ingredients to make this a true grilling experience. The best time to feast on grilled salads, of course, is when local vegetables come to market with their freshest flavors. Corn, peppers, zucchini, onions, sweet potatoes, and eggplant are all superb when grilled and blend with greens in a main course salad. Chicken, salmon, steak tips, shrimp, scallops, and other meat, fish, and seafood are terrific when grilled and added to salads.

Grilling salad ingredients is one of the easiest tasks for the outdoor chef. A zucchini or eggplant can be sliced lengthwise and laid on the grill for a few minutes. Skewers can be used to grill small ingredients like shrimp, chicken, peppers, onion, or even small, preboiled potatoes that can be tossed in a great salad.

Almost any grilled vegetable can become an ingredient, as well as a side dish or main course, so look back at Chapter 10 while you're getting inventive about your next salad. The same can be said for poultry, meats, fish, seafood, and even game. Salad is not only healthy, tasty, and attractive in a bowl or on a plate, it is infinite in its variety.

Caesar Salad with Smoky Grilled Tofu

SERVES 6 (SIDE-DISH SERVINGS)

- 14 ounces (400 g) extra-firm tofu
- 3 tablespoons (45 ml) olive oil
- 1½ tablespoons (23 ml) balsamic vinegar
- 1 large head romaine lettuce
- 1 medium egg
- 2 cloves garlic, minced
- 3 tablespoons (45 ml) freshly squeezed lemon juice
- 1 tablespoon (15 ml) Worcestershire sauce
- ½ cup (120 ml) extra-virgin olive oil
- 1 cup (40 g) croutons
- ½ cup (50 g) finely grated Parmesan cheese

PREHEAT:

Preheat grill to medium-high with a smoker box in place.

PREP:

Drain the tofu and cut the slab in half width-wise to create two pieces. Place each piece on a paper towel and cover with another towel. Place a heavy skillet on top to press the excess water from the tofu. After 15 minutes, place the tofu between fresh paper towels and repeat the process. In a bowl, whisk together the olive oil and balsamic vinegar, and pour into a rimmed baking pan. Again, cut the tofu slabs in half width-wise and soak each side in the oil-and-vinegar mixture. In a large bowl, whisk together the egg, garlic, lemon juice, and Worcestershire sauce. Gradually add the extra-virgin olive oil in a thin stream, whisking as you do. Continue to whisk for 1 to 2 minutes, until emulsified.

GRILL:

Place the tofu on the hot grill. Grill for about 10 minutes, turning several times. Remove the tofu from the grill and set aside to cool slightly. When the tofu is cool enough to handle, cut into thin strips. Set aside.

SERVE:

Wash and dry the lettuce, then tear it into bite-size pieces and briefly set it aside in the refrigerator to keep cold and crisp. Add the lettuce to dressing mixture and toss well to coat. Add the croutons and Parmesan cheese, and toss again. Arrange equal amounts on chilled salad plates. Top with the strips of tofu.

Iceberg Lettuce with Grilled Figs and Creamy Blue Cheese Dressing

SERVES 6

- ¾ cup (175 g) mayonnaise
- ¾ cup (90 g) crumbled blue cheese
- ¼ cup (60 g) sour cream
- 2 tablespoons (28 ml) red wine vinegar
- 1 tablespoon (13 g) sugar
- ½ teaspoon (1.5 g) crushed garlic
- 1 head iceberg lettuce
- 12 firm, ripe green figs

PREHEAT:

Preheat grill to medium-high.

PREP:

Place the mayonnaise, blue cheese, sour cream, red wine vinegar, sugar, and garlic in a bowl and whisk together to make the dressing. (There will be lumps of blue cheese in the creamy mixture.) Set aside in the refrigerator. Remove the center core from the lettuce and discard. Tear the rest into bite-size pieces, placing equal amounts of lettuce on six chilled salad plates. Set aside in the refrigerator. Cut off and discard the stem ends and slice the figs in half lengthwise

GRILL:

Place the figs cut side up (skin side down) on the grill and grill for about 4 minutes, until the centers are soft.

SERVE:

Remove the figs from the grill and arrange four halves on top of the lettuce on each plate. Spoon equal amounts of blue cheese dressing on each plate.

Grilled Endive Salad with Golden Raisins

SERVES 4

- ¼ cup (35 g) pine nuts
- 3 tablespoons (45 ml) extra-virgin olive oil
- 1 tablespoon (15 ml) balsamic vinegar
- ½ teaspoon (4 g) honey
- ½ teaspoon (2.5 g) Dijon mustard
- Pinch salt
- Several grindings black pepper, to taste
- 2 Belgian endives, halved lengthwise
- 1 tablespoon (15 ml) olive oil
- 6 cups (170 g) loosely packed torn red lettuce leaves
- ¼ cup (35 g) golden raisins

PREHEAT:

Preheat grill to medium-high.

PREP:

In a small bowl, whisk together the extra-virgin olive oil, balsamic vinegar, honey, mustard, salt, and black pepper. Set the dressing aside.

COOK:

Place a single layer of pine nuts in a small cast-iron skillet on the stovetop over medium-high heat. Shake the pan frequently. (The nuts will become slightly golden and emit a nutty aroma.) Remove the nuts from the pan and set aside until needed.

GRILL:

Use a pastry brush to brush both sides of the endive with some of the olive oil. Place the endive on the grill, cut side down. Cook for about 2 minutes, baste with some more of the oil, and turn with tongs. Continue to cook for about 2 more minutes. (The endive will wilt slightly and develop grill marks.) Remove the endive from the grill.

SERVE:

Place the lettuce in a large bowl and drizzle with the dressing. Toss to combine. Distribute among four salad plates. Place one grilled endive half atop the lettuce on each plate. Sprinkle with equal amounts of raisins and pine nuts.

Mixed Greens with Grilled Summer Vegetables and Blue Cheese

SERVES 4 (SIDE-DISH SERVINGS)

- 1 medium yellow crookneck squash
- 1 medium zucchini
- 1 Japanese eggplant
- 1 tablespoon (15 ml) olive oil
- 1/4 cup (60 ml) extra-virgin olive oil
- 2 tablespoons (28 ml) red wine vinegar
- 1 teaspoon (5 g) Dijon mustard
- 1/2 teaspoon (1.5 g) crushed garlic
- Several grindings black pepper, to taste
- 6 cups (170 g) mixed greens
- 1 medium tomato, sliced
- 1/4 cup (30 g) crumbled blue cheese

PREHEAT:

Preheat grill to medium-high.

PREP:

Remove the ends from the crookneck squash and zucchini, and discard. Slice the squashes lengthwise. Remove the end from the eggplant and discard. Slice the eggplant lengthwise. Place the squashes and eggplant in a plastic bag and drizzle with the 1 tablespoon (15 ml) olive oil. Twist the bag to seal, allowing some air to remain in the bag. Toss gently to coat the vegetables evenly. Place the extra-virgin olive oil, red wine vinegar, mustard, garlic, and black pepper in a bowl and whisk to combine.

GRILL:

Remove the squashes and eggplant from the bag and place them on the grill. Grill for 8 to 10 minutes, turning frequently. Remove the squashes and eggplant from the grill and place on a cutting board. Cool for several minutes, then cut into matchstick pieces.

SERVE:

Place the mixed greens in a large bowl and drizzle with half of the dressing, reserving the remaining dressing. Toss well to coat the leaves. Distribute the greens equally among four chilled salad plates. Arrange the tomato slices around the edge of each plate and place equal amounts of matchstick vegetable pieces over the top. Drizzle with the remaining dressing. Top with the blue cheese.

Fresh Greens with Grilled Hearts of Palm

SERVES 4 (SIDE-DISH SERVINGS)

- 1 (7.75-ounce [220 g]) can hearts of palm
- 1 tablespoon (15 ml) olive oil
- 2 tablespoons (28 ml) freshly squeezed lime juice
- 2 teaspoons (2.7 g) minced fresh oregano
- 8 cups (225 g) loosely packed mixed salad greens
- 1 lemon cucumber, peeled and chopped
- 12 cherry tomatoes, halved
- 1/4 cup (60 ml) extra-virgin olive oil
- 1 tablespoon (4 g) minced fresh flat-leaf parsley
- 1 teaspoon (5 g) Dijon mustard
- Pinch granulated garlic

PREHEAT:

Preheat grill to medium-high.

MARINATE:

Drain the hearts of palm and place in a shallow dish. In a separate bowl, whisk together the olive oil, 1 tablespoon (15 ml) of the lime juice, and 1 teaspoon (1.3 g) of the oregano. Pour over the hearts of palm and marinate for about 15 minutes. Roll the hearts of palm to coat as they marinate.

PREP:

Place the greens in a medium bowl. Add the cucumber and tomatoes. In a small bowl, whisk together the extra-virgin olive oil, the remaining 1 tablespoon (15 ml) lime juice, the parsley, the remaining 1 teaspoon (1.3 g) oregano, the mustard, and garlic to make a dressing. Set aside.

GRILL:

Place the hearts of palm in a grill basket on the grill and grill for about 5 minutes, turning frequently, until heated through and seared with grill marks. Remove from the grill to a cutting board and cut into thick slices.

SERVE:

Toss the salad greens with the dressing and distribute equally among four salad plates. Top with equal amounts of grilled hearts of palm.

Red Lettuce Salad with Grilled Beets and Goat Cheese

SERVES 4

- 1 pound (455 g) small fresh beets
- 1/3 cup (80 ml) Raspberry Vinegar Marinade (page 50)
- 6 cups (170 g) loosely packed torn red lettuce leaves
- 3 tablespoons (45 ml) extra-virgin olive oil
- 1 tablespoon (15 ml) raspberry vinegar
- 2 ounces (55 g) soft goat cheese

PREHEAT

Preheat grill to medium.

MARINATE:

Peel the beets and cut them into 1/4" (.6 cm) slices. Place them in a bowl with the Raspberry Vinegar Marinade and toss to coat. Allow the beets to marinate for about 45 minutes, tossing occasionally.

PREP:

In a small bowl, whisk together the olive oil and raspberry vinegar. Place the lettuce in a shallow bowl.

GRILL:

Grease a large sheet of foil, and place on grill. Remove salmon steaks from marinade, and place on grill. Cook for 5 to 7 minutes per side, depending upon thickness and desired doneness.

SERVE:

Place salad on a large serving platter, and place steaks around edge (slightly overlapping salad).

Spinach Salad with Spiced Walnuts and Fire-Roasted Red Bell Pepper

SERVES 4 (SIDE-DISH SERVINGS)

- ■ I medium red bell pepper
- ■ 6 cups (180 g) loosely packed baby spinach leaves
- ■ ¹/₃ cup (40 g) chopped raw, unsalted walnuts
- ■ 2 teaspoons (10 ml) freshly squeezed lime juice
- ■ ¹/₄ teaspoon (0.8 g) granulated garlic
- ■ ¹/₄ teaspoon (0.7 g) chile powder
- ■ ¹/₄ teaspoon (1.5 g) salt
- ■ 2 tablespoons (28 ml) orange juice
- ■ I tablespoon (15 ml) apple cider vinegar
- ■ I tablespoon (15 ml) olive oil
- ■ ¹/₂ small red onion, sliced thinly
- ■ Several grindings black pepper, to taste
- ■ 2 tablespoons (8 g) minced fresh cilantro

PREHEAT:

Preheat grill to high.

PREP:

Wash the spinach and discard the stems. Dry the spinach and tear into bite-size pieces. Place the spinach in a large bowl and set aside. Whisk together the orange juice, apple cider vinegar, olive oil, and the remaining ¹/₈ teaspoon (0.8 g) salt in a small bowl.

COOK:

Heat a dry heavy-bottomed skillet over medium heat on the stovetop and toast the walnuts for about 5 minutes, shaking the pan frequently. When the walnuts are golden brown, place them in a small bowl and toss with the lime juice while they are still warm. Sprinkle on the garlic, chile powder, and ¹/₈ teaspoon (0.8 g) of the salt. Toss to distribute evenly and set aside.

GRILL:

Place the bell pepper directly on the grill and cook for 10 to 15 minutes, turning frequently. Cook until the skin is charred black. Transfer the pepper to a plastic or paper bag, close the bag, and set aside for about 15 minutes. When the pepper is cool enough to handle, peel off the charred skin and discard the seeds, stem, and white membrane. Slice the pepper into 1" (2.5 cm) strips and set them aside.

SERVE:

Toss together the spinach, onion, and orange juice mixture. Distribute evenly among six chilled salad plates. Top the spinach with the bell pepper strips and sprinkle with the spiced nuts. Grind a little black pepper on each one and sprinkle evenly with the cilantro.

Grilled Tomato Salad with Fresh Mozzarella Cheese

SERVES 4 (SIDE-DISH SERVINGS)

- ■ 2 tomatoes
- ■ ¹/₂ teaspoon (1.3 g) mild chile powder
- ■ ¹/₂ teaspoon (1.5 g) granulated garlic
- ■ 2 balls fresh mozzarella (about 8 ounces [225 g])
- ■ 2 tablespoons (28 ml) extra-virgin olive oil
- ■ I teaspoon (5 ml) balsamic vinegar
- ■ 16 fresh basil leaves
- ■ ¹/₄ teaspoon (1.5 g) salt
- ■ Several grinding black pepper, to taste

PREHEAT:

Preheat grill to medium with a smoker box in place.

PREP:

Core the tomatoes and quarter them. Sprinkle the tomatoes with the chile powder and the garlic.

GRILL:

Place the tomatoes on the grill and grill for 2 to 3 minutes, then turn them and continue to grill for 2 to 3 minutes more. Carefully remove the tomatoes from the grill and set aside.

SERVE:

Cut the mozzarella into ¹/₄" (.6 cm) slices. Arrange the grilled tomato wedges on serving plates and place equal amounts of mozzarella slices on each plate. Drizzle with the olive oil, then with the balsamic vinegar. Stack the basil leaves and cut them crosswise into thin strips. Distribute them on top of the tomato and cheese. Sprinkle with the salt and black pepper, and then serve at room temperature.

Spinach Salad with Grilled Peaches and Gorgonzola Cheese

SERVES 4

- 3 tablespoons (45 ml) extra-virgin olive oil
- 1 tablespoon (15 ml) raspberry vinegar
- ¼ teaspoon (0.8 g) crushed garlic
- Pinch salt
- Several grindings black pepper, to taste
- ¼ cup (30 g) chopped pecans
- 6 cups (180 g) loosely packed baby spinach leaves
- 2 medium yellow peaches, pitted
- 1 ounce (28 g) crumbled Gorgonzola cheese

PREHEAT:

Preheat grill to medium-high.

PREP:

Place the olive oil, raspberry vinegar, garlic, salt, and black pepper in a small bowl and whisk to combine into a dressing. Set aside. Wash the spinach and discard the stems. Dry the spinach and tear into bite-size pieces.

COOK:

Place the pecans in a small skillet on the stovetop over medium-high heat. Shake the pan frequently until the pecans emit a roasted aroma. Remove the pecans from the pan and set aside until needed.

GRILL:

Place the spinach in a shallow bowl and toss with the dressing just before serving. Cut each peach into eight slices. Place the slices in a grill basket and put it on the grill. Grill for about 2 minutes, then turn and grill for about 2 more minutes.

SERVE:

Put equal portions of spinach on four salad plates. Top the spinach with peach slices, arranged around the perimeter of the plate. Sprinkle each salad with equal amounts of Gorgonzola cheese and pecans.

Corn, Black Bean, and Avocado Salad

SERVES 12 (SIDE-DISH SERVINGS)

- ¼ cup (60 ml) olive oil
- ¼ cup (60 ml) freshly squeezed orange juice
- 3 tablespoons (45 ml) freshly squeezed lime juice
- 1 teaspoon (3 g) crushed garlic
- ¼ teaspoon (.6 g) ground cumin
- ½ teaspoon (3 g) salt
- 2 ears yellow corn, unhusked
- 4 cups (860 g) canned black beans
- 2 Haas avocados, peeled, pitted, and diced
- 2 cups (240 g) peeled and diced jícama
- 6 green onions, diced
- ½ cup (30 g) chopped fresh cilantro

PREHEAT:

Preheat grill to high.

PREP:

To prepare the dressing, whisk together the olive oil, orange juice, lime juice, garlic, cumin, and salt in a small bowl. Set aside. Place the corn in a plastic bag and fill the bag with water to soak the husks for about 15 minutes.

GRILL:

Remove the corn from the bag of water and place the corn on the grill. Turn the corn every few minutes to evenly blacken all sides of the husks. Grill for 18 to 22 minutes. (The kernels will steam in the husks.) Remove the corn from the grill. Allow the corn to cool for a few minutes, then peel off the husks and remove the silk. Cut the corn from the cob and place in a large bowl.

SERVE:

Drain and rinse the black beans and add them to the corn. Toss in the avocado, jícama, green onions, and cilantro. Drizzle with the dressing and toss. Refrigerate until needed.

Pasta Salad with Grilled Radicchio and Sweet Peppers

SERVES 8 (SIDE-DISH SERVINGS)

- 1 head radicchio
- 1 small yellow bell pepper
- 1 small red bell pepper
- 2 tablespoons (28 ml) olive oil
- 1 teaspoon (3 g) crushed garlic
- 12 ounces (340 g) penne pasta
- 2 tablespoons (28 ml) extra-virgin olive oil
- 1 tablespoon (15 ml) balsamic vinegar
- ⅛ teaspoon (0.4 g) mild chile powder
- 2 teaspoons (2.7 g) minced fresh oregano
- 3 green onions, minced
- Parmesan cheese (optional)

PREHEAT:

Preheat grill to medium.

PREP:

Cut the radicchio into quarters, removing the core section. Core and seed the bell peppers, cutting them into quarters. Place the radicchio and bell peppers in a plastic bag and drizzle with the olive oil and garlic. Twist the bag to seal, allowing some air to remain in the bag. Toss gently to coat the radicchio and peppers evenly. Remove from bag when ready to grill.

COOK:

Fill a large stockpot with water and place on the stovetop over high heat. Bring to a boil and add the pasta. Cook for 6 to 8 minutes, until al dente. Drain into a colander and rinse with cold water. Drain well and transfer to a shallow serving bowl.

GRILL:

Place the radicchio and peppers on the grill. Grill the radicchio for 5 to 7 minutes, turning carefully to slightly char all sides. Grill the peppers until limp and slightly charred, 6 to 7 minutes. Remove the radicchio and peppers from the grill and coarsely chop.

SERVE:

In a bowl, whisk together the extra-virgin olive oil, balsamic vinegar, chile powder, and oregano. Drizzle over the pasta and toss to coat. Add the green onions and the grilled radicchio and peppers, toss to combine. Pass grated Parmesan cheese, if desired.

Warm Corn-Noodle Salad

SERVES 6

- 1 pound (455 g) egg noodles
- 1 1/2 cups (245 g) cooked corn kernels
- 1/2 cup (112 g [1 stick]) butter, melted
- 1/2 cup (50 g) grated Parmesan cheese
- 1/4 cup (30 g) shredded Cheddar cheese
- 8 ounces (225 g) cream cheese, cut into 1" (2.5 cm) cubes
- 1/2 cup (120 ml) milk, or as needed
- Kosher salt and freshly ground pepper

PREHEAT:

Preheat grill to medium.

PREP:

Cook noodles according to package directions; drain. In mixing bowl, stir together noodles, corn, butter, and cheeses; mix well. Stir in milk a little at a time, adding just enough to moisten mixture. Add salt and pepper to taste; mix well. Spray disposable pan with nonstick spray. Spoon noodle mixture into pan; cover loosely with foil.

GRILL:

Place pan of noodles on grate away from heat. Cover grill and cook for 20 to 30 minutes, or until mixture is hot throughout.

Summer Squashes with Lemon Basil

SERVES 6 (SIDE-DISH SERVINGS)

- 3 medium yellow crookneck squashes
- 3 medium zucchini
- 2 tablespoons (28 ml) olive oil
- 1 teaspoon (3 g) crushed garlic
- 1 tablespoon (15 ml) extra-virgin olive oil
- 1 tablespoon chiffonaded strips fresh lemon basil

PREHEAT:

Preheat grill to medium.

PREP:

Remove and discard the stem ends of the squashes and zucchini, and then cut them lengthwise into 1/4" (.6 cm) slices. Place the yellow squashes and zucchini in a plastic bag and drizzle with the olive oil and garlic. Twist the bag to seal, allowing some of the air to remain in the bag. Toss gently to coat the squashes and zucchini evenly. Remove from bag when ready to grill.

GRILL:

Place the squashes and zucchini on the grill and grill for about 10 minutes, until grill marks appear and the slices are tender-crisp, turning twice. Remove the yellow squashes and zucchini, and place on a platter. Drizzle with the extra-virgin olive oil and sprinkle with the lemon basil. Serve immediately or at room temperature.

Asparagus with Watercress Sauce

SERVES 10 (SIDE-DISH SERVINGS)

- 3 tablespoons (45 ml) extra-virgin olive oil
- 2 tablespoons (28 ml) freshly squeezed lemon juice
- $\frac{1}{8}$ teaspoon (0.8 g) salt
- $\frac{1}{2}$ cup (17 g) watercress leaves
- 2 green onions, minced
- 2 pounds (905 g) fresh asparagus
- 1 tablespoon (15 ml) olive oil
- 1 hard-boiled egg, peeled and chopped

PREHEAT:

Preheat grill to medium.

PREP:

Combine the extra-virgin olive oil, lemon juice, and salt in a small bowl. Place the watercress and green onions in a blender. Switch on the low setting and add the lemon juice mixture in a slow, steady stream. Blend until you have a smooth sauce. Set aside. Wash the asparagus carefully to remove any traces of soil. Snap off and discard the tough ends. Place the asparagus in a plastic bag and drizzle with the olive oil. Twist the bag to seal, allowing some of the air to remain in the bag. Toss gently to coat the asparagus evenly. Remove from bag when ready to grill.

GRILL:

Place the asparagus in a grill basket on the grill. Grill for 8 to 10 minutes, turning frequently so the stalks cook but do not burn. (The asparagus should be al dente and slightly charred.) Transfer the asparagus from the grill to a serving platter. Spoon the watercress sauce over the top and sprinkle with the chopped egg. Serve hot or at room temperature.

CHAPTER TWELVE
DESSERTS

Easy Bake Apples, page 260

GRILLED DESSERTS ARE LIMITED ONLY BY ONE'S IMAGINATION

and the variety of fruits at the local stores. A grill chef can create a spectacular dessert of nectarines with orange and almond butter or lemon-baked bananas with citrus mascarpone. Grilled Pinā Colada Parcels (page 265) can give a Caribbean feeling to your patio one weekend, while Easy Baked Apples (page 260) lend a cozy, home-grown feeling to your next dinner party.

Most fruit can be grilled—whole apples, skewered chunks of pineapple, or mango can be laid on the grill, and bananas can be wrapped in tinfoil. You can apply some of the recipes and methods of grilling you'll find here to other favorite fruits to create your own, unique desserts. Ice cream is a wonderful treat on its own, but when mixed with grilled fruit or grilled slices of pound cake, it becomes magical. Marshmallows and chocolate chips can be added to bananas wrapped in foil and grilled for a few moments for an added surprise. The possibilities are endless, even if some of them aren't exactly guilt-free.

Guests are going to remember grilled desserts for a long time because they are not traditional cookout fare. They are also memorable because of the unique flavor grilling imparts to dessert ingredients. Grilling quickly caramelizes the sugars in fruit, giving desserts a flavor that is hard to duplicate on an indoor stove.

Make sure you have a clean grill before making your dessert. Fruit may pick up flavors from meat, chicken, or vegetables you cooked for the main course. Be prepared to cook dessert ingredients for much shorter times than you used for your main course. Your grill can be quite hot for grilling fruits, but the sugars will burn if the fruit is left on the grill more than several minutes. Adding alcohol to fruit does create some spectacular dishes, but be extremely careful when grilling fruit soaked in alcohol, because of the flash flame that can be result.

Grilled desserts are simple, marvelous, and memorable—the perfect end to a family meal or a party.

Easy Baked Apples

SERVES 6

- Six large apples
- I cup (200 g) sugar
- I teaspoon (2.3 g) ground cinnamon
- 8 tablespoons (112 g [I stick]) butter
- French vanilla ice cream
- I sheet heavy-duty aluminum foil

PREHEAT:

Preheat grill to medium.

PREP:

Peel, core, and slice the apples. Mix the sugar and cinnamon together. Combine with the apples and set inside the sheet of foil. Cut the butter into thin slices and put those on top of the apples. Fold the sheet of foil over the apples and seal it shut so no steam will escape.

GRILL:

Grill for 30 to 45 minutes.

SERVE:

Open the foil carefully to allow steam to escape and serve apples over ice cream.

Maple Apples

SERVES 4

- 2 large cooking apples, such as Granny Smith, Jonathan, or Braeburn
- 2 tablespoons (28 g) butter, melted
- ⅛ teaspoon (0.3 g) ground cinnamon
- ¼ cup (60 ml) real maple syrup

PREHEAT:

Preheat grill to medium.

PREP:

Core apples and cut into thick slices. Brush with melted butter; sprinkle with cinnamon.

GRILL:

Place on grate over heat and brush with maple syrup. Cook, turning and basting frequently with syrup, until nicely glazed on both sides. Serve warm.

Maple Apples

Grilled Cake with Bananas

Grilled Cake with Bananas

SERVES 4

- 5–6 medium bananas, firm and unspotted
- ¹/₂ cup (112 g [1 stick]) butter
- 1 cup (225 g) packed brown sugar
- 1 teaspoon (5 ml) rum extract
- ¹/₂ teaspoon (1.2 g) ground cinnamon
- 4 slices pound cake (1" [2.5 cm] thick)
- Vanilla ice cream, optional

PREHEAT:

Preheat grill to medium.

PREP:

Peel and slice bananas.

GRILL:

Place butter into disposable aluminum pan; place on grate over heat and cook until butter melts, stirring frequently. Add brown sugar, rum extract, and cinnamon; stir to blend. Add sliced bananas to brown sugar mixture. Cook until bananas are soft on the edges, 8 to 10 minutes, stirring frequently. Meanwhile, toast pound cake slices on both sides on the grill.

SERVE:

Place toasted cake slices on plates and spoon bananas and syrup over them. Top with ice cream, if you like.

Peaches and Cream

SERVES 4

- 4 firm peaches
- ¹/₂ cup (115 g) packed brown sugar
- 3 tablespoons (45 ml) rum
- ¹/₂ teaspoon (1.2 g) ground cinnamon
- 1 cup (235 ml) heavy cream

PREHEAT:

Preheat grill to medium.

PREP:

Peel peaches. Remove and discard pit; slice peaches into mixing bowl. Add sugar, rum, and cinnamon, stirring to coat; adjust sugar as needed based on sweetness of peaches. Divide peach mixture between two large squares of foil, shiny side up, and seal packets.

GRILL:

Place packets on grate over heat and cook for 20 to 30 minutes, or until peaches are tender and heated through, turning packets occasionally. Remove from grill and open packets carefully. It is a good idea to open into a bowl or serving dish in order to capture all the juices. Serve warm, topped with cream.

To peel peaches, drop individually into a saucepan of boiling water and cook for 1 minute. Remove with slotted spoon and hold under cold water; the skin should slip off easily.

Grilled Pineapple Topped with Ice Cream and Rum

SERVES 4

- ¹/₂ cup (100 g) sugar
- ¹/₄ teaspoon (0.6 g) ground cinnamon
- 4 thick slices fresh pineapple
- 2 tablespoons (28 g) butter, melted
- 1 pint (288 g) vanilla or rum raisin ice cream
- 3–4 tablespoons (45–60 ml) rum (gold, dark, or spiced)

PREHEAT:

Preheat grill to medium.

PREP:

In flat dish, stir together sugar and cinnamon. Brush pineapple with melted butter and then dip into sugar mixture, coating both sides. Shake off excess.

GRILL:

Place on grate over heat and cook until brown and sizzling, 5 to 8 minutes per side.

SERVE:

Serve at once, topped with ice cream and drizzled with 2 to 3 teaspoons (10 to 15 ml) of rum per serving.

Grilled Pineapple with Honey Glaze

SERVES 4

- 1/4 cup (85 g) honey
- I tablespoon (15 ml) dark rum
- I unpeeled medium pineapple, quartered, core removed
- Toasted coconut (optional)

PREHEAT:

Preheat grill to medium.

PREP:

In small bowl, stir together honey and rum.

GRILL:

Place pineapple quarters on grate over heat, with one of the cut sides down. Sear that side, then rotate the pineapple quarters slightly and sear the second cut side. When both cut sides are nicely seared, turn quarters rind side down and brush cut sides with honey mixture. Cook for about 20 minutes longer, turning fruit several times.

SERVE:

Remove from grill and sprinkle with coconut, if you like; serve warm.

Blueberries and Grilled Pound Cake

SERVES 8

- I purchased or homemade pound cake loaf (about II ounces [312 g])
- 2 tablespoons (28 g) butter, melted
- 2 cups (240 g) whipped cream
- 2 cups (290 g) fresh blueberries
- 1/2 cup (100 g) sugar

PREHEAT:

Preheat grill to high. Lightly oil insides of hinged grilling basket or cake-cooling racks.

PREP:

Cut pound cake into 8 equal slices. Brush with melted butter; place in grilling basket or between cake-cooling racks.

GRILL:

Place pound cake on grate away from heat and cook until golden, 1 to 2 minutes per side.

SERVE:

Place each grilled pound cake slice on a plate. Top with a large dollop of whipped cream. Top that with 1/4 cup (36 g) blueberries and sprinkle with sugar.

Grilled Glazed Fruit Compote

SERVES 6

- 1 banana, peeled, cut into chunks
- 2 cups (310 g) fresh pineapple chunks
- 1 cup (140 g) peeled papaya chunks
- 1 cup (165 g) peeled mango chunks
- 2 large kiwifruits, peeled and quartered
- $^2/_3$ cup (115 g) honey
- 3 tablespoons (45 ml) lemon juice
- 1 teaspoon (2.7 g) grated fresh gingerroot
- 1 tablespoon (4 g) snipped fresh mint
- 2 tablespoons (9 g) shredded coconut

PREHEAT:

Preheat grill to medium-high.

PREP:

Skewer fruit chunks on 12" (30 cm) skewers. Combine the honey, lemon juice, and gingerroot in a small bowl till well combined.

GRILL:

Grill the fruit, turning and basting with the honey mixture frequently till nicely coated, about 6 to 8 minutes.

SERVE:

Divide the fruit among six dessert bowls and sprinkle on the mint and coconut, then drizzle with the rest of the honey syrup.

Grilled Marsala Cantaloupe Balls

SERVES 4

- 1 cantaloupe
- $^1/_2$ cup (100 g) sugar
- 2 teaspoons (12 g) salt
- 2 cups (470 ml) Marsala wine
- 1 lemon, juice and zest
- Mint sprigs, for garnish (optional)

PREHEAT:

Preheat grill to medium-high.

PREP:

With a melon baller, scoop cantaloupe into balls and place in a large bowl. Sprinkle sugar and salt on top of cantaloupe and toss to coat. Add wine and lemon juice and zest to bowl, and carefully toss to coat. Set bowl aside at room temperature for 30 minutes, carefully tossing fruit every 10 minutes. Drain excess liquid from bowl, then thread cantaloupe balls onto lightly oiled skewers.

GRILL:

Place cantaloupe on oiled grill grates for about 20 to 30 seconds per side. Remove from grill and remove from skewers.

SERVE:

Place cantaloupe on large platter and garnish with mint sprigs if desired.

Grilled Piña Colada Parcels

SERVES 6

- 3 cups (465 g) cubed fresh pineapple chunks
- I ripe large plantain (peel is black, speckled), peeled and sliced thinly
- I cup (74 g) sweetened coconut flakes
- ²/₃ cup (160 ml) sweetened coconut cream
- 2 tablespoons (28 ml) rum
- I teaspoon (5 ml) vanilla extract
- 6 tablespoons (85 g) butter, melted
- 6 scoops vanilla ice cream

PREHEAT:

Preheat grill to high.

PREP:

In a bowl, mix pineapple, plantain, coconut flakes, coconut cream, rum, and vanilla.

Cut six 15" x 12" (37.5 x 30 cm) pieces of heavy-duty foil. Brush foil with butter.

Place one-sixth of fruit mixture on half of one piece of foil. Fold over other half and seal edges well. Make sure it does not leak. Leave some room between edge and fruit filling. Repeat process with remaining ingredients till finished.

GRILL:

Place fruit parcels on grill and bake about 15 minutes. Let each person open his or her own parcel, being careful to avoid the escaping steam. Serve with ice cream if desired.

English Muffin Pies

SERVES 4

- 4 English muffins
- 3 tablespoons (42 g) butter or margarine
- I can (about 20 ounces [560 g]) apple, blueberry, or other fruit pie filling

PREHEAT:

Preheat grill to medium.

PREP:

Tear off four pieces of foil, each about 12" (30 cm) square. Split English muffins. Butter the outsides generously, then place a muffin half, buttered side down, on the shiny side of each piece of foil. Spoon about 3 tablespoons (50 g) pie filling onto each muffin; refrigerate any remaining filling for another use. Top filled muffins with remaining buttered muffin halves, buttered side up, and seal packets.

GRILL:

Place packets on grate over heat and cook for about 15 minutes, turning several times. The outsides of the muffins should be nicely browned. When done, remove from grill and open packets. Be careful, because the filling will be extremely hot; allow to cool for several minutes before serving.

Apricot and Blackberry Pizza with Camembert and Sweet Ricotta Cheese

SERVES 6

- I recipe Sweet Pizza Dough (page 207)
- Olive oil for brushing dough
- ½ cup (160 g) apricot preserves
- 6 apricots, peeled and sliced
- ½ pint (145 g) fresh blackberries
- 4 ounces (115 g) Camembert cheese, sliced thickly
- Sweet Ricotta Cheese (below)

Sweet Ricotta Cheese:

- ½ cup (115 g) ricotta cheese
- 2 tablespoons (40 g) honey
- 3 tablespoons (20 g) confectioners' sugar
- ⅛ teaspoon (0.25 g) ground nutmeg

PREHEAT:

Preheat grill to high.

PREP:

Combine Sweet Ricotta Cheese ingredients in a small mixing bowl. Cover and refrigerate until ready to use.

COOK:

Preheat broiler. Heat preserves in a saucepan over low heat. Spread preserves over top of dough, then top with Sweet Ricotta Cheese.

GRILL:

Stretch dough to a large rectangular shape. Oil and grill one side at a time until golden and crisp, about 3 minutes per side. Transfer to flat surface and let cool.

SERVE:

Arrange apricots and blackberries over ricotta cheese and top with Camembert. Place under broiler to melt and brown the cheese approximately 5 minutes.

Mixed Berries on Grilled Pizza Shell with Mascarpone Spread

SERVES 6

- 16 ounces (455 g) mascarpone cheese
- 4 ounces (115 g) cream cheese, at room temperature
- ¼ cup (25 g) sifted confectioners' sugar, plus extra for garnish
- 1 tablespoon (7 g) ground cinnamon
- 1 teaspoon (2.2 g) ground nutmeg
- 1 teaspoon (5 ml) vanilla extract
- 1 teaspoon (5 ml) lemon extract
- 1 tablespoon (5 g) lemon zest
- 2 tablespoons (40 g) honey
- 1 recipe Sweet Pizza Dough (page 207) at room temperature
- 1 pint (357 g) strawberries, washed, hulled, and sliced in half
- 1 pint (312 g) red raspberries
- 1 pint (312 g) blackberries
- ½ pint (402 g) blueberries (optional)
- ½ cup (120 ml) Strawberry Glaze (right)
- Fresh mint, for garnish

PREHEAT:

Preheat grill to medium-high.

PREP:

Combine mascarpone cheese, cream cheese, confectioners' sugar, cinnamon, nutmeg, vanilla extract, lemon extract, lemon zest, and honey in a small mixing bowl and whip until smooth.

GRILL:

Stretch dough out to a moderately thin round. Dust a pizza peel with flour or cornmeal. Oil and grill one side of dough at a time until browned and crisp, about 3 minutes per side. Remove from grill and set aside to cool.

SERVE:

Spread cheese mixture evenly on grilled dough, leaving a 1" (2.5 cm) clean border around shell. Top with mixed berries. (For an artful arrangement, form strawberries into a ring around the outside and work into the center with the raspberries in the middle.) Brush berries with strawberry glaze. Chill dessert for a least 1 hour. Sprinkle with confectioners' sugar and garnish with mint.

Strawberry Glaze

SERVES 6

- 1 pint (357 g) strawberries, stemmed and chopped
- 1 tablespoon (15 ml) water
- ¼ cup (50 g) granulated sugar

PREP:

Place all ingredients in a medium-size saucepan. Bring to a boil to dissolve sugar. Reduce heat to a simmer. Continue to cook, stirring occasionally, until strawberries are cooked down and sauce is thickened, about 15 minutes. Remove from heat and pass through a medium-gauge strainer into a bowl, using a rubber spatula to press against the sides of the strainer. Discard the pulp.

Grilled Strawberry and Mango Pizza

SERVES 6

- 1 recipe Sweet Pizza Dough (page 207)
- 1 (8-ounce [225 g]) container mascarpone cheese, softened
- 2 tablespoons (13 g) confectioners' sugar
- 2 tablespoons (40 g) honey
- 1/2 teaspoon (2.5 ml) vanilla extract
- 1 tablespoon (15 ml) orange liqueur (such as Grand Marnier)
- 2 tablespoons (40 g) orange marmalade
- 2 pints (714 g) large strawberries, washed, dried, and hulled
- 1 tablespoon (15 ml) olive oil
- 1 mango, pitted, peeled and sliced into thin strips
- Cabernet Chocolate Sauce (below)

Cabernet Chocolate Sauce:

- 1/2 cup (120 ml) heavy cream
- 8 ounces (225 g) semisweet chocolate, finely chopped
- 1 tablespoon (15 ml) Cabernet Sauvignon wine

PREHEAT:

Preheat grill to high.

PREP:

Stretch dough to a rectangular shape about 16" x 24" (40 x 60 cm). Oil and grill one side at a time until toasted, about 3 minutes per side. Let cool. Place mascarpone cheese in a mixing bowl with sugar, honey, vanilla, orange liqueur, and orange marmalade, then stir to combine.

GRILL:

Cut strawberries in half from top to bottom, then place in a bowl and toss with 1 tablespoon (15 ml) olive oil. Grill for about 7 minutes, turning each berry as they cook. (Take care not to overcook the strawberries, as they will become too soft and difficult to handle.) Remove strawberries from grill and transfer to a bowl.

SERVE:

Spread mascarpone cheese mixture evenly over the top of the grilled dough. Top with strawberries and mango in an artful manner. Slice and place on serving plates. Using a fork or a plastic sandwich bag with a tiny hole cut in one corner, drizzle the slices with chocolate sauce.

CONCLUSION

GRILLING IS THE CENTERPIECE OF MANY SOCIAL ACTIVITIES IN

our modern society. While it's wonderful to have a superb grill and a collection of marvelous recipes, it's even better to share all this with family and friends whenever you can. A grill is not only an outdoor kitchen, it's party central whenever the chef feels like putting his or her skills to the ultimate test. So, depending on your party site, here's some advice for socializing while you're grilling:

- Clean the area thoroughly of dog droppings, broken glass, stones, splintered wood, or thorny branches, and rope off your roses.
- Stake out any public party area early, and check to see if you need a party permit in a park, playground, or beach. Creating a website with party details is a plus for large events.
- Consider invitations for large happenings, or if you need to provide a map to the party, set ground rules, provide telephone and cell numbers, or exclude pets—politely, of course.
- Create a website with party details for larger events.
- Limit the number of people you have on a terrace or balcony for safety reasons and for space, making it possible for guests to move easily from indoors to outdoors.
- Be sure to invite neighbors if they might otherwise be disturbed by the hubbub and check with the landlord, if you have one, to make sure you're meeting the building's rules.

Consider a potluck party where everyone brings his or her own cookables suitable for grilling. And, on a Vermont Castings grill, that leaves a lot of room for imaginative recipes. Here's how to fine-tune your menu and gastronomic expectations of your guests:

- Sit-down or stand-up? Let your guests know well ahead of time if your BBQ is buffet style or a sit-down affair, so they'll know what to wear and when to show up.
- If you're going with the popular buffet style, offer sturdy paper plates and lots of napkins. And don't forget plastic knives, forks, and spoons, with responsible recycling of the waste, instead of washing dishes all night.
- Do some research into the likes and dislikes of your guests. If you're having a large party, consider categories of food, like red meats, poultry, seafood, and vegetarian offerings. For smaller groups, plan something for each person, if possible. And don't forget the kids' menu—smaller portions with less spice and little or no sugar.

COOKING TIME CHART Courtesy of Vermont Castings

TYPE OF FOOD	WEIGHT or THICKNESS	COOKING TEMPERATURE	COOKING TIME
BEEF			
Burgers	1 inch (2.5 cm)	400°F - 450°F (200°C - 230°C)	Rare: 4 - 7 min. Medium: 7 - 10 min. Well Done: 10 - 12 min.
Roasts			
Blade, Sirloin Tip		350°F (180°C)	Rare: 18 - 20 min./lb. Medium: 20 - 25 min./lb. Well Done: 25 - 30 min./lb.
Steaks			
Porterhouse, Rib Ribeye, Sirloin, T-Bone	1 inch (2.5 cm)	Max. (to sear) 400°F - 450°F (200°C - 230°C) (to finish)	Rare: 4 - 7 min. Medium: 7 - 10 min. Well Done: 10 - 12 min.
Filet Mignon	2 inches (5 cm)	Max. (to sear) 400°F - 450°F (200°C - 230°C) (to finish)	Rare: 15 - 17 min. Medium: 17 - 19 min. Well Done: 19 - 22 min.
POULTRY			
Chicken, Parts		325°F - 350°F (170°C - 180°C)	30 - 45 min.
Chicken, Whole	3 - 4 lbs. (1.4 - 1.8 kg)	325°F - 350°F (170°C - 180°C)	20 min./lb.
Chicken Breasts, Boneless	1 - 2 lbs. (0.5 - 0.9 kg)	325°F - 350°F (170°C - 180°C)	12 - 15 min.
Cornish Hens	1 - 1 1/2 lbs. (0.5 - .07 kg)	325°F - 350°F (170°C - 180°C)	45 - 60 min.
Duck	4 - 5 lbs. (1.8 - 2.3 kg)	325°F - 350°F (170°C - 180°C)	18 - 20 min.
Turkey	13 - 25 lbs. (5.9 - 11.3 kg)	325°F - 350°F (170°C - 180°C)	20 min./lb.
FISH & SEAFOOD			
Fish			
Fillets	1 - 1 1/2 inches (0.5 - 0.7 kg)	400°F - 450°F (200°C - 230°C)	10 - 15 min.
Steaks	1 - 2 lbs. (0.5 - 0.9 kg)	325°F - 350°F (170°C - 180°C)	20 - 30 min.
Whole Fish	2 - 4 lbs. (0.9 - 1.8 kg)	325°F - 350°F (170°C - 180°C)	30 - 50 min.
Seafood			
Lobster	1 - 1 1/2 lbs. (0.5 - 0.7 kg)	400°F - 450°F (200°C - 230°C)	15 min.
Shrimp	Large	325°F - 350°F (170°C - 180°C)	5 - 6 min.
PORK			
Chops	1 inch (2.5 cm)	400°F - 450°F (200°C - 230°C)	25 - 30 min.
Ham			
Steak	1 inch (2.5 cm)	400°F - 450°F (200°C - 230°C)	12 - 15 min.
Whole Ham	12 - 14 lbs. (5.4 - 6.4 kg) (Bone-in)	325°F - 350°F (170°C - 180°C)	Medium: 20 - 25 min./lb. Well Done: 25 - 30 min./lb.
	4 - 5 lbs. (1.8 - 2.3 kg) (Boneless)	325°F - 350°F (170°C - 180°C)	50 - 60 min.
Ribs Back, Side	5 - 6 lbs. (2.3 - 2.7 kg)	325°F - 350°F (170°C - 180°C)	Medium: 25 - 27 min./lb. Well Done: 27 - 30 min./lb.
Roasts Butt, Loin, Shoulder	3 - 5 lbs. (1.4 - 2.3 kg)	325°F - 350°F (170°C - 180°C)	1 - 1 1/2 hrs.
Tenderloin		375°F - 400°F (190°C - 200°C)	Medium: 30 - 35 min./lb. Well Done: 35 - 40 min./lb.

TYPE OF FOOD	WEIGHT or THICKNESS	COOKING TEMPERATURE	COOKING TIME
PORK, cont'd			
Sausage	1/2 - 1 inch (1.3 - 2.5 cm)	325°F - 350°F (170°C - 180°C)	12 - 20 min.
LAMB			
Chops			Rare: 7 - 9 min. Medium: 10 - 13 min. Well Done: 14 - 17 min.
Loin, Rib, Shoulder	1 inch (2.5 cm)	400°F - 450°F (200°C - 230°C)	
Roast			
Crown Roast	2 - 4 lbs. (0.9 - 1.8 kg)	325°F - 350°F (170°C - 180°C)	40 - 45 min./lb.
Leg	5 - 9 lbs. (2.3 - 2.7 kg)	325°F - 350°F (170°C - 180°C)	30 - 35 min./lb.

TYPE OF FOOD	COOKING TEMPERATURE	COOKING TIME
VEGETABLES		
Asparagus	325°F - 350°F (170°C - 180°C)	6 - 8 min. Cut off ends of stems. Lay across the grill.
Beans	325°F - 350°F (170°C - 180°C)	30 - 35 min. Wrap in foil with butter or margarine. Turn over once.
Carrots	325°F - 350°F (170°C - 180°C)	20 - 30 min. Cook directly on the grill.
Corn on the Cob	325°F - 350°F (170°C - 180°C)	25 - 35 min. Soak in cold water for 15 minutes. Cook with husk on.
Eggplant	325°F - 350°F (170°C - 180°C)	6 - 8 min./side Cut into slices and coat with oil.
Mushrooms	325°F - 350°F (170°C - 180°C)	6 - 8 min. Cook directly on the grill.
Onions	325°F - 350°F (170°C - 180°C)	40 - 45 min. Wrap in foil. Turn over once during cooking.
Peppers	400°F - 450°F (200°C - 230°C)	15 - 20 min. Remove charred skin before eating.
Potatoes	325°F - 350°F (170°C - 180°C)	50 - 60 min. Wrap in foil. Turn over once.
Roasted Garlic	325°F - 350°F (170°C - 180°C)	30 - 40 min. Cut off top of bud and lightly coat with olive oil. Wrap in foil.
Tomatoes	325°F - 350°F (170°C - 180°C)	5 - 7 min. Cut in half and coat with olive oil.
Zucchini	325°F - 350°F (170°C - 180°C)	6 - 8 min./side Cut into slices and coat with olive oil.

Appendix B:
Menus for Entertaining

Try any of these menus with your choice of vegetables.

MENU 1: DINNER

Appetizer: Basil-Pesto Stuffed Mushrooms (page 83)

Salad: Spinach Salad with Spiced Walnuts and Fire-Roasted Red Bell Pepper (page 252)

Entrée: Flank Steak (page 96)

Dessert: Grilled Glazed Fruit Compote (page 264)

MENU 2: DINNER

Appetizer: Crostini with Grilled Zucchini and Eggplant (page 86)

Salad: Grilled Endive Salad with Golden Raisins (page 249)

Entrée: Italiano Greek Steaks with Grilled Fresh Salsa (page 98)

Dessert: Vanilla Ice Cream with Fresh Blueberry Sauce (page 45)

MENU 3: DINNER

Appetizer: Purple Figs Stuffed with Blue Cheese (page 85)

Salad: Red Lettuce Salad with Grilled Beets and Goat Cheese (page 251)

Entrée: Barbecued Smoked Ribs (page 108)

Dessert: Easy Baked Apples (page 260)

MENU 4: DINNER

Appetizer: Crostini with Fresh Tomatoes, Basil, and Garlic (page 87)

Salad: Corn, Black Bean, and Avocado Salad (page 254)

Entrée: Apple-Ginger Quail (page 159)

Dessert: Grilled Marsala Cantaloupe Balls (page 264)

MENU 5: DINNER

Appetizer: Lettuce Wraps with Grilled Red Peppers and Kalamata Olives (page 92)

Entrée: Grill-Roasted Rosemary Pork Loin (page 106)

Vegetables: Grilled Red Potatoes (page 240)

Dessert: Maple Apples (page 260)

MENU 6: DINNER

Appetizer: Mushrooms Stuffed with Couscous, Mint Pesto, and Walnuts (page 82)

Salad: Fresh Greens with Grilled Hearts of Palm (page 250)

Entrée: Grilled Lamb with Port Glaze (page 119)

Dessert: Peaches and Cream (page 261)

MENU 7: DINNER

Appetizer: Aussie Chips with Sweet Chile Sauce (page 91)

Entrée: Caribbean Chicken with Pineapple-Cantaloupe Salsa (page 129)

Vegetables: Peas in a Packet (page 239)

Dessert: Grilled Pineapple Topped with Ice Cream and Rum (page 262)

MENU 8: DINNER

Appetizer: Crusty Grilled Bread with the Works (page 90)

Salad: Iceberg Lettuce with Grilled Figs and Creamy Blue Cheese Dressing (page 248)

Entrée: Grilled Artichoke Stuffed Chicken Breasts (page 131)

Dessert: Grilled Glazed Fruit Compote (page 264)

MENU 9: DINNER

Appetizer: Zesty Pita Crisps (page 91)

Salad: Grilled Tomato Salad with Fresh Mozzarella Cheese (page 252)

Entrée: Simple Vegetable Grill (page 243)

Dessert: Grilled Cake with Bananas (page 261)

MENU 10: DINNER

Appetizer: Dove Breast Appetizers (page 92)

Salad: Warm Corn-Noodle Salad (page 255)

Entrée: Glazed Salmon with Mango Salsa (page 168)

Dessert: Grilled Piña Colada Parcels (page 265)

MENU 11: DINNER

Appetizer: The Real Bruschetta (page 88)

Salad: Grilled Tomato Salad with Fresh Mozzarella Cheese (page 252)

Entrée: Ham Steak with Peach-Mustard Glaze (page 117)

Dessert: Easy Baked Apples (page 260)

MENU 12: DINNER

Appetizer: Guacamole (page 71) with Zesty Pita Chips (page 91)

Salad: Fresh Greens with Grilled Hearts of Palm (page 250)

Entrée: Fabulous Fajitas (page 124)

Dessert: Grilled Pineapple with Honey Glaze (page 263)

MENU 13: DINNER

Appetizer: Grilled Vegetables and Pasta (page 89)

Salad: Red Lettuce Salad with Grilled Beets and Goat Cheese (page 251)

Entrée: Rubbed Hot Venison Steaks (page 154) and White Corn with Chile Butter (page 233)

Dessert: Blueberries and Grilled Pound Cake (page 263)

MENU 14: DINNER

Appetizer: Grilled Spinach Rolls stuffed with Tofu and Feta (page 82)

Salad: Grilled Endive Salad with Golden Raisins (page 249)

Entrée: Grilled Salmon with Sweet Maple Glaze (page 165)

Dessert: Maple Apples (page 260)

MENU 15: BRUNCH

Appetizer: Crusty Grilled Bread with the Works (page 90)

Salad: Warm Corn-Noodle Salad (page 255)

Entrée: Brunch Pizza with Scrambled Eggs and Tasso Ham (page 216)

MENU 16: LUNCH

Appetizer: Lettuce Wraps with Grilled Red Peppers and Kalamata Olives (page 92)

Entrée: Wood-Grilled Chicken Pizza with Radicchio and Feta (page 209)

MENU 17: LUNCH

Appetizer: Aussie Chips with Sweet Chile Sauce (91)

Entrée: Pizza Margherita (page 225)

MENU 18: LUNCH

Salad: Caesar Salad with Smoky Grilled Tofu (page 248)

Entrée: Grilled Summer Sandwiches (page 196)

Dessert: Peaches and Cream (page 261)

MENU 19: PARTY TIME

Appetizer: Mushrooms Stuffed with Couscous, Mint Pesto, and Walnuts (page 82)

Salad: Corn, Black Bean, and Avocado Salad (page 254)

Entrée: Jamaican Triple Burgers with Jerk Sauce and Orange-Chipotle Mayonnaise (page 103)

Dessert: Grilled Pineapple Topped with Ice Cream and Rum (page 262)

MENU 20: PARTY TIME

Appetizer: Zesty Pita Crisps (page 91)

Salad: Spinach Salad with Spiced Walnuts and Fire-Roasted Red Bell Pepper (page 252)

Entrée: The Everything Grill (page 124) with Grilled Vidalia Onions (page 237) and Russet Potato Wedges (page 239)

Dessert: Grilled Pineapple with Honey Glaze (page 263)

INDEX